Private Higher Education and the Labor Market in China

Institutional Management Efforts & Initial Employment Outcomes

Yingxia Cao

DISSERTATION.COM

Boca Raton

Private Higher Education and the Labor Market in China:
Institutional Management Efforts & Initial Employment Outcomes

Dissertation.com
Boca Raton, Florida
USA • 2008

ISBN-10: 1-59942-663-3
ISBN-13: 978-1-59942-663-1

PRIVATE HIGHER EDUCATION AND THE LABOR MARKET IN CHINA:

Institutional Management Efforts and Initial Employment Outcomes

by

Yingxia Cao

A Dissertation

Submitted to the University at Albany, State University of New York

in Partial Fulfillment of

the Requirements for the Degree of

Doctor of Philosophy

School of Education

Educational Administration & Policy Studies

2007

PRIVATE HIGHER EDUCATION AND THE LABOR MARKET IN CHINA:

Institutional Management Efforts and Initial Employment Outcomes

by

Yingxia Cao

ABSTRACT

The proliferation of demand-absorbing and commercial private higher education institutions is one of the most extraordinary developments reshaping the landscape in the worldwide higher education of the latest decades. With the growth, however, has come considerable debates and skepticism. One key area of controversy involves efforts and performance regarding graduate employment. China is a major case epitomizing the international trends. This research thus investigates how and how well private colleges in China have managed efforts to link private higher education to the labor market.

The research finds that Chinese private colleges have made major efforts to link private higher education to the labor market and that their efforts are well received by the labor market and their graduates. A mixed methods research design triangulates and validates the findings, with both quantitative and qualitative data. The analysis of qualitative data focuses on mission, provided fields of study, educational delivery, and career services. It reveals that the private colleges not only include meeting labor market demands in their mission, they also improve student employability and bridge graduates and employers through providing job-oriented fields of study, educational delivery, career services, and networking. The analysis of self-reported quantitative data by their graduates examines employment status, starting salary, job and educational level match, job and field match, job and skills/knowledge match, job satisfaction, as well as graduate feedback on the worthiness of private higher education and satisfaction with various management efforts. Both initial employment outcomes and graduate feedback reflect positive picture about the appreciation of institutional efforts by the labor market and the graduates.

Yet the research also finds wide variations in efforts and outcomes among the colleges. In examining the outcome variations and possible related factors, it identifies two likely relevant efforts: the existence of separate offices for career services and niche-field designation. The former is positively, whereas the latter is negatively associated with various outcomes. Based on summarized effort and outcome variations, this study builds a conceptual model to distinguish serious demand-absorbing colleges from those low quality mere demand-absorbers, with eight criteria on the "effort" dimension and seven criteria on the "outcome" dimension.

To my husband, Lang Zhang; son, Andy Zhang; and daughter, Angie Zhang.

ACKNOWLEDGEMENT

As my doctoral study comes to an end, I cannot stop thinking: Dr. Daniel C. Levy, if it were not for your scholarship and for the Ford Foundation grant for PROPHE (Program for Research On Private Higher Education), I probably would not have come to the University seven years ago; if it were not for your efforts, this dissertation would not have happened. You are fabulous, in serving as both my advisor and my mentor! Your tremendous care, encouragement and praise, and even sometimes admonishment have certainly transformed me and I will always treasure them in my future. You will always be the model for my journey.

So fortunately, I not only have Dr. Levy, the best scholar on private higher education, as the chair of my dissertation committee, I also have Dr. Alan P. Wagner, one of the best scholar on higher education and the labor market and with a lot of experience on relevant work from OECD, and Dr. Fengqiao Yan, certainly one of the top scholars on private higher education in China, as members of the committee. I am grateful for their generosity and help, all through the intellectual challenges of my dissertation research and writing. Without Dr. Wagner, I would have not been able to examine the complexity of the relationships between private higher education and the labor market so comprehensively. Without Dr. Yan, my fieldwork and exploration on Chinese private higher education would not have been accomplished amid the daunting difficulties.

I would like to express my sincere appreciation to many other members of the Department of Educational Administration & Policy Studies. Dr. Kevin Kinser offered insightful comments on my dissertation proposal and thoughtful guidance on my

PROPHE work. Mrs. Carmelinda M. Colfer has given me enormous help and she is always there when I need her. You are an extraordinary professional, Carm! The "PROPHE Troika", with Makoto Nagasawa and Prachayani Praphamontripong, and many other fellow graduate students have always been supportive. I wish them all the best in their journey. Last, but not least, a special person, Dr. Irene Harbison, wife of late dean Dr. Ralph Harbison, has invested a lot of her energy and care for the department and for the graduate students.

My thanks also go to the Initiative for Women for a fieldwork grant, and to my colleagues at the University of La Verne, who have given their support for my administrative work and encouragement for my dissertation writing. Special thanks to Dr. Alfred Clark, Mr. James Schirmer, and Mr. Guangjian Hou. I appreciate their editing assistance. I am thankful to Dr. Mark Nelson, who has given advice and enabled flexibility for my dissertation completion.

My gratitude also goes to many people who helped my fieldwork in China. The presidents, vice-presidents, and other administrators of the private colleges examined permitted this study on their campuses and offered their time, resources, and insights. Several employers, current students, and alumni also offered their knowledge. Though I keep them anonymous for confidentiality purposes, all of them really deserve my special thanks. Two Chinese scholars, Mr. Dong Shengzu and Mrs. Lili Liu, shared their expertise on private higher education in China and helped for my fieldwork.

Very fortunately, I have the unbounded support of my big and small families. Mom and dad, brothers and sisters, your consistent asking and jokes about my dissertation surely have kept reminding me that I still have a mission to accomplish. I am deeply indebted to my small family, my husband Lang, son Andy, and daughter Angie, for their love, support, and sacrifice. Lang, you are a splendid husband and thanks for taking care of the kids while I wrote the dissertation on weekends and at night. Andy, thanks for your "massage" and I did feel much better for your hard work and understanding. Angie, I love you very much, even when you climbed on my lap and sat between me and the computer. I also thank my parents-in-law, sisters-in-law, and brothers-in-law for taking care of Andy and Angie as well as me during our stay in China.

TABLE OF CONTENTS

LIST OF TABLES

LIST OF FIGURES

CHAPTER ONE: INTRODUCTION

One of the most fascinating phenomena in the past several decades' higher education development is the rapid and controversial growth of its private sector in China and many other countries. By the late 1970s and early 1980s, private higher education appeared, re-emerged, or took new forms in many countries. It has expanded enormously worldwide since then. This private growth has been commonly accompanied by controversies over its institutional practices and performance. The controversy is strong and heated with regard to graduate employment, which makes it necessary to approach the research question of this study on how and how well private higher education institutions have made efforts to link private higher education to the labor market.

This first chapter introduces the study. It first highlights the controversial international private higher education growth and analyzes how the Chinese case chosen for this study echoes certain international patterns. It proceeds to state the research question and hypotheses. After defining several key terms and delimiting the research scope, it pinpoints some of the limitations and the significance of this research. Lastly, it briefs the organization of this dissertation.

Private Higher Education Worldwide: New Development and Controversies

Private higher education, defined in this study primarily by its private official judicial status, has achieved spectacular growth since the 1980s in both countries with no previous history or existence of the sector as well as those with a relative long history of its existence (Altbach, 1999; Levy, 2002b, 2005, 2006b).The first category has widespread examples in each geographic region worldwide, where private higher

education appeared or re-emerged around the early 1980s.[1] The second category includes

the United States and some Latin American countries, where the private sector takes new

forms or new roles. A striking case in the United States is the increasing number of for-

profit institutions, such as the University of Phoenix (Kelly, 2001; Tooley, 1999).

Nevertheless, as will be explained later, the worldwide numerically dominant form is a

demand-absorbing type, legally nonprofit, but often with "commercial" and sometimes

"entrepreneurial" characteristics.

Controversies are common and frequent over the practices and performance of the

newly developed demand-absorbing private higher education, hereafter called "the new

private higher education". With evidence or alleged evidence of institutional malpractice,

[2] opponents accuse it of being low quality, often profiteering without accountability,

being irresponsible and untrustworthy, and cherry-picking several most lucrative fields.

Proponents often counter that it has grown with no or little cost to the general public,

providing higher education access to thousands who otherwise may never have had a

chance. Admitting that some of what opponents charge might be true in some private

institutions, they argue that the majority make serious efforts and fill special niches by

providing certain particular types of higher education, including market-needed

specialized programs that are not provided or sufficiently provided by the public sector. [3]

The controversy over institutional practices and performance regarding graduate

employment is a vital case in point. With evidence of graduate unemployment and

underemployment, some complain that the new private higher education has low value in

---

[1] See relevant references in Maldonado, Cao, Altbach, Levy, and Zhu (2004) for examples in various regions.
[2] See criticisms reported by several (Brender, 2004; Gong, 2004; Mok, 1997a).
[3] See arguments reported by several (James, 1993; Levy, 1992; Newman and Couturier, 2001; Sosale, 1999).

employment and its institutions provide little or no career services to graduates seeking employment. [1] To refute this and similar other criticisms, many private institutions argue that their graduates are well employed and some are even better and more quickly employed than their public counterparts. They attribute their success to institutional efforts, such as assessing labor market demand and soliciting feedback from employers and graduates. [2] Some of the institutions go even further by promising job placement and guaranteeing money back if graduates cannot find a job in a certain period of time after graduation. [3]

In short, the impressive growth of the new private higher education is accompanied by frequent and heated controversies, over its practices and performance in general and those of its graduate employment in particular. For the latter, the focus is mainly on how and how well private institutions have met labor market demands, while providing higher education access and being managed commercially.

Private Higher Education in China: Resurgence and Controversies

The growth of Chinese private higher education and its relevant controversies epitomize the prominent worldwide trends highlighted above. First, China is indeed a major case of private sector expansion in contemporary worldwide private higher education growth. The initial private higher education reappeared in 1978, [4] but it was

---

[1] See such claims reported by Sapatoru, Nicolescu, and Slantcheva (2003) .
[2] Such arguments are often made by administrators and publications of private institutions, as shown by several (Ellerinton, 2004; Kelly, 2001; Mok, 1997a; Sperling, 2000; Sperling and Tucker, 1996).
[3] Two German private institutions promised students money back if they could not find jobs within four or six months of graduating (Brookman, 1997).
[4] The private sector was an important part of Chinese higher education before 1952. All 89 private institutions, 39 percent of the higher education, were transformed into public ones by the communist government in 1952. Private higher education, along other private enterprises, was prohibited in China for several decades. Its reappearance and growth since 1978 are mainly related to market development (Lin, 1999; Qin, 2000).

not until the 1980s that major growth began to surge. It has grown conspicuously in size, speed, and scope shortly after (Liu, 2002; Qin, 2000; Yan and Wu, 2004). By 2000, about 1280 private institutions existed, with a total enrollment estimated to be around one to two million, or about one fourth of entire higher education enrollment. [1] The total number of accredited private institutions, defined as being recognized by the Ministry of Education to grant associate or/and bachelor degrees, has jumped several folds, from 43 in 2000 to 278 in 2006. Among them, the number of the four-year colleges has jumped from one to 25. [2][3]

China is also a country where private higher education profiteering is prominently alleged and assailed, along with perceived low quality and reported frauds. In a country where philanthropic and religious actions seen in other countries are rare, profit-making is seen as a major motive and practice in many, if not most, private institutions (Kwong, 1997; Mok, 1997a; Mok and Wat, 1998), despite laws prohibiting the establishment of for-profit educational institutions. Profit-making Chinese private institutions have been described and denigrated as "typifying the times" and "a way to cash in on the increasing desire for degrees" while producing little value in employment and providing little help for graduates seeking jobs by one *Washington Post* report (Goodman, 2003). Of course, malpractices have taken place in the private sector (Gong, 2004). Additionally, as in

---

[1] The two million figure was cited by Daguang Wu in his presentation "Development and Issues in Chinese private higher education" in SUNY at Albany 2003 from the report of Yandong Qu on *Minban Education Development and Research* conference in Ningbo, China. April 2002.

[2] The 2000 figure was reported by Wu, as cited above. "278" was reported the Ministry of Education, 2006 Educational Statistics (http://www.moe.gov.cn/edoas/website18/level3.jsp?tablename=2233&infoid=33446, accessed 11/09/2007). "25" was reported by China Education and Research Network, online at http://www.edu.cn/20060717/3200140.shtml (accessed 11/09/2007). The rest 253 colleges are three-year colleges and can only grant associate degrees.

[3] In addition to these independent private institutions, 318 privately managed but publicly-affiliated colleges are also recently defined as part of the private sector. The Ministry of Education announced a list on April 4, 2007 at http://www.gov.cn/zfjg/content_566290.htm, accessed on 11/09/2007). But as will be explained later, this research does not study them. Hereafter, except where special notes are given, all private numbers refer only to the real independent ones.

many countries outside the United States, the Chinese private institutions occupy the low level of academic hierarchy, with lower standards of admission, higher part-time faculty and student-faculty ratios, and less equipment, laboratories, and libraries than their public counterparts. Its quality is thus also often doubted.

Despite criticism and doubts, the new private higher education in China is sometimes officially praised for its salient job preparation efforts and widely advertised for its good employment outcomes. For example, the Ministry of Education, along with five other important governmental agencies in China, conducted a joint study on graduate employment and lauded the private sector. According to their study the graduate employment rate of the 171 private colleges surveyed had higher employment rates than their public counterparts. Some private colleges even had 100 percent job placement through several consecutive years. [1] In China, some officials criticize the privates in one way or another, others have repeatedly expressed satisfaction with the graduate employment efforts and performance by some colleges. They have even encouraged public institutions and other privates to follow such practices. The privates also publicize their higher initial employment rates and assert superior job preparation practices and efforts in newspaper and admission brochures. [2] As a matter of fact, however, such praises and claims are sustained by serious studies. [1]

---

[1] See news "Schools: Aids Students Seeking Jobs", Guo Nei, *China Daily*, July 5, 2004, at http://www.chinadaily.com.cn/english/doc/2004-07/05/content_345480.htm; "Seminar on the Sustainable Development of China's Minban Higher Education was Held", Guo Yan, *China Net*, July 5, 2004, at http://edu.china.com/zh_cn/1055/20040705/11765441.html (accessed, 11/9/2007). However, a caution that I would drop on here is: when I sought the final report from the key officials of the Ministry of Education on private education, I found that they had not heard about it and never seen the report. Thus, it was suspected that such a report was probably not serious study, if not just an advertisement of the private colleges.
[2] See a news series on management efforts and employment rate in four private colleges, *China Daily*, 8/11/2003, p.4: Yi Feng, "How to Ensure High Employment Rate #1: Beijing City College – Start and End Point"; Ke Wenying and He Yu, "How to Ensure High Employment Rate #2: Jianqiao Vocational & Technical Colleges – Vocational Graduates Become Popular Targets"; Huang He, "How to Ensure High

Overall, what China has experienced, in its private higher education growth and relevant controversies, strikingly echoes these described international patterns. The private institutions are usually commercially managed and often focus on some low-cost but profitable disciplines, while also receiving complaints and criticisms. Nevertheless, in a country where demand for private academic elite and culturally or religiously differentiated private sector is rare, meeting differentiated labor market demands becomes the only area in which the new private higher education in China can make unique and continued contributions, in addition to providing higher education access. Thus, China is an ideal case for studying the new private higher education from the perspective of institutional efforts and graduate employment.

Research Question and Hypothesis

The context highlighted above illustrates huge concerns and major claims about the practice and quality of the new private higher education worldwide. The concerns and claims are: a). Does the new private higher education largely fit critics' charges of low quality, rip-offs and even being interested only in profit by merely providing higher education access and absorbing excess higher education demand? Or b) does it aim at some serious academically non-elite ends, notably pursuing substantial job goals albeit not of the elite, high status, or purely academic variety, while providing higher education access opportunity for those who otherwise would not have? And c) how and how

Employment Rate #3: Huanghe Technical College – Establishing High Effective Employment System"; Lan Tian Xuan "How to Ensure High Employment Rate #4: Lantian Vocational & Technical College – Meeting Company's Demand and Broader Employment Pathway".
[1] No serious research, not even the joint-study by several governmental agencies, has been released to sustain either governmental or institutional claims of success. A study, such as this dissertation, can reveal how some governmental positions and institutional claims are sustained; the study can do this through describing the patterns of institutional practices in linking private higher education to the labor market, initial graduate employment outcomes, and graduate feedback on institutional practices.

commonly do private institutions undertake efforts to move from something like (a) toward something like (b)? An overarching research question to address the concerns and claims around its graduate employment in particular is: How and how well have private higher education institutions made efforts to link the new private higher education to the labor market?

To answer the research question, several interwoven sub-questions must be pursued: What efforts have private institutions made in linking the new private higher education to meet labor market demands? How good are their employment outcomes and how satisfied are their graduates with their management efforts? Do managed efforts correspond with employment outcomes? What variations in efforts and outcomes exist among the private sector? Answers to these questions can shed light on the role of the non-academic or modestly-academic non-elite private higher education in meeting labor market demands. They can also provide responses to the controversies over private institutions' graduate employment practices and performance in particular and the private sector's management and quality in general.

However, understanding based upon studies about the relationship between the new private higher education and the labor market is limited. Globally, the relationship between the two has just recently become prominent in many countries and only begins to catch the attention of some scholars. Very few studies on private higher education and the labor market have been done and the existing handfuls of such studies are often limited in scope. [1] Neither the private higher education literature nor the higher education and the labor market literature can adequately address the research question on the new

---

[1] Only several such publications are available (Monks, 2000; Sapatoru, Nicolescu, and Slantcheva, 2003; Yonezawa and Baba, 1998). Among them, only Sapatoru, Nicolescu, and Slantcheva (2003) is about the new demand-absorbing private higher education.

private higher education and the labor market. The private higher education literature seldom studies the labor market (as *Private Higher Education: An International Bibliography* reveals); the literature on higher education and the labor market seldom studies private higher education in particular or as focus. Even where studies on graduate employment of private institutions exist, they largely use the private cases like the public ones and rarely take the distinctive nature of private higher education into consideration. Existing empirical studies on private higher education and graduate employment in China are also few.[1] Many of them lack vigorous research methodology and analysis. The criticisms, the doubts, and even the praises and advertisement mentioned above are more based on ad hoc impression and incomplete institutional disclosure than on robust empirical research.

And yet a review of literature provides guidance on how to approach the research question. First, many studies on private higher education identify meeting labor market demands as a major niche of the new private higher education (Cohen, 2003; Levy, 2003b; Sharvashidze, 2002; Stetar and Berezkina, 2002). And in reality, although most demand-absorbing private institutions do not achieve academic standing and they do not make such a claim (whereas some do and even achieve some kind of superiority), many of them do claim that their efforts and outcomes in job training and preparation are differentiated and even superior, even though such training and preparation may not be conventionally academic-oriented and even are widely labeled or dismissed as low quality (Levy, 2003b). Factors cited in explaining such niche, efforts, and outcomes include branded or different programs, specialized areas and courses with strong market demands, new programs attuned to the market, high-demand occupational or professional

---

[1] Only a few studies exist (Bao, 2005, 2006b; Cao, 2000; Wu, 2003; Zhou, 2003).

fields, jointed professional training and practicum with employers, emphasis of job related skills, job placement, career counseling, other intermediary services, etc. [1] Additionally, field of study can be a fundamental link between private higher education and jobs (Levy, 1986a). Moreover, studies on higher education and the labor market uncover how institutions may influence employment outcomes through managing various structures, policies, and activities in educational/ field of study provisions (Finnie, 1999a), career services (Chesler, 1995; McGrath, 2002), and networking (Villar, Juan, Corominas, and Capell, 2000).

Therefore, this research hypothesizes that private higher education institutions have managed major efforts to link the new private higher education to the labor market; their graduates are well employed and satisfied with institutional management efforts related to graduate employment; their efforts correspond with initial employment outcomes. In approaching the hypothesis, this research studies institutionally managed structures, policies, and activities in educational provisions, career services, and networking. It also reveals initial employment outcomes of the graduates and explores the associations of these management practices with initial employment outcomes, while considering the distinctive nature of the new private higher education.

Definition of Terms

Several key terms need to be defined before testifying the hypothesis and pursuing the answers to the research question of this study.

---

[1] See the aforementioned series in *China Daily*, 8/11/2003 and several others (Cohen, 2003; Giesecke, 1999b; Kwong, 1997; Levy, 2003b; Mok, 1997a; Pritchard, 1992; Sharvashidze, 2002; Stetar and Berezkina, 2002).

Private Higher Education

This research uses official judicial status to distinguish private institutions from public ones, which follows the conclusion of Levy's meticulous examination and comprehensive definition. In defining the term, Levy notices that the private and public higher education sectors increasingly blur in reality and also "private higher education" is a term often taken for-granted in higher education practice and research. After identifying the status of private higher education sector along the "privateness" and "publicness" spectra in terms of criteria such as mission, function, finance, governance, founder, and ownership, he concludes: empirically, only the current judicial/legal ownership status can exhaustively separate the identification of the two sectors (Levy, 1986b, 1987, 1992). That is, an institution cannot legally be both public and private at a specific time, and it can only be either a private, or a public institution. Thus, this research follows the criterion of judicial status in referring to private higher education and its institutions.

New Private Higher Education

"New private higher education" is a term coined in this research to refer to the private higher education sector or part of the private higher education sector that has appeared, re-emerged, or taken new forms of development after the 1970s and 1980s. The word "new" is used to distinguish the private sector (or part of the private sector) with newly-established private institutions from the "old" or those with a long history and existence of private institutions. Its predominant role is revealed by literature as absorbing excess higher education demand, in the sense that its appearance and growth have taken advantage of a sort of "public failure", in that the public sector cannot provide enough higher education access to keep up with increased demands (Levy, 1982, 1986a).

Also its institutions are operated entrepreneurially or commercially, often adopting business management styles, picking up some demand, and providing access generally at low cost (Kelly, 2001; Kwong, 1997; Moses, 2000; Nicolescu, 2001; Wolff and Castro, 2001). Naturally, there is overlap between the "new" and the "old" private sector, especially when the older institutions take commercial and demand-absorbing characteristics, as many Liberal Art colleges and non-selective private colleges in the United States do (Breneman, 1994), and when the new institutions take serious interests and efforts in research, as with some of the top private institutions in Central and Eastern Europe (Sapatoru, Nicolescu, and Slantcheva, 2003) and Asia (Praphamontripong, 2004) do.

Differences also exist between the institutions within the new private sector. If listed along a spectrum of seriousness on many criteria, the merely demand-absorbing ones can be placed on one pole and the commercial but serious demand-absorbing ones on the other, with most private institutions between the two, as suggested by Levy. A rough comparison around eight criteria can be constructed to indicate possible major differences between the two types, as shown in Table 1.

China is a major case of the new private higher education re-appearance and growth. It currently has about 1300 such institutions. As mentioned above, most private institutions have a commercialized purpose or commercialized operation. Almost all of them serve as demand-absorbers. In terms of admission standards, the private sector as a whole recruits the less academically competent student population. Based on their accreditation status, private institutions in China can be roughly classified into two types:

accredited and unaccredited. [1] Based on the criteria listed in Table 1, my fieldwork

suggests that many accredited institutions can probably be classified as "Serious

Demand-Absorbers", albeit with varying degrees of "seriousness" on the criteria. The

Table 1: Comparing Private Institutions Using Eight Criteria*

Dimension	Serious Demand-Absorbers	Mere Demand-Absorbers
Accreditation	Being Accredited or Aspiring for Accreditation by Trying to Meet Accreditation Standards	No Aspiration for Accreditation or No Action Taken to Meet Accreditation Standards
Program Provision and Student Catering	One or More Niche/Brand Fields; Proactively Catering for Student Demand Appropriate to Institutional Mission	No Niche/Brand Field; Negligence of Student Demand or Just Relying on there being sufficient demands
Curriculum Provision	Feedback-Based Innovations and Revisions	Pale Emulation
Job Concern	Labor Market Scanning and Concern about Labor Market Demand	Lack of Concern about Labor Market Demand
Faculty Qualification and Composition	Major Efforts or at least Concern to Hire Reputable and Qualified Professors/ Professionals; A Core of Qualified Full-Time Faculty for All or a Majority of Programs	Few or No Reputable and Qualified Professors/Professionals; No Core of Qualified Full-Time Faculty for All or Most Programs
Administration	Coherent Administrative Policy & Rules	No Institutionalized Administrative Policy or Rules
Employer Contact	Various Networking Efforts and Follow-Ups with Employers	No or Few Networking Efforts and Follow-Ups with Employers
Alumni Feedback	Various Networking Efforts and Follow-Ups with Graduates	No or Few Networking Efforts and Follow-Ups with Graduates

Note: This table uses and revises Levy's listing in a memo sent to PROPHE Group in April 2005. In the memo, he listed 20 things that we might see in serious non-elite private higher education institutions.

---

[1] Accredited private institutions are recognized by the Ministry of Education to grant bachelor and/or associate degrees. Their degree program students must meet government college entrance examination requirement, although those of their non-degree programs do not. Unaccredited private colleges are basically Self-Study Facilitating Institutions that offer non-degree certificate programs. Their students must pass all courses in National Adult Self-Study Examinations to get degrees (in this sense, these institutions serve as students' tutors). Accredited institutions provide two types of higher education programs: general programs (Type I) and vocational programs (Type II). And unaccredited institutions provide Self-Study Facilitating Programs (Type III) as well as the transitional Pilot Examinations and Certificates Programs (Type IV, such programs were not permitted to enroll new students since 2004).

picture is less clear for the unaccredited institutions. It appears that some are seriously pursuing high standards along several or most of the criteria, while others are not. Nevertheless, no empirical study exists to differentiate them and give an accurate picture. Distinguishing the serious demand-absorbing institutions from those merely demand-absorbers is thus still a challenge to scholars, accreditation bodies, and policy-makers. This study on institutional management efforts attempts to respond to this challenge. By identifying how and how well private institutions have made efforts on the aforementioned dimensions in linking private higher education to the labor market, it may shed some light on how to distinguish them.

Labor Market

This study adopts the general definition of labor market used in labor economics, which refers to both labor demand and labor supply. It specifically focuses on the graduate labor market regarding the production of college graduates and the demand of highly educated labor. As general labor markets, graduate labor markets are segmented. The segmented markets can often be classified by geography (i.e. local, regional, national, and international), industry (business, education, science, agriculture, etc.), educational requirement (manual, secondary education, higher education, etc.), occupation (doctor, lawyer, teacher, etc.), and job stability (primary and secondary). [1] Higher education institutions and their sub-structures (i.e. school, department, and program) may define specific labor markets with certain classification criteria in accordance with their purposes to specialize strategically in producing a workforce for certain defined labor markets. For example, many higher education institutions in Europe

---

[1] See such classification in books on labor market and also at http://www.des.calstate.edu/labor.html.

broadly define the labor market as an international labor market because of the reality of graduate mobility throughout the continent. In contrast, some Chinese private institutions have defined their targeted labor market at the local level, even as narrowly as several employers. Nevertheless, it claims that a narrowly defined labor market can sometimes be "particularly useful for job seekers and recruiters because it allows qualified job hunters to easily search for openings and for potential employers to get information to potential applicants". [1] Thus, this study pays special attention to elements surrounding how private institutions have defined their targeted labor markets, what efforts they have made accordingly, and how their definitions and efforts are associated with initial graduate employment outcomes.

Institutional Management Effort

In this study, the term "institutional management effort" is used to refer to consciously devised structures, policies, and activities by higher education institutions, for accomplishing certain purposes. These purposes may be multiple. In regard to graduate employment, literature on higher education and the labor market reveals two perspectives: improving student employability and connecting students with potential employers (Brennan, Kogan, and Teichler, 1996; Little, 2001). It also identifies three main types of efforts: providing certain field of study and curricula, facilitating graduate employment, and networking with other organizations. This study also uses terms like "institutional efforts" and "institutional management practices" to indicate similar meanings.

---

[1] See how labor market can be narrowly defined for the purpose of higher education, please go to http://www.des.calstate.edu/labor.html.

14

Graduate Employment Outcome

"Graduate employment outcome" is a rather loose but functional term used in this study, referring to both monetary (i.e. salary, bonus, wages) and non-monetary (e.g. job satisfaction, employment status, job match etc.) results of actual employment and transition from college to the labor market. As the literature review in Chapter Two identifies, graduate employment outcomes are mainly indicated by employment status, earnings, job-education match, and job satisfaction (Brennan, 2000; HEFCE, 2001; Koskinen, 2005). Although graduate employment has both initial and long-term outcomes and the literature has rich findings on both, this study only examines its initial outcomes due to various constraints. Nevertheless, little research indicates that short-term and long-term employment outcomes are significantly and consistently different for over college graduates. Furthermore, Silver, Lavallée, and Pereboom (1999) find that the patterns of major employment outcomes are consistent in both long-term and initial employment.

Identification of the Research Scope

The study scope of this research is limited in several ways. First, although this research analyzes initial employment outcomes of private college graduates in detail, its priority is to describe the patterns of institutional management practices in the private sector. The analysis of initial graduate employment outcomes is complementary to the exploration of institutional employment outcome variations and the correspondence of management practices with employment outcomes. The reason is: Graduate employment outcomes, especially initial outcomes, have often been a major part of empirical studies on the relationship between higher education (both private and public) and the labor market. In contrast, various institutional management practices are seldom systematically and comprehensively studied and reported. In other words, while both topics are important, only one has been much studied, so this study focuses on the other.

This research does not study affiliated private colleges. The exclusion of affiliated private colleges in this research is mainly due to their short history: the official private ownership was not clarified by the Ministry of Education until 2003; and most such colleges have too short a history to reveal any patterns in institutional management effort regarding graduate employment. Nonetheless, likely much of what the study finds about independent private institutions would apply to the affiliated private colleges or at least serve as hypotheses for prospective studies of them.

This research does not survey public colleges, either. The aim of this study is not to compare private institutions with public ones, but to explore the private sector's practices. There are already numerous studies (though they may not be robust empirical studies with rigorous research designs) on graduate employment of Chinese public institutions. Those studies have revealed essential facts about employment outcomes and institutional management efforts that can be utilized for certain useful comparison.

Limitations of the Study

Beyond the limitations in study scope, other limitations that pose challenges to the generalization of findings are also present in this study.

Due to resource and other constraints, the total number of studied private higher education institutions in this research is small, and all of which are located in four cities and most are in Shanghai. Even though the selected institutions from the four cities were based on major criteria, such as level, region (east, middle, and west China), and province income (high-income, middle-income, and low-income provinces), the sampling is too small to represent the complexity of the widespread Chinese private institutions in terms of type, geography, size, and history, even within the accredited sub-sector.

As in most graduate surveys, bias can happen because many graduates do not respond and graduate surveys are not consistently conducted. It is often said that graduates who are satisfied with their jobs or job offers are more likely to respond and their responses tend to be positive, while many of those who have not found jobs may choose not to respond at all. This research tried to use techniques to minimize the bias [1] by improving the response rate to 50.1 percent as well as comparing student profiles of the graduates with those who responded to the survey to diagnose the extent of bias. However, possibl bias cannot be ruled out because it is difficult to identify. Additionally, because colleges have high stakes in releasing graduate employment information because the government sanction those with low employment rates. Many private institutions did not accept my study and only two of the six surveyed let the author control the survey. Bias may have taken place if any of the rest four colleges had selected certain graduates with desirable employment outcomes.

Additionally, the fact that this study catches private higher education and the labor market in China at a time of extraordinary economic expansion and transition has two limitations. On one hand, while the supply and demand of the labor market as well as private and public higher education sector in China are unique because of economic and higher education expansions as well as transitions, this research applies what has been studied on tertiary graduates (mainly public graduates) in rather stable higher education

---

[1] Porter (2004) has reviewed how techniques can be used to improve response rate of mailed questionnaire.

17

and labor markets outside of China. It thus may not be able to accommodate some features of the Chinese context. On the other hand, because of the dynamic and fast-changing nature of the current Chinese case, the generalization of the findings of this study to private higher education in other countries or even to private higher education in China at a different period of time may be limited in one way or another. The findings of the research thus have to be examined within the current context of China and its various institutions.

Above all, key limitations derive from the lack of good guidance from prior work, particularly on how private higher education relates to the labor market. The lack of literature, especially well-developed research designs, as guidance to develop this study, makes it difficult to assess whether the exploration is effectively conducted and how convincing the descriptions and explanations are. Solid guidance would assume ample prior efforts, critiqued and honed through scholarly norms. Instead, this study has to originally fashion how to apply the literature on higher education and the labor market not only to the Chinese case, but, notably, to the new private higher education.

Significance of the Study

Despite its limitations, this research has significance in both scholarship and possible practical implications of its findings.

To date, the literature on private higher education rarely deals with the labor market, just as the literature on higher education and the labor market does not deal with private higher education. As a pioneer study on private higher education and the labor market, this research can advance our knowledge about private higher education through three contributions. First, it identifies important institutional practices in providing education to meet labor market demands and in promoting graduates to jobs. Second, it systematically analyzes and reports initial graduate employment outcomes of a half dozen Chinese private colleges. Lastly, it explores the associations between institutional practices and initial employment outcomes. The three contributions help clarify the role of the new private higher education and discern the practices and performance of its institutions.

By studying the path of college graduates to jobs, this research addresses the arguably foremost concern in China, for students going to college, for the industries general supporting higher education, and for the colleges and universities undertaking education and training. Its findings thus can inform relevant decision makers in China – students, employers, and administrators alike, with its findings on what some private institutions do. The information can serve as feedback for institutions to help guide their program provisions, curriculum designs, career services, and networking efforts. Also, knowing the differences in institutional practices and employment outcomes of various private and public institutions will help inform students so that they can make more appropriate college choices based on their interests, as well as assisting employers in choosing the best institutions to recruit employees appropriate to their needs.

This research may also help policymakers adjust to certain public agenda and policies on accreditation, quality assurance, financing, and especially on graduate employment. Since graduate employment practices and outcomes are important indicators of institutional quality, relevant findings about different types of private institutions can serve as guidance for future accreditation. For example, latitude should be given to institutions that seriously make major efforts and those that are aspiring to effect a transition from "mere demand-absorbers" to "serious demand-absorbers". Policymakers may also make better policy in choosing what private institutions to finance and which ways to finance if they are informed about institutional practices and outcomes. Above all, the research is of special importance for China now. As college graduate population increases at an unprecedented speed, [1] improving immediate job placement is an urgent matter for the sake of the welfare of graduates and the stability of the society. As the Ministry of Education prioritizes institutional efforts to improve college graduate employment, paying special attention to improvement within private and vocational colleges, [2] the findings on institutional efforts and initial graduate employment outcomes in private colleges, mostly vocational, as well as the associations of the efforts with outcomes, can point out strategies to improve graduate employment outcomes through institutional management efforts.

Organization of the Dissertation

Besides this introduction chapter, this dissertation has five chapters. Chapter Two presents the literature review of two strands of literature: one on private higher education and the other on higher education and the labor market. The former reviews the distinctive nature of private higher education and suggests why the new private higher education may be linked to meet labor market demands. The latter indicates how the issue about private higher education links to labor market demands may be examined through studying institutional efforts and graduate employment outcomes. Lastly, it

---

[1] In 2006, total college graduates were 4.13 millions, increased 0.75 million from 2005. The estimated number for 2007 will be 4.95 million (See news at http://www.moe.edu.cn/edoas/website18/info23261.htm).
[2] See strategies proposed by the Ministry of Education at Work Conference on 2007 Regular College Graduate Employment was Held in Beijing, online at http://www.moe.edu.cn/edoas/website18/info23261.htm.

reviews existing empirical studies on private higher education and the labor market and reveals the necessity of this research in terms of scholarship.

Chapter Three describes the research methodology, including data collection methods, research procedures, instruments, sampling techniques, data analysis methods, respondent characteristics, as well as limitations of the study in terms of research methodology. Mixed research methods are adopted for this research. Interview and document analysis were used to obtain qualitative data on institutional management efforts and graduate surveys were conducted to obtain quantitative data about initial graduate employment outcomes.

Chapter Four analyzes the qualitative data. To explore whether private colleges commit to meet labor market demands in their mission and where the mission meets the labor market, it compares the institutionally declared or published mission/goals as well as fields of study between the investigated private colleges and their selected public counterparts as well as within the private colleges. It also describes how mission meets labor market demands through educational delivery and career services, along with relevant networking efforts.

Chapter Five analyzes the quantitative data. It examines several major initial employment outcomes (employment status, starting salary, job and education match, and job satisfaction) and, reports graduate feedback on institutional worthiness and management efforts. It also examines factors related to outcomes and identified two major such institutional efforts described in Chapter Four, niche-field designation and the existence of separate offices for career services.

Chapter Six concludes the research, pinpoints its contextual limitations, highlights major practical implications, and points out directions for further research.

CHAPTER TWO: REVIEW OF LITERATURE

Very few empirical studies pertain to institutional management practices and graduate employment outcomes of the private higher education sector (Bao, 2005, 2006b; Cao, 2000; McMahon and Wagner, 1981; Sapatoru, Nicolescu, and Slantcheva, 2003; Yoshimoto and Yonezawa, 1994; Zhou, 2003). [1] This study thus refers to two strands of relevant literature – works on private higher education and works on higher education and the labor market. Together these two strands of literature form the content of this literature review, along with the few empirical studies specifically on private higher education and the labor market. Highlighting the Chinese case as it proceeds, the literature review in this chapter is divided into the following sections:

- Review of the literature on private higher education;

- Review of the literature on higher education and the labor market; and

- Review of empirical studies on private higher education and the labor market.

The integration of this review yields rich knowledge for the research design in Chapter Three and for the analysis of collected information thereafter. The synthesis is presented at the end of this chapter. It concludes that private higher education literature indicates why private higher education may be linked to meet labor market demand and literature on higher education and the labor market points out major elements of institutional management efforts to explore for conducting this study in China.

---

[1] Only four (Bao, 2005, 2006b; McMahon and Wagner, 1981; Sapatoru, Nicolescu, and Slantcheva, 2003; Yoshimoto and Yonezawa, 1994)) are formally published.

Review of the Literature on Private Higher Education

This section reviews literature on private higher education. It suggests reasons that the new private higher education, by its distinctive nature, may be linked to the labor market and meet labor market demands through institutional management efforts.

<u>The Distinctive Nature of Private Higher Education</u>

With ample theoretical underpinnings and international comparisons, Levy finds private higher education – while far from always distinctive or distinctive in every important aspect – is often distinctive in key ways. Moreover, his works show how the new private higher education may fill certain special niche in preparing human resources for the labor market because of its distinctive nature (Levy, 1999, 2002c, 2003b, 2004). He analyzes this distinctiveness in respect of several variables, including mission/function, finance, and governance (Levy, 1986a, 1986b, 1987, 1991, 1992). Mission/function is the variable that is most obviously pertinent to the efforts in linking private higher education to the labor market, but finance and governance also fit in pivotal respects. Examining and comparing the differences between the public and private higher education sectors, he argues that the mission of private institutions is usually tuned to specific constituencies more than to diverse, general, and broad ones, as public institutions are; that their student clientele tend to be narrow, selective, and specialized; and that their concentrations or fields of study tend to be more focused. He also observes that private higher education tends to depend on private tuition and sometimes other private financial sources much more than their public counterparts do. This is partly decided by mission and partly by being resource-dependence, and lack of alternatives. In addition, the private sector is found to generally have less state control and often more institutional flexibility than the public sector. In referring to cases like China, South Africa, Mexico, Brazil, Argentina, the United States, as well as many other countries, Levy suggests that the new private higher education is often more oriented to private, business, and labor market (Levy, 2002a, 2002b, 2003a, 2003b, 2004, 2006a).

Among the variables utilized, field of study stands out in these works as a fundamental link of private higher education's orientations to private, business, and labor market demand (Levy 1986: 100-108; 210-215; 259-280). In his analysis of the function of Latin American private higher education, Levy notes: "In fields of study the two sectors show divergent patterns, with the private sector much more oriented toward business-related and especially toward inexpensive fields" (Levy, 1986a: 259). Many other studies in individual countries collaborate the generalizations as they report that most private institutions usually only concentrate on several popular fields of study provision, mainly in term of job prospects (Banya, 2001; Burke and Al-Waked, 1997; Thomas Owen Eisemon, 1992; Giesecke, 1999b; Gulosino, 2003; Huong and Fry, 2002; Kelly, 2001; Mabizela, 2004; Nagy-Darvas and Darvas, 1999; Roane, 2000). The tendency may be particularly stark in the early years of institutional functioning and often seen as clear contrast with the public sector's decreased quality, out-of-dated curricula, and impractical program provision (Levy, 1986a; Kruss, 2004; Mok and Wat, 1998). In China, such private-public contrast in field of study provision is said to be one main reason why some students admitted to secondary-tier public institutions opt instead to attend some rather prestigious private institutions. A few famous employers are reported to recruit graduates mainly from several private institutions instead of from their public counterparts for similar account. [1]

Studies and data generally confirm the existence of the distinctive nature of the new private higher education sector, not only rather generally, but also specifically in regard to these job-related points. For example, a perusal of several country-wide datasets and miscellaneous statistics accumulated by PROPHE on fields of study provided by the sector provision can affirm its distinctiveness. The fields mostly concentrate on several "soft" sciences (e.g. education, social sciences, business, and law), humanities, as well as certain types of technology or engineering. This is especially true in countries whose private higher education sectors are heavily demand-absorbing. [2]

Economic Analysis of Private Educational provision

James brings economic analysis to private education research. Her studies (James, 1987, 1993) about why and how private education meets excess and differentiated demands in developed and developing countries generally confirms what the leading literature says about the private higher education sector on its distinctiveness and demand-absorption. With a comprehensive theoretical model, abundant official data across country and education level, and well-controlled regression analysis, she examines private educational provision against public spending, while considering political coalitions. Her empirical analysis has several conclusions. First, the excess-demand-driven private sector in many countries, such as Japan, Brazil, and Philippines, is a result

---

[1] A group of Chinese doctoral students visiting private institutions (e.g. Guangzhou Baiyun Vocational & Technical College) reported such information in workshops.
[2] For country datasets and miscellaneous statistics about private higher education, please go to http://www.albany.edu/dept/eaps/prophe/data/data.html.

of both public choice of limited public spending and the coalitions of upper-income class'

government control. Second, differentiated private provisions are results of private

choices for product variety and quality, for the reason of geographical dispersion,

uniform or low quality public products, and group preferences. Third, disguised profits,

benefits, and ideology are reasons for entrepreneurial nonprofit private supply. James

(1993) also observes that the higher stake the education is—such as for access to jobs, the

more likely the private parties will have interest to invest.

Although more rigorous investigation remains needed at the higher education level,

the soundness of the model and the validity of different data sources of James's economic

analysis make it reasonable to expect that private higher educational provision may also

meet labor market demands while being demand-absorbing, which is further confirmed

by some publications on private higher education. Lacking public financing and failing to

meet the quality and quantity of industrial workforce needs in the public sector are often

cited as reasons for the growth of the new private higher education sector in general

(Bollag, 1999; Levy, 1992, 2003a, 2006a; Wolff and Castro, 2001) and in some specific

countries (Catterall and McGhee, 1996; Dima, 1998; Gulosino, 2003; Hopper, 1998;

Kwong, 1997; Nagy-Darvas, 1997; Sharvashidze, 2002). For example, in China, the

limited public spending and advantageous groups' preference to a small public sector

resulted in the appearance of demand-absorbing private sector at the early 1980s. And

some private institutions seem to have been entrepreneurial enough to take up those fields

with excess labor demands than the public sector can provide and fill in profitable areas

that the public sector has neglected, as some scholars suggest (Ke, 2001; Liu, 2002; Mok,

1997b).

The New Demand-Absorbing Private Higher Education

Absorbing excess higher education demand and meeting labor market demands are often mentioned in literature about the new private higher education.

The New Private Higher Education in Absorbing Excess Higher Education Demands

The dominant role of the new private higher education sector is often described as meeting excess higher education demands in many countries (Castro and Navarro, 1999; Galbraith, 2003; Kwong, 1997; Levy, 2006a; Mabizela, 2004). The private sector in these countries mostly fits the demand-absorbing (non-elite) type as classified by Levy (1986a) in his "three wave" analysis of private growth. Levy examined the revolution of private higher education development, with intensive case studies in three Latin American countries, Mexico, Brazil, and Chile. He found that regionally the Wave III demand-absorbing non-elite private institutions tend to appear and grow after Wave I Catholic/Religious and Wave II Elite private institutions, which were established to meet differentiated cultural or religious demand and demand for better quality or status, respectively (Levy, 1986a:27). [1] The demand-absorbing private institutions fill in a gap of accommodating excess demand left unfilled by the public, though also by the private religious and elite sub-sectors (Levy, 1986a: 60). His further works suggest that institutions established basically through demand-absorbing may also take certain religious and semi-elite elements (Levy, 1986a: 59-65, 2002b). [2]

---

[1] He also notes that is "three wave" classification is "easier to apply to the causes of growth than to the institutional characteristics that have ensured" (Levy, 1986a: 61).

[2] Demand-absorbing private growth has salient occurrences in Africa, Asia, Central and Eastern Europe, and Latin America (Burke and Al-Waked, 1997; Catterall and McGhee, 1996; Duczmal, 2005; Thomas Eisemon,

In China, the demand-absorbing nature of the private higher education sector is paramount. The establishment of various types of private institutions is often seen as the private sector's reaction to perceived "public failure" of meeting extraordinarily increased demands for higher education from a growing population of secondary education graduates and an accelerated economic growth (Cao and Levy, 2005; Kwong, 1997; Liu, 2002; Mok, 1997a). For high school graduates, private higher education is usually regarded as "the second" choice, an alternative when they cannot be admitted by the public sector (Wang and Secombe, 2004). The most obvious evidence is that the private higher education sector as a whole has enrolled a less academically competent population, although some of the best accredited private institutions are said to have attracted a certain number of academically well-prepared students. [1]

The New Private Higher Education in Meeting Labor Market Demand

Along with exemplified efforts, private higher education literature suggests that the demand-absorbing private institutions may do more than merely grasp excess higher education demand through meeting labor market demands. Although many non-scholarly and scholarly-limited studies document the demand-absorbing private institutions as being of low quality and only self-interested, the literature indicates that serious, different, and even better job preparation may be found in some of these institutions. This may just be one of the most salient characteristics of the new private higher education

---

1992; Giesecke, 1999b; Hopper, 1998; Huong and Fry, 2002; Jalowiecki, 2001; Kolasinski, Kulig, and Lisiecki, 2003; Nagy-Darvas, 1997; Nicolescu, 2002, 2005; Stetar and Berezkina, 2002).

[1] It is reported that certain programs in Xi'an Translation College have enrolled students who have higher entrance scores than many of their public counterparts. See "Upgraded Private Higher Education Institution Having Three Types of Programs: Abnormal or Innovation" (in Chinese, Minban gaoxiao shengben bian santiaotui zoulu, Jixing haishi chuangxin). Source: Sohu.com, 6/28/2005, re-posted at http://www.mb-edu.com.cn/2005-6/2005628102704.htm, accessed 7/12/2005.

sector in many individual countries (Bollag, 1999; Caplánová, 2003; Cohen, 2001; Fehnel, 2001; Giesecke, 1999b; Kelly, 2001; Mok and Wat, 1998; Sharvashidze, 2002; Sperling, 2000). Niche fields, practical and updated courses, and timing career services are cited as main institutional efforts that may have contributed to such job preparation (Cohen, 2001, 2003; Giesecke, 1999b; Kwong, 1997; Levy, 2003b; Mok, 1997a; Sharvashidze, 2002; Stetar and Berezkina, 2002; Pritchard, 1992). Even more specifically in relation to the concerns of this study, some studies find that the new private institutions may make major management efforts to build relationships with employers or scan labor market demands, in order to link private higher education to industry needs and to facilitate graduate employment. For example, the for-profit two-year institutions in the United States are said to "work assiduously" on building relationships with employers to facilitate graduate job placement, whereas community colleges rely on their public and accreditation status in their communications with employers (Deil-Amen and Rosenbaum, 2004). Furthermore, for the new private higher education sector in the US as well as in other countries, experts on the new private higher education regard such relationship-building and job-preparation as important sources towards legitimacy (Kinser, 2007; Kinser and Levy, 2005; Slantcheva and Levy, 2007; Suspitsin, 2007).

In a series reported by the most circulated official education newspaper, *China Education Daily*, administrators of four private colleges assert that serious institutional efforts have been made in linking private higher education to the labor market. They sketched how their institutions have managed to maintain high and even higher employment rates than their public counterparts. The management efforts they quoted include: establishing special committees working on labor market surveys and field of study provision, arranging employment services at the institutional level and program sites, hiring and inviting employment professionals, contacting employers for course and program advices and employment contacts, collecting and disseminating job vacancy information, building a network of co-operate bases, and even setting-up Labor and Talent Exchange Markets on campus. While most strategies are also seen in the public sector, some of the practices are seldom seen or unheard in China's public colleges, such as establishing Labor and Talent Exchange Market on campus. [1]

In reading the sketchy reports about Chinese private higher education, one may wonder: Have the mentioned institutions really done what the administrators report? What specific structures, policies, and activities are utilized in each listed effort? What patterns can be generalized about such efforts in the private sector? How likely have the efforts actually contributed to employment outcomes? However, such questions cannot be adequately answered by existing publications. Even when institutional efforts are mentioned, most publications merely list or allude to the efforts, or they have a limited thematic range by focusing on only one type. The patterns of such efforts and the associations between various efforts and employment outcomes in the private sector are still left unrevealed. Therefore, this study aims to fill that gap.

The review of private higher education literature points out important directions for filling in the gap. It suggests that the new private higher education may be linked to meet labor market demands through various institutional efforts, given its distinctive nature in mission/function, finance, governance, etc. A salient link involves fields of study. Other links may be through institutional services and connections. Of course, the demand-

---

[1] See the series in *China Daily*, 8/11/2003, p.4, as previously noted.

absorption and the job focus are often heavily intertwined, as the latter can be very instrumental in attracting students interested in higher education.

Review of the Literature on Higher Education and the Labor Market

This section reviews literature on higher education and the labor market around three topics: First, dimensions that higher education institutions can approach the labor market from; Second, elements and practices that institutions can grapple with in linking private higher education to the labor market and in influencing employment outcomes; Third, initial outcomes of graduates in the labor market that institutions might influence.

Approaches to Institutional Management Efforts from Two Dimensions

With scientific research designs, considerable data, quantitative analysis, and analytic logic, dozens of empirical studies and analyses of higher education and the labor market in Europe and Japan conclude that the relationship between higher education and the labor market has three dimensions: the relevance of higher education to work, the linkage between higher education and work, and the relevance of work to higher education. These studies note that higher education institutions can actively or proactively manage the relationship from the first two dimensions while the third dimension mainly defers to employers' initiatives (Brennan, 2004; Brennan, Johnston, Little, Shah, and Woodley, 2001; Brennan, Kogan, and Teichler, 1996; Little, 2001; Paul, Teichler, and Van Der Velden, 2000; Teichler, 1989, 1994, 1995, 1996, 2002, 2003).

Dimension#1 – the relevance of higher education to work emphasizes labor market demand factors related to quantitative and structural education development, curricular, training and socialization, as well as educational provisions and services (Brennan, Kogan, and Teichler, 1996: 2). On this dimension, scholars find that institutions can manage to improve high education's contribution to graduate employability. They can do so by improving job-related knowledge, skills, abilities, and personality presentation through curricula and services, and by selecting appropriate students for future jobs through differentiated types of education and fields of study (Little, 2001: 123-125).

Dimension#2 – the linkage between higher education and work emphasizes bridging employers and graduates and eliminating the information asymmetry between them. On this dimension, institutions can manage to facilitate the transition of graduates from college to the labor market, by coaching students for job-hunting, networking for job opportunities and identifying obstacles, cooperating with intermediary agencies and public transitional services, lobbying for a favorable regulatory system, and providing lifelong education to workers (Brennan, Kogan, and Teichler, 1996; Little, 2001).

Accordingly, in managing the relationship between higher education and the labor market, institutions may accomplish relevant tasks mainly through two approaches: enhancing graduate employability (mainly via program and curriculum provision), as revealed by dimension #1; and bridging employers and graduates (mainly via career services and networking), as revealed in dimension #2. Of course, the managed specific elements and practices among institutions may vary.

Three Major Types of Institutional Management Efforts

Systematic and comprehensive analysis of various management practices at the institutional level is scanty. Most studies on the relationship between higher education and the labor market address only macro labor market demand and graduate supply, patterns of transition from college to the labor market, as well as employment outcomes (Schomburg, 2000). Even though studies focus on management practices exist, most of them only examine one type of management efforts and analyze the effects of the particular efforts at the individual level. In other words, existing research has limited thematic scopes. Study that can reveal the patterns of institutional management practices is still lacking. Nevertheless, albeit subject to further investigation, three major types of institutional practices are found to be associated with graduate employment outcomes: educational/field of study provision, career services, and networking.

Educational/Field of Study Provision

Of educational provision, field of study is particularly important, in the sense of building academic knowledge. The longitudinal studies of Statistics Canada (Finnie, 1998, 1999a, 1999c) find that field of study consistently affects graduates' early employment (from two to five years after graduation) in terms of earnings, employment status, job-field match, and job satisfaction. Other studies confirm the importance of field of study in determining employment outcomes (Bryant, 2001; Schomburg, 2000; OECD, 1992). Two major reasons are adopted to explain the consistent employment differences across fields of study. Structure differences in labor market demand or supply are said to be the main reason: quantitatively variations of labor market demand or supply affects short-term differences; compensation differentials characterize different sectors and industries; and general scarcity of skills exists in certain market (Finnie, 1998, 1999a, 1999c). On the other hand, institutionally managed constraints, such as admission, examinations, and certifications, create fields (e.g. law, accounting, and medicine) with limited qualified graduates, which functionally improve the employment condition of qualified graduates but deter the employment of unqualified ones (Aamodt and Arnesen, 1995).

In improving graduate employability, what skills are to be developed through educational provision is one of the most debated and studied (Brennan, 2000, 2004). Many studies focus on generic or core skills that are deemed to be sustainable, transferable, and required by workplace (Bennett, Dunne, and Carré, 1999; Business/Higher Education Round, 2002; Clanchy and Ballard, 1995; Tait and Godfrey, 1999). Most such studies broadly agree that some general courses should build student generic skills, such as basic literacy and numeric skills, conceptual thinking skills, interpersonal communication skills, teamwork skills, good personal characteristics and attributes, and skills towards community and citizenship (National Centre for Vocational Education Research, 2003). Some argue that such skills are more effectively delivered through disciplinary courses than the general study courses (De La Harpe, Radloff, and Wyber, 2000). However, a well-sustained empirical study shows that a broader curriculum with focus on generic skills does not seem to be more rewarded by the employers in the UK (Dolton and Vignoles, 2002). More recently, professional skills (Coimbra Group of Universities, 2006), practical skills, information technological skills, and competency in foreign languages gain special attention (Akoojee, 2003; Fuller and Unwin, 2003; Team of Economic Research Foundation of Turkey, 2007).

Institutions are said to manage educational provisions in responses to the changing labor market differences and institutionalized constraints through: 1) adjusting existing curricula and programs as well as creating new specializations and degrees with labor

market information and graduate employment feedback (de la Fuente, 1995); 2)

prioritizing employer needs and interests in program and course adjustment to labor

market demand (de la Fuente, 1995); 3) optimizing institutional mission to cater to

student choice and advise students on their choices of programs and curricula; and 4)

breaking the constraints by serving students in admission, examinations, and

certifications (Brennan, Kogan, and Teichler, 1996; Maoscati and Rostan, 2000; OECD,

1992; Paul and Murdoch, 2000; Paul, Teichler, and Van Der Velden, 2000; Teichler,

1989).

Career Services

Career services have become a vital type of institutional efforts in bridging

graduates and employers during graduates' transition from colleges to the labor market,

as observed in many countries. Although the specific elements of career services and

their functions still need systematic and comprehensive research, various career-oriented

or employment-oriented services are mentioned in works on higher education and the

labor market. They are found to affect graduate employment in employment status, job

search length, the nature of employed job, and job satisfaction (Chesler, 1995; McGrath,

2002) .

Three types of career services are reported to influence graduate employment,

ranging from career advices to job placement (McGrath, 2002). The major type of such

services is career counseling, which includes career planning assessment and assistance

in job searching, such as resume and cover letter writing, interview guidance, and job fairs arrangement. Also important is pre-employment work experience or opportunity provision by institutions, which includes experiences and opportunities in apprenticeships, internships, field experience, and volunteer work. Finally, job placement closely relates to graduate employment. Elements of job placement are specified as gathering information about job vacancies, dissemination of employment information, nominations and recommendations of job positions (Rosenbaum, Kariya, Settersten, and Maier, 1990). It also includes the institutionalization of graduate employment contacts between companies and higher education institutions (Paul and Murdoch, 2000). Chesler's (1995) survey in the US found that jobs through institutional career services paid graduates more at the start, continued to pay more after acquiring experiences in the job, and appeared to provide opportunities for careers.

Networking

Like other markets, the graduate labor market is not perfect because of information dissymmetry and other reasons. Networking or institutional linkages are intended to help graduate employment by increasing information dissemination and building trust between graduates and employers. Networking, at both individual and institutional level, is shown as an important factor affecting graduate employment in both industrialized countries (Rosenbaum, Kariya, Settersten, and Maier, 1990; Villar, Juan, Corominas, and Capell, 2000) as well as less-developed countries, particularly in China (Agelasto, 1996). At the *individual level*, relatives and other social ties can serve as intermediaries in job search and entry (Villar, Juan, Corominas, and Capell, 2000). Notably, department faculty's networking efforts with potential employers is found to consistently result in most of institutional effects on employment outcomes, in terms of chance of being unemployed for less than 3 months, chance of acquiring a job which matches the educational level attained, and gross monthly wages (Bosker, Velden, and Loo, 2001). Individual networking may work well in trust-embedded government jobs (Brown and Scase, 1994) and in medium and small-size firms with hidden jobs (Kivinen and Ahola, 1995). At the *institutional level*, institutionalized liaisons are found to affect graduate employment. Research indicates that employers are more likely to hire from institutions where they have stronger connection (The Institute for Research on Higher Education, 1998). Various rapprochements, agreements, partnerships (for teaching, program revision, student practicum, or job placement) between institutions and employers can facilitate graduates' transition from colleges to the labor market (de la Fuente, 1995), often through job information distribution, employers' instruction resources and field exercise opportunities, and job recommendations (Rosenbaum, Kariya, Settersten, and Maier, 1990: 287-288). Government efforts can also be utilized to build school-employer partnerships, in which government offices provide liaisons among relevant parties, in addition to providing counseling and placement, apprenticeships, training, and examinations, as having taken place in Great Britain and the former Western Germany (Rosenbaum, Kariya, Settersten, and Maier, 1990: 285-287).

All in all, educational/field of study provision, career services, and networking are the three major types of efforts that higher education institutions have made in meeting labor market demands and enhancing the relationship between higher education and the labor market. Exploring the three types and disclosing their specific elements are thus the main foci of the study's research design and thereafter data analysis.

Indicators and Patterns of Graduate Employment Outcomes

Graduate employment patterns are usually the major focus of most empirical publications on higher education and the labor market. Being common and relatively-easy-to-collect (Brennan, 2000: 20), they are often sought after for comparisons across disciplines, institutions, and countries. The most-often agreed upon indicators include employment rate, earnings, job-education match, and job satisfaction.

Common Indicators of Employment Outcomes

Among the several often used indicators, employment rate is the only one that has been used solely in distinguishing one institution and one field from another. For instance, *Indicators of Employment* analyzes the first destinations of UK students graduating in the 1999-2000 academic year. It calculates both actual and benchmark values for employment rate. These values are then used to compare the performance of all the institutions surveyed in graduate employment as a whole and in that of different fields (HEFCE, 2001).

Brennan (2000: 19-20) discussed methodological problems and issues regarding comparing higher education supply with employers' demand as well as comparing the current situation in UK with its past as well as with that in US and other European countries. As a result, he defines graduate employment indicators along two dimensions: obtaining a job and preparing for a job. The variables he listed include: speed into employment, earnings, job and occupation level, job and education match, and self-perception of knowledge/skill.

Though with little theory or supporting data, Koskinen (2005) picks out employment status, earnings, occupation level, job-education match, and job satisfaction. He summarizes the advantages and shortcomings of having them as indicators. He argues: employment placement should be included because it is not self-evident; salary (earnings) is the obvious sign of the success of job placement, though the connection between earnings and jobs is not always straightforward; occupation levels can be one indicator for its strength in comparing one graduate's position in occupation hierarchy against others', though occupations are changing and often too general; work and education correspondence should be defined from the perspective of degree level, discipline, and skills and knowledge; and job satisfaction is a mixed perception of job challenges, self-competency, and future job and education advancement.

In brief, employment status, earnings, job-education match, and job satisfaction are the most commonly used indicators of graduate employment outcomes. They figure prominently into this study for China in its research design and analysis.

Patterns of Graduate Employment Outcomes

Relevant statistics and analysis on initial employment outcomes are very often reported. Nevertheless, longitudinal research does exist and has the advantages of revealing information with depth. Some of the longitudinal studies suggest certain consistency among some short-term and long-term employment outcomes, such as employment rate and earning levels. For example, Silver, Lavallée, and Pereboom's (1999) analysis of the National Graduate Survey in Canada of three cohorts two and five years after graduation has four important findings in this regard. First, it finds that the employment among university graduates, and, increasingly, among college graduates, are consistently stable and at high levels for 1990 graduates in both two years and fives years after graduation. Second, being male and having more education are the two factors consistently having positive association with employment among the three studied cohorts: 1982, 1986, and 1990. Third, obtaining employment soon after graduation and remaining employed is found to be associated with higher earnings than obtaining employment only after some time lag. Fourth, those who find early success in the labor market following completion of post-secondary studies are more likely than others to remain with the initial employer and to achieve higher earning levels over the post-graduation period. These findings suggest surprisingly high consistency in near-term and long-term employment patterns. Thus, with an emphasis on describing initial employment outcomes, this sub-section synthesizes general patterns of graduate employment outcomes around the above-mentioned common indicators.

College graduates are found to be more likely to be employed and less likely to experience long-term unemployment than people with less education, though actual status may vary (Boesel and Fredland, 1999; Brennan, 2000; OECD, 1992; Teichler, 1989, 2002). Institutional differences in employment rate may mainly be due to field of study and level of education differences (Teichler, 1989). Statistics shows that the higher the degree, the more likely the graduates will be employed in good or bad time and across countries (Haapakorpi, 1995; Smyth, Gangl, Raffe, Hannan, and McCoy, 2001; Vincens, 1995). Employment status is highly related to field of study (Teichler, 1989). In time of higher education expansion, although the transition from higher education to the labor market tends to last longer (Brennan, 2000: 1) and the unemployment rate is increasing

(Vincens, 1995) , college graduates are less likely to be unemployed than other groups (Haapakorpi, 1995). Finnie's (1998, 1999a, 1999b, 1999c, 2000) longitudinal study in Canada finds that unemployment rates were quite low for all college graduates, lower (and considerably lower than the non-postsecondary graduates) and tended to be lowest at the more advanced degree and certain disciplines through three college-cohorts in the 1980s and 1990s.

With strong evidence, college graduates are found likely to earn substantially more than people with less education, though actual earnings may vary (Boesel and Fredland, 1999; Brennan, 2000; OECD, 1992; Teichler, 2002). College location (Paul and Murdoch, 2000), field of study, and degree level (Finnie, 1998, 1999a, 1999c, 2000) are reported to be three important determinants of earnings. Moreover, James's economic analysis of the US case finds that fields and courses explain more of the variations in earnings than institutional characteristics, ability, and family background combined (James, 1989) can. In addition, based on cohort data of 11 European Countries, Brunello and Comi (2004 419) find that earnings grow with experience significantly faster for the more educated, and grow faster in the countries with higher productivity. Even in time of higher education expansion, graduates may not endure much harm in terms of earnings (Vincens, 1995). Across three cohorts of the class of 1980, 1986, and 1990, earning levels are consistently different among disciplines (Finnie, 1998), higher at the more advanced degrees, increase substantially in the early five years or so in the labor market, and then either hold steadily or show some decline (Finnie, 1999b: 41).

The majority of college graduates are likely to be employed in jobs corresponding to their education though actual degree of correspondences of job may vary with degree level, disciplines, and courses taken (Brennan, 2000; Teichler, 1989). Fiorito's (1981) examines of the US case with national data and comprehensive labor supply and demand model. He finds that major is a crucial factor in determining occupation and education match along degree level. Despite numerous claims about over-education and underemployment (Chevalier, 2001; Dolton and Silles, 2001; OECD, 1992; Rubb, 2003; Rumberger, 1981; Wielers and Glebbeek, 1995), Gottschalk and Hansen (2003) find that the number of college graduates in non-college jobs declined from the mid-1980s to the mid-1990s in the US. They conclude that the aggregated proportion of such graduates may not necessarily increase, but can even decrease, because skill-biased technology changes. Citing others, Teichler argues that overeducation claims may neglect the possibility that the previous non-college jobs may be more suitable for college graduates (Teichler, 1989: 234).

College graduates are likely to experience high level of job satisfaction for the challenges and opportunities that their jobs have (HEFCE, 2000). Job satisfaction is often included in graduate surveys as an overall subjective assessment of graduate employment (Sapatoru, Nicolescu, and Slantcheva, 2003; Teichler, 2002), though it is less analyzed in depth than other indicators in empirical studies. Nevertheless, it is said that students who get their jobs through institutional networking are more likely to be satisfied (Bosker, Velden, and Loo, 2001; Villar, Juan, Corominas, and Capell, 2000).

By and large, as criticized by (Schomburg, 2000: 196), existing studies on higher education and the labor market often only focus on certain quantitative aspects of graduate supply and demand, employment outcomes, and major factors affecting outcomes. Little research has been done on management practices at the institutional level and with qualitative approaches. Research on institutional practices or the associations between such practices and employment outcomes seldom has depth and breadth. The structures, policies, and activities of various institutional practices are still mostly ill-informed, although some new efforts are undertaken in many European countries (Directorate for European and International Relations and Cooperation, 2006). Consequently, a large and important lacuna is left in exploring the patterns and elements of institutional efforts in linking higher education and the labor market.

Empirical Studies on Private Higher Education and the Labor Market

This section reviews empirical studies on private higher education and the labor market. According to their research topics, it classifies relevant studies into three types: institutional management efforts, graduate employment outcomes, and the combination of the two. As already noted, the research on private higher education and the labor market is, overall, very limited.

Institutional Management Efforts in the Private Sector

As reviewed in the previous section, research on institutional management efforts with regard to graduate employment at the institutional level is scanty, and concentrates even less on that of the private sector. The only known published study focusing on institutional management efforts for graduate employment in the private higher education sector is Yoshimoto and Yonezawa's (1994) study in Japan. With scientific research design, they surveyed the employment guidance and equivalent organizations in all universities and compared institutional job placement efforts in private and public institutions. [1] Their study finds that only private universities have school job placement divisions and good employment guidance activities. Job placement and employment guidance facilitates private university graduates in getting jobs from large companies. The school job placement division of private universities thus becomes the third most important route to employment in addition to the two traditional routes: free application and school laboratory/faculty's recommendation.

Employment Outcomes of Private College Graduates

Compared to studies on institutional management efforts, more studies exist on the employment outcomes of higher education institutions, even private ones, in both developed and developing countries. This juxtaposition is particularly important in regard to this dissertation, which prioritizes institutional management efforts. McMahon and Wagner's (1976, 1982) extensive studies in the US are among the few well-known studies that specifically identify private institutions. They compared rates of return across institutions with a sample of 2,776 freshmen. Their carefully-controlled work shows that the perceived and actual rates of return of private college graduates are generally higher than their counterparts, but private liberal art college graduates do not fare as well as community colleges and junior colleges where technical courses yield high return. Their findings about rates of return of private institutions are confirmed by Monks's (2000) analysis of 734 samples from the National Longitudinal Survey of Youth. On the other hand, the private and public higher education sectors in the US notably blur (Levy,

---

[1] Private institutions in Japan are considered inferior to public ones academically, though some private ones lead certain public ones.

1986b; Miller, 2000). Its private and public distinction is generally not nearly as salient as it is seen in most other countries. So the studies cited in this paragraph do not have the same sort of private and public distinction that will characterize the studies on China.

Although the best ranked private institutions may perform better than their public counterparts, [1] studies in Central and Eastern European's transitional countries have not had enough evidence to confirm what has been found in developed countries, but findings are emerging. They suggest that private higher education may be as good as their public counterparts in employment, if not better. Sapatoru, Nicolescu, and Slantcheva's (2003) study on Romania and Bulgaria is the only known systematically conducted research about the new private college graduates. [2] They secured reasonably large national samples of students and graduates in Romania (210 students) and Bulgaria (1,457 students) in 2001. They analyzed several employment outcomes: employment rate six months after graduation, type of contract, earnings, job and education match. After controlling variables related to personal characteristics, academic performance, and field of study, they found no significant difference between private and public college graduates in employment rate, earnings, job-field match, or type of contract. [3] These findings are startling because this is a region where the better perceived and academically best institutions are public, and private higher education is only recent.

Moreover, given the new private higher education is often regarded as the "second choice" by high school graduates (Nicolescu, 2007) and is perceived negatively as "low

---

[1] For example, Sharvashidze (2002) reported that the average job placement rate immediately after graduation in five highly-ranked private higher education institutions in Georgia is several times higher than that of the highest job placement rate reported for state higher education institutions, 86% v. 26%.
[2] The Bulgaria case is one in which there are not numerous tiny private higher education institutions, but the Romania case is one where there are and, in particular, were in the early 1990s.
[3] But descriptive statistics show slightly more private college graduates are unemployed and have manual jobs, though not statistically significant. The difference in employment rate between private college graduates and public ones is 3 percent; and that in manual jobs is 6 percent.

quality" by the general public and the business community (Nicolescu, 2003), it is interesting to see three important findings to the advantages of the private sector. First, when comparing to public college graduates, the individual probability of being employed for private college graduates is significantly higher (one half to two thirds, said to depend on specification of explanatory variables). Second, private college graduates have significant fewer limited-period contracts (7%). Lastly, they also have slightly higher level of job-degree match. [1] The three findings thus refute arguments about private college graduates' willingness to take jobs without necessary match with their education or reasonable contracts. In explanation, the authors revert to unobserved characteristics, such as proactive spirit, entrepreneurship, and networking, which are found to be rewarded in job hunting. Some of the factors are not directly about institutional management but others are. Also, it is possible that some aspects of institutional management tend to attract certain kinds of students.

However, one of few published studies in China (Wu, 2003), seems to produce a different picture for the new demand-absorbing private institutions. It suggests that private college graduates may have far inferior initial employment outcomes than their public counterparts. With a sample of 953 students of three private junior colleges and 847 students of four public junior colleges in three provinces shortly before graduation, Wu (2003) found that private college graduates have much worse employment outcomes than their public counterparts do. They are less likely to get job offers upon graduating (33% v. 67%); they have to try harder through more job applications before getting offers (5.05 v 4.40 applications per job offer); they have significantly lower levels of job-field

---

[1] Controlled variables includes type of high school, field of study, academic performance, gender, marital status, residence and parental education, usual monthly hours of work on the main job, and firm ownership, size, industry, and existence before 1990.

match; and their starting salary is significantly lower than their public counterparts ($150 v. $180). Similarly, they have significantly lower job expectations in starting salary, job-field match, and type of employment. Additionally and directly related to our concerns about institutional management efforts, Wu found that private institutions provide far less internships for their students than public institutions do (14% v. 50%). Also, fewer private college graduates get job offers through school job placement divisions or school-provided job vacancy information (40% v. 56%). [1]

Bao (2005, 2006b) examines the function of the new demand-absorbing private higher education in China from the perspective of graduates' employment labor market. With 1624 valid graduate samples from six "key" and ordinary public institutions, two affiliated private colleges, four accredited private colleges, and six unaccredited private colleges, her study suggests that graduates from accredited vocational and unaccredited private colleges are more likely to be employed in newly established but disadvantageous "city-but-free-contract labor markets" and "non-city labor markets", than graduates from public colleges, affiliated private colleges, and regular private colleges who are mostly employed in "city-but-institutionally-contracted" market. Using multinomial logistic analysis, it also finds that: within private college graduates (total 430 samples, including 103 graduates from private affiliated colleges), those students graduated from unaccredited colleges, having lower family/parental income, but higher preference and aptitude towards practical knowledge and skills are more likely to enter the new labor market than those from accredited or public colleges, who have higher family/parental income, but lower preference and aptitude towards knowledge and skills. The study also

---

[1] The study uses employers' negative perception of private higher education and unwillingness to disseminate vacancies in private colleges to explain the phenomena.

examines the characteristics of private higher education in educational provisions. It finds that the characteristics of regular private colleges are similar to those of public colleges, but the characteristics of accredited vocational and unaccredited private colleges are different from those of public college. The accredited non-vocational and unaccredited private colleges emphasize practical contents in their educational provisions, using low tuition and seeking new admission market. Her studies also find that the students in private colleges are more oriented towards skills and careers. Nevertheless, although Bao's study reveals major facts about the private higher education sector against the public one in regard to the labor market and student characteristics, the selected private institutions are not comparable to the selected public ones and their graduates are not comparable to graduates of the selected graduates of the public institutions. Of course, her studies do not aim at it or claim so, nor does it reveal findings on major employment outcomes.

Nevertheless, while Bao's studies does not support or refute what other studies have found on initial employment outcomes of private college graduates, Wu's study on China, presenting a picture different from others, may be questioned and much less reliable than Sapatoru, Nicolescu, and Slantcheva's (2003) study on Romania and Bulgaria. First, her sampling of graduating seniors in three private colleges of a big country like China is much less likely to reveal employment outcomes than sampling of alumni with large samples, as Sapatoru, Nicolescu, and Slantcheva's (2003) study does. [1] Besides, Wu's survey of on-campus seniors a couple of months before graduation neglected institutional arrangement differences between public and private institutions:

---

[1] The sample in Bulgaria is especially large, given that it only had 4 private universities (24,898 students) and 6 private colleges (2,516 students) at the time of survey (Slantcheva, 2001).

public institutions generally require their seniors to be on campus after they receive job offers while the private ones permit, encourage, even ask such students to get apprenticeships somewhere else. Likewise, her analysis of employment outcomes uses only descriptive statistics or simple regressions and does not control many variables as the Bulgaria and Romania study does. On the other hand, Wu's study claims that there are very strong private and public differences in employment outcomes, all favoring the public side, whereas Sapatoru, Nicolescu, and Slantcheva (2003) find much more private and public parity but with certain private advantages. Moreover, as will be reported in the next subsection, the findings of two other unpublished studies in China (Cao, 2000; Zhou, 2003) reinforce the doubts about Wu's study. In short, this research is pursued for lack of disagreements and pertinent studies on employment outcomes of private college graduates.

Management Practices and Initial Employment Outcomes in the Private Sector

Both Cao (2000) and Zhou (2003) have studied Chinese private colleges and dealt heavily with institutional management efforts, in addition to initial employment outcomes. Their findings about initial employment outcomes are closer to the favorable ones reported by Sapatoru, Nicolescu, and Slantcheva (2003) on Bulgaria and Romania, than to the unfavorable ones of Wu on China. Moreover, their findings about institutional management efforts are close to the findings of the Japanese study.

With complementary analysis of institutional marketing strategies, Cao's study focuses on initial employment outcomes. Compared to statistics reported by studies about the public sector, [1] it concludes that the overall employment of private college graduates is as good as that of their public counterparts. She surveyed alumni (112 samples, return rate 31.4%) in four private colleges and found only a small percentage of graduates are either unemployed six months after graduation (15%), [2] or dissatisfied with their jobs (7.2%), or employed in field-mismatched jobs (18.1%). Similarly, private college graduates also perceive themselves to be as good as their public counterparts in labor market competition, salary, and job advancement. Its analysis of four administrator interviews and relevant documents reveals that private institutions respond to market changes and orient graduates to employers through activities such as market scanning and niche specification, program changes and curricular revision, graduate job placement, and connections with employers.

Yet key weaknesses hamper Cao's study. First of all, her sampling of colleges is not representative. Convenient sampling was used in which three of the surveyed colleges were located in cities within a single province. While one of the four colleges surveyed was located in a rural area, 99 percent of the private institutions are located in urban areas. In terms of institutional type, the sampling is dominated by accredited institutions [3] and the only accredited bachelor-degree-granting college then is selected. Second, its graduate sampling was not consistently executed among institutions. In one institution, graduates (1997, 1998, and 1999) were sampled and the questionnaire was distributed by the institution with the president's signed cover letter, following the paper instruction on

---

[1] The study refers to "public counterparts" as public colleges/graduates of similar programs to the privates.
[2] But almost all graduates are employed within 6 month after beginning their job search. Given that some private college students have to take self-study examinations to get their degrees and thus must postpone their job search, time used for job search seems to be more reliable. And Schomburg and Teichler (2005) also regard duration of the job search as more reliable for comparison than employment rate upon graduation.
[3] One selected Type III institution was accredited shortly after Cao's survey.

51

stratified sampling method. Graduate employment outcomes of this college are found to be more favorable than those of the other three institutions, where only 1999's graduates were surveyed and stratified sampling method was strictly followed. Third, it lacks solid research design and analysis. Its comparison of public and private college graduate employment is weak and mainly based on subjective perception. Its analysis mainly uses simple statistics techniques and does not control various variables. Moreover, although it analyzes institutional marketing strategies and tries to associate them with employment outcomes, the analysis was mostly based on superficial newspaper reports, with little fieldwork and only a few interviews.

Zhou's (2003) study has even more encouraging findings about institutional efforts and initial employment outcomes in the private sector than Cao's study, though mainly based on institutionally provided information. The information provided during interviews of administrators of two private colleges and a comparable public college in the study shows that private college graduates have higher starting salaries than their public counterparts do. They also have higher employment rates upon graduation in three consecutive years (2000, 2001, and 2002). The analysis of 533 senior students before graduation from the three colleges surveyed finds that private college students have participated in more practices and are more satisfied with college career services than their public counterparts. With information from fieldwork, the study suggests that private colleges endeavor to update curricula and set-up unique programs, provide more internships and other practice opportunities than the surveyed public college. They have more stable institutionalized structure and activities for student career services.

Nevertheless, Zhou's (2003) study also has several major limitations. First, the survey of seniors was done several months before graduations, when most students did not have job offers yet. Thus, little data about graduate employment outcomes are generated by the study. Second, the analysis of graduate employment outcome and institutional management practices uses only sketchy description and descriptive statistics and the findings are weak. Third, the study only conveniently uses institutionally-reported employment rate, graduate starting salary, and institutional management practices, which makes its findings vulnerable because the validity of the information sources is questionable. [1] Above all, its analysis of institutional management efforts lacks depth. It does not overcome the usual shortcomings of listing practices that most news reports and non-scholarly publications do. Also related to the limited sampling of institutions is that the analysis of institutional management efforts lack breadth. The patterns of various management efforts in different private institutions cannot be ascertained.

To conclude, even though public institutions remain the perceived leading institutions, often get better students, and certainly get the overwhelming majority of the best students, the findings of the reviewed studies on private higher education and the labor market suggest: private college graduates do not necessarily fare worse than their public counterparts in the labor market, assuming initial academic standing and certain non-institutional variables are controlled and various indicators of employment outcomes are considered. On balance, the new private higher education institutions may make more

---

[1] Students and graduates of private colleges told journalists that their colleges have cheated initial employment rates and exaggerated what they have done in facilitating graduates to the labor market (see Duan Chaohua and Yan Lina, Minban Higher Education Institutions: Where is the Future for Their Graduates. Online at http://www.sina.com.cn 2003/08/21).

efforts in job placement than their public counterparts, which have a favorable public image on their behalf. However, the scope and reliability of the studies on private higher education and the labor market remain extremely limited, compared to the importance of the subject matter, especially as private higher education continues to grow so much in China and globally.

Synthesis of the Literature Review

This chapter reviews two strands of literature – literature on private higher education and on higher education and the labor market. It reveals that both have strengths and shortcomings for a study on the relationship between private higher education and the labor market. The literature on private higher education has the strength of providing possible explanations from the distinctive nature in institutional mission, function, finance, and governance. It suggests that the new private higher education in general and Chinese private higher education in particular may be linked reasonably well to labor market demands; institutional management efforts for the linking may be formidable. However, except for a few studies, very little private higher education research has been done on labor market related issues outside the United States. This lack is even more acute if we focus on institutional management. Nor is any account available in private higher education literature about the relationship between institutional management practices and initial graduate employment outcomes, though we might have thought that the private higher education literature in particular would have dealt with management. On the other hand, the latter seldom focuses on private higher education. Even though several studies do, they have generally studied private higher education as they have studied public higher education. In other words, they use the same methodology and analysis for both private and public sector without identifying the basic private higher education characteristics and the sector's distinctiveness in mission, function, finance, governance, etc. Without considering the distinctiveness, they have not studied private higher education institutions as private ones, but just taken some institutions that happen to be private and studied some topics that just happen to take place in institutions with private judicial status. Fortunately, this literature has the strength of guiding us to show how private higher education can be linked to the labor market through institutional practices and to demonstrate how institutional practices can be associated with initial graduate employment outcomes.

Moreover, the strengths of the two strands of literature are complementary to each other for analyzing the relationship between private higher education and the labor market. Literature on higher education and the labor market suggests that the linkages between private higher education and labor market demands can be analyzed through major institutional management practices in educational provision, career services, networking, as well as the association of these practices with initial graduate employment outcomes. The distinctiveness of private higher education sector in mission, function, finance, and governance can further explain its distinctive practices and associations between these practices and employment outcomes. Thus, a combination of the two literatures serves as rich basis for the research design and analysis of this study.

CHAPTER THREE: RESEARCH METHODOLOGY

This chapter presents the research design to approach the research question stated in Chapter One: how and how well have private higher education institutions made efforts to link private higher education to the labor market? First, a mixed methods research design is adopted and explanation of reasons is given. After describing major methods used to collect quantitative and qualitative data for the design, this chapter reports how institutional selection and interviews with administrators were executed for this research, and describes major demographic and other background characteristics of graduates who responded to a questionnaire graduate survey. Finally, it addresses data analysis techniques and the limitations of the research execution.

Research Design

In order to answer the research question on how and how well private higher education institutions have made efforts to link private higher education to the labor market, the main task of the research design was to collect information and address specific questions regarding initial employment outcomes and institutional efforts. As the literature review suggests, questions about educational/field of study provision, career services, and networking should focus on managed structures, policies, and activities; questions about initial employment outcomes should focus on major employment indicators.

To successfully carry out the main task, this study embraces a combination of qualitative and quantitative research approaches. It makes major qualitative data analysis in identifying patterns of institutional management practices in linking private higher education to the labor market. On the other hand, quantitative methods and analysis are important in approaching graduate employment outcomes and in asking graduates feedback on institutional management efforts. Moreover, exploring the associations of initial employment outcomes with institutional practices, something the literature has not extensively or compellingly studied, needs both quantitative and qualitative data analysis.

Thus, this research adopts mixed methods with two phases of data collection (Johnson and Christensen, 2004): one for interviews and the other for questionnaire surveys. The surveys were done before interviews in two colleges and after the interviews in four colleges. Still, in the other four colleges, interviews were carried out without successfully securing access to the surveys. Administrators were interviewed to gather information about institutionally managed structure, policies, and activities in linking private higher education to the labor market. Graduates were surveyed with questionnaires to provide information about their employment outcomes and their satisfactions with institutional practices to verify the authenticity of administrators' reports about relevant efforts. Additionally, document analysis is conducted in interpreting first-hand data and describing institutional practices for verification and comparison. Such verification and comparison with both qualitative and quantitative elements are said to enhance the breadth and depth of qualitative research and thus improve its validity through triangulation and complementarity (Patton, 2002).

Data Collecting Methods

Three data collecting methods were used to gather information about institutional management efforts and initial graduate employment outcomes.

The core component of this research execution was the interviews with presidents or vice-presidents who handled student affairs, or with any other senior administrators who had authority and influence over policies, directions, and activities regarding graduate employment. Securing authoritative administrators with knowledge about the interested topics as key informants is a common research practices. Of course, selecting them as informants has limitations. First, accessibility can be a major problem and the authoritative figures may not readily accept the interview. For example, three interviewed presidents or vice presidents only permitted part of my interviews, mostly due to time constraints. Besides, it is questionable whether such authoritative administrators might have provided as much information as ex-presidents or other lower ranking administrators might be able to. Notwithstanding, since the purpose of the interview was to gather information about specific elements of presently managed structures, policies, and activities, the ex-presidents or junior administrators probably knew much less about the details of present decision-making processes and various management practices. Nevertheless, the study could only study the institutions with authoritative administrators' permission and willingness to participate. Also, the authoritative administrators know the institutions well and speak for the institutions. Or, at least, given their official positions, they may be better positioned to help guide what we explore for and against which we can compare *actual* efforts.

The second component was a questionnaire survey of graduates just before their graduation ceremony or within weeks after the ceremony, which is a common practice of empirical studies on graduate employment (Teichler, 1989: 225). The purpose is to get data about their initial employment outcomes and reflections on their experiences with their Alma Maters' career and job placement services, program provision and curriculum update, as well as networking efforts. The selection of such graduates, rather than on-campus seniors or past years' alumni, has several advantages: they just experienced or were experiencing the transition from college to the labor market and had clear memory about the process and institutional practices; their experiences in employment and in institutional efforts were close to the *present* situation in a dynamic and ever-changing society; for comparison across institutions, the starting-point of graduate employment has less influence due to various labor market and individualized reasons.

The last component was the analysis of miscellaneous available documents regarding institutional management practices and institutional, student, and labor market characteristics. The documents about institutional practices are used to enrich and verify the information that administrators provided in the interviews. The characteristics are used to verify, explore, and interpret institutional management efforts, initial employment outcomes, and the associations between the two. For example, institutional affiliations (e.g. with industry groups) may influence management practices and thus outcomes (Bernasconi, 2004a); Sapatoru, Nicolescu, and Slantcheva (2003) found various student characteristics are also related to outcomes; and local and regional labor market demand is also a well-known factor affecting graduate employment outcomes (Schomburg and Teichler, 2005).

Selection of Cases

It is impossible for an individual to survey all or a majority of the private institutions, even if the survey is only limited to the accredited institutions. This is partially due to the exploratory and qualitative nature of the topic and partially to my resource constraints. China has a large and quite widespread private higher education sector, complex across different regions, types, and levels. To make the dissertation research design feasible, the author purposefully limited the studies to focus on ten or so private colleges in four cities, six colleges in Shanghai, two in Xi'an, one in Zhengzhou, and one in Hefei (see Appendix A). [1] Purposeful sampling was adopted because a priori knowledge is important to study the interested topic (Patton, 2002).

The case selection was intentionally limited to be institutions from four cities that were deemed to be representative as well as feasible. The four cities, Xi'an, Zhengzhou, Shanghai, and Hefei, [2] are all capital cities where the private higher education sector develops the most and has all types of private institutions. In at least some ways, they are also typical in China. Most Chinese private institutions are in cities, especially in capital city. The development of the private sector in the capital city of each province usually represents the province's level of private development. Furthermore, statistics show that a majority of capital cities have the biggest number of accredited private colleges of their provinces (see Appendix A). The four cities are no exception. In 2004, Xi'an had all the 14 (one bachelor) accredited private colleges of the whole Shaanxi province; Zhengzhou had seven (one bachelor) of the eight accredited colleges in Henan province; Shanghai has 15 accredited colleges; and Hefei has five of the eight accredited colleges in Anhui

---

[1] It had proposed to select five colleges in only Shanghai, Xi'an, and Zhengzhou.
[2] After unsuccessful access to many proposed private colleges in Xi'an and in Zhengzhou, this study selected Hefei as an alternative and completed interviews in one college there.

province. All three cities have at least one four-year accredited college and Xi'an is China's only city that has four such institutions. [1] Furthermore, nationally, Shanghai and Xi'an are the two cities with the most number of accredited private institutions while Zhengzhou ranks the seventh (see Appendix A). Equally important, the four cities represent considerable breadth of China in geography and income. Xi'an, Zhengzhou, and Shanghai reside in provinces of three different geographical regions – West China, Middle China, and East China. Their economic development represents three different levels: low-income, middle-income, and high-income provinces in China (Yan & et. al, 2003). And Hefei of Anhui Province represents Middle China but low-income regions. Within low-income provinces, the total number of private institutions in Hefei is second only to Xi'an.

Private higher education development in the four provinces where the four cities are located is also among the provinces that have the most private institutions, [2] which suggests that the local and provincial government agencies may give the private sector the chance to make its efforts. In some other provinces and cities, local government has been more hostile and conservative, which is probably one reason (there are other reasons) why the private sector is not prevalent there, as the fieldwork tends to suggest. Excluding such places is certainly a limitation of the study, but a reasonable one. An open-minded or supportive local and provincial government is important for institutional leaders to comfortably give relatively accurate data.

---

[1] Xi'an had one four-year universities in 2004. Three were added on June 1, 2005.
[2] According to Yan and et. al (2003), Shaanxi had 96, Henan had 83, and Shanghai had 187 private institutions, which were respectively the third, sixth, and first province where had the most total number of private institutions in 1999 (see Appendix A)

This research emphasizes accredited private colleges in the institutional selection. On one hand, accredited institutions often have a longer history than unaccredited ones and thus may have sufficient documentation about curriculum and program updates and changes, and even mission establishment and change. On the other hand, such institutions have secured accreditation and may be less likely to hide unfavorable information than the unaccredited private institutions. They have the information and they have already made some public. Many unaccredited private institutions, particularly the mere demand-absorbers, may not have the resources and ability to accumulate needed data. Essentially, this study selected a couple of unaccredited institutions to get an idea of the contrast to our portrayal of the accredited private institutions.

After the decisions on targeted and preferred cities as well as emphasis on accredited colleges were made, this research selected and investigated private colleges in accordance with professional recommendation and fieldwork accessibility. [1] The author asked about five experts on Chinese private higher education to recommend five representative colleges of the first three cities for the purpose of study on institutional management efforts and graduate employment. The author then approached key administrators of the recommended colleges and pursued their permits for my fieldwork access. In Shanghai, all of the five recommended colleges were willing to participate in the study and four of them also executed the graduate survey. A sixth college was interviewed and surveyed for special personal reference. In Xi'an, the author interviewed two colleges of the three agreed colleges and only one interviewed college executed the graduate survey. In Zhengzhou, only one college agreed to participate in the study at the

---

[1] This research was originally proposed to select one accredited four-year, two accredited three-year, and two comparable size unaccredited colleges in each of the first three cities.

time and the author only managed to interview two of its administrators without the graduate survey. After unsuccessful attempt in Zhengzhou, Hefei was selected as an alternative because its similarity to Zhengzhou in geographical location, income level, and private higher education scale. As a result, the study interviewed the administrators of ten private colleges and surveyed the graduates of six of them, though only three of the interviews and one of the graduate surveys were of unaccredited colleges (see Table 2 for institutions selected by city).

Table 2: Selection of Private Higher Education Institutions

	Xi'an	Zhengzhou	Hefei	Shanghai
Location	West China	Middle China	Middle China	East China
Income Level	Low	Middle	Low	High
Institutions	✓ One 4-Year College without Bachelor Degree * ✓ One Unaccredited 3-Year College	One 4-Year College with Bachelor Graduates	One 3-Year College	✓ One 4-Year College with Bachelor Graduates* ✓ One 4-Year College without Bachelor Graduates* ✓ Two 3-Year College* ✓ Two Unaccredited 3-Year**

Note: In Xi'an, a self-study examination private college affiliated to pubic university was interviewed. Despite its official private status, all employees the author contacted, except the president, regarded it public and reported their public employee status. Some, including the president, lamented that its public nature hinders necessary efforts for graduate employment. For its affiliation nature, this research will not analyze its practices in detail. * indicates graduate surveys were also executed in the college; ** indicates graduate surveys were executed in one of the two colleges.

Interview Instrument and Procedures

The purpose of interviewing administrators was to collect information about institutional management efforts and to procure access to their most recent year's graduates. The information about institutional management efforts was not only used for revealing institutional practices regarding graduate employment, but also for interpreting the quantitative data gathered via graduate questionnaire surveys.

The instrument was an interview guide with open-ended questions. It has four sections (See Appendix F). Section I is on management mechanism in field of study provision. Field of study provision is one major link to labor market demands for higher education in general (Finnie, 1999a, 1999c) and for private higher education in particular (Levy, 1986a). The aim of this section is not to get data about how each field is related to labor market demands (the questionnaire survey and certain document analysis help with that), but to collect information about the mechanism used by institutions in enhancing the relevance of private higher education to labor market demands through field of study and curriculum changes, which is mostly unknown. Section II and III focus on mechanism used by institutions in building linkages with the labor market and in connecting graduates and employers through career services and networking. Finally, a probing question is asked to inquire any neglected or unknown issue to the interviewer, such as other types of institutional practices.

The informants of the interview were authoritative figures who knew the operation of the surveyed institutions their in general and student affairs in particular. Three types of administrators were interviewed: 1). Four presidents, who had most knowledge about the institutions' operation and have more knowledge about field of study provision and institutional networking; 2). Four vice-presidents handling student affairs, a position that has best expertise in career services, institutional networking, and much of program provision; 3). Three directors who handled graduate employment related career services and networking while also having certain knowledge about the institution's program provisions were chosen, as an alternative when neither of the first two types of informants were available in four institutions; 4) One director in the president's office, who had close knowledge about both student affairs and general institutional management efforts. The decisions on whom to be interviewed were admittedly based in part on accessibility.

The interview process had three steps. At the beginning of each interview, the informant was given a consent form (see Appendix B) to sign, along with explanations of the purpose of the interview and the background of the consent requirement. And the interviewee were permitted to ask any question he or she would like before the interview started. During the interview, the author asked the questions listed in the Interview Guide (Appendix F), recorded the interview, took notes, and collected provided documents. After the interview, the author reviewed the notes, wrote down observations, and made a follow-up call to some of the interviewees to express my appreciation and clarified any area of vagueness and uncertainty (Patton, 2002). Three interviews lasted about half an hour and two about fifty minutes. Eight interviews were around one to one and a half hour. Only one lasted more than two hours.

Questionnaire Survey Instrument, Sampling, and Procedures

The purpose of conducting graduate questionnaire survey was to ask graduates to report their employment outcomes around graduation and to reflect on institutional management efforts regarding graduate employment. As mentioned above, the resulted data are used for describing initial graduate employment outcomes as well as for triangulation – verifying and comparing with the information provided by administrators about institutional management efforts.

Graduate Sampling. Graduates were selected from the latest graduates in July 2006, as given by or sought after via selected private institutions. The timing of conducting such surveys upon graduation is commonly used to study the initial transition of college graduates to the labor market internationally. 200 graduate survey questionnaires were given to six institutions with the intention to get a similar number of returned surveys for statistical comparison. Within each institution, the author tried to use or asked the person who administrated the survey to use stratified proportionate sampling and randomly surveyed graduates from different programs while also considering gender composition. Graduates of major programs were selected from six institutions, which covered a broad range of fields of study similar to current program provision in China's private higher education institutions. [1] Three colleges distributed all 200 questionnaires; one college distributed 125 questionnaires, and for various reasons, the other two colleges only distributed about 100 surveys the author gave. Thus, 925 questionnaires were actually distributed, which resulted in 463 valid samples from private college graduates. The numbers of questionnaires distributed and valid samples resulted in are shown by Table 3.

Table 3: Response Rates in Surveyed Colleges

	Valid Samples	Distributed Questionnaires	Response Rate
College A	58	125	46.40%
College B	96	200	48.00%
College C	28	100	28.00%
College D	145	200	72.50%
College E	79	200	39.50%
College F	57	100	57.00%
Overall	463	925	50.10%

---

[1] This research was intended to send out 1600 questionnaires and had a target of 384 returned samples (384 is the recommended sample size for a population under 10,000 at 95% confident level by Krejecie and Morgan (1970: 608)) using mailing survey and the response rates of most graduate surveys via mailing are around 25%.

Instrument. A three-page mailing questionnaire was developed and used for collecting information about initial graduate employment outcomes and graduates' reflection on institutional management practice (see Appendix H). It had three sections and asks similar questions to most graduate surveys, but overcomes the pitfalls of the previous survey in neglecting asking institutional graduate employment-related practices. [1] The questions asked were around the following themes: a). socio-biographic and early education background variables; b). initial employment during the transitional period; c). reflection and report on studied field and courses; d). reflection and report on alma mater's career services, and; e). reflection and report on alma mater's networking efforts. The questions under theme #a aimed at graduates' background information, with an intention to control certain variables (e.g. high school education, family background, gender, age, etc.) in analysis as Sapatoru, Nicolescu, and Slantcheva (2003) do. The questions under theme #b targeted at information about several major employment outcomes. Questions under the other three themes sought graduates' reflection on major institutional practices regarding graduate employment as revealed by literature. In addition, an open-ended question was designed to let graduates write down whatever else they choose to say regarding their Alma Mater and their jobs. Altogether, 8 questions are asked about graduates' reflection and report on their fields of study and their experiences in their Alma Mater; 12 questions were asked on job-hunting and initial employment outcomes as well as graduates' feedback on institutional management efforts. 6 questions were asked about graduates' demographic and background information.

---

[1] The questions designed in this questionnaire have the same or similar appearances as those in the survey questionnaires for Finnie's (2000) study in Canada, Sapatoru, Nicolescu, and Slantcheva's (2003) study in Romania and Bulgaria, Teichler's (2003) study in 12 European Countries and Japan, NCES's Recent College Graduate Survey in US, or Ball State University Graduate Survey in US.

Survey procedures. Although this study was initially intended to use only mailing surveys, [1] it actually adopted both mailing and face-to-face surveys in its execution. The choice of methods was made in accordance with specific situations. Specifically, mailing surveys were used in one college and face-to-face surveys were used in the other five. In College B, the author passed out the questionnaires to students in different classrooms (with different majors), and graduating students filled out the questionnaires during their graduation ceremony, and then the author collected the questionnaires after the ceremony. In College A, questionnaires were passed out to graduated students one by one selectively when they went to an office desk to get their leaving-form to be stamped in a graduation-facilitating session conference room with a dozen of such desks during a period of about four hours, and students returned the survey to the same desk voluntarily after they left the room. In College G, questionnaires were mailed to graduates through presidents' office, and the VP collected the returned questionnaires and mailed to me. In College F, graduates who went for graduation were asked to complete the questionnaires in their career service office, and the director of career service office collected and mailed completed questionnaire to me. In College E graduates who went back to their individual departments for leaving procedures were asked to complete the survey. One staff member of the college's institutional research office collected the completed questionnaires from

---

[1] The following was the initial designed procedures: I will obtain mailing addresses through administrators, alumni clubs, or other sources. After selecting graduates, I will send questionnaire along with one stamped return envelope and a cover note signed by presidents to their mailing address. The return address will be my mailing address in China. Each sent-out questionnaire and envelop will be assigned a code to identify institutions and students name for aggregation, for follow-up, as well as for attacking the problem of response bias. The 15 institutions will be coded by letters from "A" to "N"; the majors will be coded by two digit numbers; then followed by first letter of students' last name and a numeric number assigned for the student in the his or her major. The total number of returned undelivered questionnaire will be counted and the information of responded questionnaires will be coded and input in SPSS. A follow-up with questionnaires and stamped return envelops will be mailed to non-respondents one month after the first letter is sent if the response rate is less than 25%.

departmental office and sent them to the author by mail. In College C, questionnaires were passed to deans of four colleges through the secretary of the president's office. The deans in turn asked students to voluntarily fill out the survey during their graduation ceremony and the completed questionnaires was collected by designated staff member and mailed to me. [1]

The Demographic and Background Characteristics of Survey Respondents

This section describes demographic and other background characteristics of the 463 graduates who responded to the survey in age, gender, length of study (educational level), type of program pursued, nature of graduated high school, family location, mother's and father's highest education..

Age and Gender. As expected, respondents are similarly in their twenties, because almost all Chinese undergraduate students enter college immediately after their high school or secondary vocational schools, and then graduate after three or four years' full-time study. The private colleges are no exception. [2] Gender composition of the survey respondents is close to that of the targeted population, with 53.2 percent of the surveyed 463 respondents being female. See Table 5 for detail.

Field of Study. Table 4 gives detailed information of each reported discipline within five major fields of study. Organized according to China's Ministry of Education's definition of major fields of study, [3] 67.6 percent of the graduates are of business and social sciences, which are composed of administration (30.7%), economics/business

---

[1] Most Chinese private colleges encourage their graduates who have found jobs to start work before graduation ceremony, but ask them to come back to school for ceremony and other purposes.
[2] Although some adults who have left high school or secondary vocational schools for jobs and then go back to college for further education after passing national college examinations or examinations specially designed for vocational high school graduates, it rarely happens to regular private or public colleges.
[3] A copy of the Field of study classification from China's Ministry of Education can be accessed at http://jxgl.fimmu.com/Article/UploadFiles/200604/20060413113437434.doc (Accessed 10/22/2006).

(18.8%), and literature (18.1). Most of the programs are either newly-developed or popular disciplines, such as foreign languages, art & design, logistics, and international business & trade. The other 32.4 percent of the survey respondents majored either in science or in engineering. It indicates that private colleges have begun to endeavor in science and engineering, although still within a limited range of program provision, such as computer science and electronic engineering. Even though respondent composition by field of study reflects overall trends of private higher educational provision's dominance in business and social sciences, the sampling is convenient and does not warrant sample representativeness. The fields of study provided by all of the ten interviewed private colleges, along ten comparable public colleges, are analyzed in detail in Chapter Four.

Length of Study and Graduated College/Program Type. 96.3 percent of the 463 graduates surveyed (446 students) had studied for three-year programs in colleges before graduation, whereas the remaining 3.7 percent had studied for four or more years and pursued bachelor degrees. 84.0 percent of the three-year program had their higher education in accredited private colleges, while 12.3 percent of them studied in unaccredited private colleges (for detail, see Table 5).

High school origin. Of all the graduates surveyed, four fifths had graduated from academic high schools before entering the private colleges, and one fifth had graduated from vocational high schools or technical secondary schools (For detail, see Table 5). The high school origin composition of the private colleges surveyed is similar to what Bao (2006a) reports. [1] The private colleges are different in student high school origin. Of the graduates from technical or vocational school origin, 54 percent were from one

---

[1] The high school origin composition of surveyed private colleges in this and Bao's (2006) study are both different from that of public colleges, which only have about 0.2% students from vocational/technical schools.

unaccredited college and 25 percent were from one accredited college prominent in engineering. The differences are probably due to the limited access of vocational/technical school graduates to accredited colleges and to compatibility differences among colleges to fields in vocational and technical schools.

Family Location. Because most private colleges surveyed are in Shanghai and most private colleges in China recruit students locally, for regulatory and voluntary reasons, most survey respondents reported that they originated from high income urban areas. [1] In terms of family location's province income, 83.4 percent respondents were of high-income provinces, 11.6 percent from low-income province, and 5.0 percent from middle-income province (for detail, see Table 5). [2] In terms of family location's urbanity, 256 of the 399 (64.2 percent) survey respondents were from urban areas, 104 (26.1 percent) from suburban areas, and 39 (9.8%) from rural areas.

Father's and mother's education: The fathers and mothers of the graduates responded received similar amounts of education. Over 70 percent of both parents entered secondary education, though significantly fewer mothers have received postsecondary education. 21.2 percent of the fathers or male guardians and 11.6 percent of the mothers or female guardians received higher education. 4.8 percent of the mothers or female guardians only had elementary education; 25.4 percent had middle school; 56.0 percent had high school or secondary vocational school; and 2.2 had no formal education at all. As for fathers or male guardians, the comparable numbers are 4.5 percent, 24.1 percent, 49.2 percent, and 1.1 percent (see Table 5).

---

[1] Except the top public universities, second-tier colleges/universities often recruit most of their students locally.
[2] Bao (2006a) reported that 30.6% private college respondents and 28.0% public college respondents were from rural area.

Table 4: Detailed Field of Study of Survey Respondents

Administration		Frequency	Percentage
Business Administration		6	1.3
Community Management		47	10.2
Conference Arrangement and Management		4	0.9
Hotel Management		1	0.2
International Transportation & Customs		8	1.7
Investment Management		14	3.0
Logistics		54	11.7
Marketing Management		3	0.6
Project Management		2	0.4
Real Estate Management		1	0.2
Tourism		2	0.4
	Subtotal	**142**	**30.7**
Economics (Applied)			
Accounting		12	2.6
Electronic Commerce		19	4.1
Insurance		5	1.1
International Business		51	11.0
	Subtotal	**87**	**18.8**
Science (Computer)			
Computer Science & Application		36	7.8
Information Management and Computer Application		54	11.7
	Subtotal	**90**	**19.4**
Engineering			
Architecture		15	3.2
Building Automation		4	0.9
Electronic Equipment Repair		2	0.4
Electronic Manufacturing		38	8.2
Mechanic and Electronic Engineering		1	0.2
	Subtotal	**60**	**13.0**
Literature (Art and Foreign Language)			
Advertisement & Design		9	1.9
Art & Design-Environment		5	1.1
Art & Design-Interior		4	0.9
Commercial English		20	4.3
Commercial French		2	0.4
Commercial German		10	2.2
Commercial Japanese		19	4.1
Journalism		15	3.2
	Subtotal	**84**	**18.1**
	Total	**463**	**100.0**

Source: The graduate survey of this study.

Table 5: Survey Respondent Demographic and Background Information

		Frequency	Percentage
Age			
24-26		18	4.1
21-23		409	94.0
19-20		8	1.9
	Total	435	100.0
Length of Study			
3 Years		446	96.3
4-5 Years		17	3.7
	Total	463	100.0
The Type of Enrolled Program & Institution			
Accredited Institutions Pursuing Bachelor-Degree Program		17	3.7
Accredited Institutions Pursing Associate Degree Program		389	84.0
Unaccredited Institutions on Three-Year Program Towards Associate Degree program - Certificate & Exam or Self-Study Facilitating or Others		57	12.3
	Total	463	100.0
The Type of Graduated High School			
General high school		335	79.6
Vocational high school		24	5.7
Technical secondary school		55	13.1
Others		7	1.7
	Total	421	100.0
Family Location: Province Income			
High Income Province		351	83.4
Middle Income Province		21	5.0
Low Income Province		49	11.6
	Total	421	100.0
Family Location: Urbanity			
Urban		256	64.2
Suburban		104	26.1
Rural		39	9.8
Mother (Father) or Female (Male) Guardian's Highest Education			
No education		9 (4)	2.2 (1.1)
Elementary school		20 (17)	4.8 (4.5)
Middle school		105 (91)	25.4 (24.1)
High or vocational secondary school		232 (186)	56.0 (49.2)
Associate or Bachelor Degree		48 (80)	11.6 (21.2)
	Total	414 (378)	100.0 (100.0)

Source: The graduate survey of this study.

Observations and Additional Documents

During the fieldwork of this study, observations about graduate employment career services and some other management efforts were made. The author also met and conversed with some faculty, alumni, and a couple of employers. Additional documents were also collected, including relevant data available via internet, newspapers, government data, institutional newsletter, and publications on institutional mission, program provision and change, alumni, graduate employment data, career development and job services, and the enrollment data and other information about 2005 graduates.

Data Analysis Strategies

For the purpose of this study, the analysis of collected data is organized into two chapters. Chapter Four presents the qualitative analysis of documents, interview records, and field observations on major institutional practices relevant to linking private higher education to the labor market. Institutional management efforts are coded and categorized and the patterns are reported around their missions, fields of study, educational delivery, and career services. Thick, rich descriptions as well as quotations about relevant institutional practices are provided, which gives room for readers' own judgment (Patton, 2002: 437-440). Chapter Five analyzes initial graduate employment outcomes and explores the associations of initial employment outcomes with management efforts, using both descriptive statistics and regression modeling. Descriptive statistics describes the initial outcomes in employment status, starting salary, job-education match, job satisfaction, and graduate feedback on institutional worthiness and management efforts. Simple correlations are used to examine the relationships between employment outcomes and relevant variables. The results of simple relationship are interpreted and illuminated along with acquired qualitative contextual information from both interviews and document collection (Patton, 2002: 563-564). In cases of significant associations, institutional effects are further examined with multivariate regression analyses. Findings are illustrated with contextual information and statistical results are considered for generalization beyond existing context (Patton, 2002: 479). [1] The examinations of the relationships between management variables and outcome variables with both qualitative and quantitative data from different sources serve as triangulation to enhance the quality and credibility of the analysis in this study (Patton, 2002: 559-563).

Limitations in Research Design Execution

Limitations were present in research design execution. First and foremost, the governmental practices of associating employment rates with permitted admission quotas posed major problems to institutional access, graduate survey completion, as well as accurate and relevant document acquirement. The author successfully accessed to ten private colleges and completed graduate surveys in only half of the colleges. Not only the total number of studied private institutions is small, most of them are in Shanghai and only one college outside of Shanghai agreed to the graduate survey. Moreover, only one unaccredited college in Shanghai participated in the graduate survey, either for lack of resource or for being uncomfortable to release their information before being accredited. Additionally, limitations are also associated with both small graduate samples and the way how graduate surveys were carried out. Only 270 of the 463 respondents of graduate

---

[1] Citing Lofland (1971:62), Patton (2002) warns that "the consideration of causes and consequences using qualitative data should be a 'tentative, qualified, and subsidiary task' ". He also states that "simple statements of linear relationships many be more distorting than illuminating." (p.480).

survey were employed and are thus eligible for major employment outcomes analysis. All of the colleges, except two, were reluctant to let the author control the graduate surveys. It is unknown how exactly the surveys were conducted and how strictly my instructions on sampling were followed by. Finally, not all the surveys had consistently used the same method. Five colleges used face-to-face surveys. One college used mailing surveys.

However, eliminating or diminishing the limitations is difficult. For one thing, the colleges of the less developed and less open-minded regions will still be reluctant to participate in research around initial employment outcomes while there is a major stake involved in releasing bad results. For another, personnel turn-over is frequent and data collecting is not institutionalized in most colleges. Consequently, the representativeness of the samples in terms of gender, field, and level for the private colleges and for general private higher education cannot be verified because complete data on graduates by gender, field, and level are not available for all of the surveyed colleges. In turn, weighting of different sample sizes among colleges cannot be used.

For the limitations, the author cautions readers to pay attention to the contexts of this research in generalizing its findings regarding initial employment outcomes and to emphasize the exploratory nature of this study instead. On the other hand, it is fair to regard this research as pioneering in a number of ways, involving China, studying the new demand-absorbing private higher education, exploring management efforts in graduate employment, and using both quantitative and qualitative data as well as key concepts from both private higher education literatures and the literature on higher education and the labor market to associate management efforts with initial employment outcomes.

CHAPTER FOUR: QUALITATIVE DATA ANALYSIS ON INSTITUTIONAL MANAGEMENT EFFORTS

While the last three chapters introduced the research question, literature, and research design, this chapter, along with the following one, analyzes collected data to approach the research question on how and how well private higher education institutions have made efforts to link private higher education to the labor market. The "how" part of the research question is addressed in this chapter through qualitative data analysis. The ensuing chapter devotes itself to answering the "how well" part of the research question by analyzing quantitative data on initial employment outcomes and graduate feedback.

Qualitative data were collected from three sources. Face-to-face interviews were the main source, which provided first-hand data on involved structures, policies, and activities relating to graduate employment. The author paid attention to curriculum as well as general and niche field establishment and changes during the interviews, and asked questions about typical practices in educational delivery, career services, and college networking with external and internal entities. The interviews led to successful access to the second source - published and unpublished documents, including campus newsletters,[1] recruiting and advertising publications, and research papers and publications. College websites are the third important source. Most college websites state institutional missions, list provided fields of study, and post information about career services. Some also show institutional structures and policies of various management efforts, including practices related to graduate employment. Still many include high

---

[1] Campus newsletters of investigated private colleges are often circulated among college communities, such as trustees, faculty, administrators, staff, and students. One college also sent them to parents and alumni.

graduate employment rates and exemplary alumni on their websites, presumably being regarded as a prominent part of institutional portfolio.

Three issues are of importance to the "how" part of the research question in qualitative data collecting, categorizing, and interpreting. First, since most high school graduates go to college to seek professional careers and the Chinese economy is in a period of rapid growth, do the private colleges say that they link or intend to link private higher education to the labor market? Second, if they do say that, do their educational provisions reflect what they say? Third, have they provided any services to build the linkages? This chapter starts the analysis by examining the most possible formal statements that the Chinese private colleges may have made, notably their mission and goal statements. It first examines major elements included in the mission statements of all the private colleges accessed, along with those of selected comparable public colleges, paying special attention to elements related to the labor market. It then investigates general and niche field of study provision and discusses how private colleges have scanned labor market demands in establishing their programs. Lastly, to show how private institutions have carried out their missions to meet labor market demands, it summarizes observed effort patterns and describes typical institutional practices for improving student employability and connecting students to employers through educational delivery and career services.

Institutional Mission/Goals in a Fast-Growing and Changing Economy

Statements of college mission, goals, and objectives generally reflect what the colleges do in their practices and stand for in their roles. As suggested by the literature review in Chapter Two (Levy, 1986b, 1992, 2002b), the mission of private colleges and universities is pertinent to their efforts to link private higher education to the labor market and to produce human resource to meet labor market demands. Analyzing the statements of mission, goals and objectives of four private and four public universities in the Middle East, AL-Omari and Obeidat seem to confirm this hypothesis with a two dimension framework. They find "many times that these universities aim[s] at producing graduates who meet [s] the demands of employers for a skilled workforce", whether they are private or public (AL-Omari and Obeidat, 2006). Borrowing their framework, this section analyzes the mission statements of Chinese private colleges, along with those of their public counterparts, to determine whether private colleges in China say they intend to link private higher education to the labor market, and if so, how much attention they have paid to issues and elements related to the labor market.

This section analyzes the statements of mission and goals of all the ten private colleges interviewed as well as eight most closely comparable public colleges in China, including five public colleges in Shanghai and one in each of the other three cities. [1] Qualitative data about college mission and goals were obtained through interview, college websites, and college brochures for admissions and public relations. It is certainly arguable to claim that the selected public colleges are compatible to the interviewed private colleges. The study failed to find even one public college close to be comparable to one unaccredited private college in Shanghai, as well as in Xi'an, with similar program offerings and student populations. Nevertheless, eight public colleges, mostly not

---

[1] The dates and nature of the analyzed colleges are similar and briefly introduced in Appendix J.

universities, seem to be comparable in certain degrees and are chosen for comparative analysis. [1]

Analysis Framework

The two dimensions used for the comparative analysis are "individual/local vs. national/general v. global/international" and "economic/labor vs. human/cultural", a further development upon a framework laid by AL-Omari and Obeidat (2006). The first dimension is about the locality of various demands that colleges try to meet in their educational provisions, which reveals how widely colleges target their education. In categorizing the mission statements of the private and public colleges, "individual" refers to individual students or other individual college constituents; "local" refers to the nearby community where a particular college is located; "regional" refers to major regions of China; and "global" or "international" refers to the rest of the world. This analysis categorizes statements about general society as "general", equivalent of "national", because such general statements often refer to things beyond individual, local community, or region, but usually not global or international. The second dimension is about the types of demands tthat educational provisions tries to meet. The demands are categorized into economic development and cultural development. This study regards the production of educated workers, for both private and quasi-private enterprises as well as national purposes, as an integral part of economic development. It organizes elements about human development and cultural development together.

---

[1] In Shanghai, two four-year colleges were selected based on discussions with local higher education experts. Three three-year ones were selected according to official listing (http://edu.sina.com.cn/exam/2006-05-10/171737605.html). Based on similarity in size and program offering, only one public four-year college was successfully selected in Xi'an; comparable public college is difficult to find in Zhengzhou and instead, a public college in a close city is selected; one comparable public college is selected in Hefei.

Analyzing the Mission Statements of Ten Private Colleges and Eight Public Colleges

Using this framework, Appendix K details the elements included by the private and public colleges in their mission statements. For further comparison, Table 6 summarizes the analysis, listing college names under each dimension.

Elements Included by Private and Public Colleges in Their Mission Statements

Three patterns appear in analyzing the elements included in the mission statements by the private colleges. First, all other private colleges, except two, include both economic and human development elements in their mission statements. At the international level, three private colleges show their concerns about economic globalization and its labor needs, international communication and exchanges, and cooperation with foreign higher education institutions for curriculum and pedagogy advances. At the national level, five colleges address economic and human development issues around producing labor to meet economic needs, developing the country through enhancing education, science and technology, contributing to the development of socialistic mass media and modernization. All of the colleges touch elements at both the local and the individual level. Their mission statements enclose topics around student careers and jobs, student program choices, student personal development, campus living and education quality, student transfers to further education, and even parents' needs.

Second, either because current economic development poses imminent challenges to advanced human resource development for private colleges, or because the private college leaders think that providing education for economic and career development may make private colleges sound more attractive or legitimate, the private colleges investigated pay more attention to economic and career development than to human and cultural development in their mission statements. Also, they are very specific about their economic and career development mission. They approach their economic development missions from the perspective of producing the right labor to meet market demands, whether the demands come from global market, China's national market, regional market, or the local community. They often declare the types of labor they want to produce and the corresponding education they deem appropriate to provide, in order to fulfill their missions. For example, College D claims a mission "to cultivate front-line professionals"; College F to "produce intermediate and advanced professionals and practical labor"; College G to "produce various types of inadequately-produced but urgently-needed advanced technical professionals"; College I, an unaccredited mass media college, to encourage students to "become multi-disciplinary artists"; and College L is set to "produce advanced practical professionals". To produce the right workers, most of them emphasize practical skills, English and other foreign languages competency, computer skills, and/or professional abilities in their teaching. Some claim that they orient their programs and curricula toward market demands. About half of them also claim that they undertake cooperation with enterprises, business, and industry. Four colleges also note that they offer help for acquiring professional certificates or multi-disciplinary education.

Third, the investigated private colleges refer more to economic/career and human development at the local and individual level than to those at the national or international level. Among the elements listed at individual/regional/local level, individual career and job prospects are the components most pinpointed. Most private colleges indicate that they enable students to become certain types of professionals and be successful in their careers. Some, such as College A, even declare that they are responsible for student career and employment. Some highlight their methods for achieving the mission of providing desirable career goals. For example, College C lists its distinguished English teaching and good computer skills training; College A claims that its educational provisions pursuing "a combination of career orientations between recruitment and career guide & recommendations; a combination of practical learning between diploma education and professional qualification certificate education; a combination of college-enterprise cooperation between theoretical education and practical training". [1]

Similar to private colleges, public colleges also include both economic development and human development elements in their mission statements. They state their goals as producing labor to meet the labor demands of the market economy, enabling students to become advanced or front-line practical professionals, and serving local community. They claim their commitment to cultivating certain types of values, ethics, and skills, and to producing a better-educated life-long learning community. Interestingly, they claim more often than the private colleges that they involve students and faculty in international communications and other academic activities related to international cultural development. Also more likely, they include scientific research, socialistic modernization, and rejuvenation of Chinese people, for the purpose of national cultural and human development. Overall and in their mission statements, the eight public colleges examined almost equally emphasize economic and human development elements.

_____

[1] Citation is from the mission statement of College A.

Like their private colleagues, the eight public colleges underscore the individual/ local/regional level economic and human development the most, although they mention such elements at all levels. Above all, the public colleges center their efforts on individual students. Their major effort is said to educate students to become specific types of workers. Aspects of student wellbeing are also mentioned, such as morale, intelligence, physical health, ethics, skills and abilities, and creativity. Some of the public colleges also state that they gear their efforts towards the local community and regional development. Still others claim that they have engaged in various activities to fulfill their goals, through demand-oriented or application-oriented educational provisions (programs, curricula, and educational delivery), cooperation with industry/business, networking with corporations, and granting multiple professional certificates.

Private vs. Public

The detailed analysis in Appendix K and the summary in Table 6 reveal interesting findings about the private and public colleges. Above all, the private and public colleges examined are similar in that they include four major themes in their mission statements, of which meeting labor market demands for individual students and for economic development are the two key themes. All of them, with the exception of one public college, claim that they exist to prepare students for successful careers and to enable them to be professionals possessing certain skills, especially practical skills. Second, by educating students to become certain types of workers, both the private and the public colleges examined claim that they intend to meet the demands of the international, national, regional, and/or local labor markets from economic, social, and/or individual purposes. The colleges also claim to educate for individual development.

Lastly, some also state that their educational provisions address international communications, national culture preservation, and/or local community learning.

Nevertheless, private colleges emphasize the mission of assuring student success in their job-seeking and meeting labor market demands much more than public colleges do. First, all ten private colleges analyzed clearly state their concerns about students' job prospects and their commitment to improving student employability through various practices. Only six of the eight public colleges analyzed indicate that they do so. Second, in their mission statements, the private colleges analyzed pay more attention to market demands in establishing fields of study and curriculum than the public colleges. Six of the ten private colleges declare that their educational provisions are directed by market demands, while only two of the eight public colleges claim this. Third, private colleges also tend to be more specific about their educational provisions in their mission statements, whereas their public counterparts state more vaguely, by referring that their educational provisions are in accord with labor market demands. For example, College F "tries to have a niche in educational provision by having new fields of study" and College L "adheres to the demands of economic and social development, and establishes hot fields of study with good employment prospects in the labor market." Additionally, more of the private colleges include partnerships with industry and business in their mission statements. Half of the ten private colleges investigated claim that they engage in certain types of formal networking with industry and business. Those non-Shanghai private ones even declare that they have dozens of such cooperative training bases for their students across the country. The fieldwork for this study found that almost all of the private colleges boasted that they had well-defined relationships with some local and national corporations. [1] In contrast, only two of the eight public colleges analyzed indicate that they have such networking with industry.

Private vs. Private

The detailed analysis and the summary also suggest that, within the private sector and at the institutional level, the private colleges investigated differ from each other in their mission statements in two major ways: How much emphasis they place on meeting market demands as contrasted with cultural and individual development elements, and how clear and unique their mission statements are. None of the colleges studied includes cultural and human elements at all three geographic levels. Only three include them at both international and national levels and one includes them at both national and individual levels. Four colleges include such elements only at the individual level. Two colleges mention no such element in their mission statements. Among those private colleges with cultural and individual development elements stated in their mission statements, some, such as College A, College B, College C, College I, College K, emphasize cultural and individual development as much as they do on meeting market demands. Other colleges, like College D, College E, and College L, clearly regard meeting market demands as their primary mission, although they include some cultural and individual development elements as well.

Among the private colleges, some have a clear mission while others follow the tide. Colleges that state their mission statements clearly include College A, College F, College G, College I, and College L. The mission statements of most of these colleges

---

[1] During fieldwork, I noticed one college held a partnership ceremony on the day of my visit and another prepared for a similar ceremony on the next day of my visit.

contain even some unique elements. For example, College A has very clearly and specially defined mission statements, by focusing primarily on individuals, specifically students and their parents and particularly about student career and overall development. It highlights college-enterprise cooperation in teaching and practical trainings. College F makes its mission statement distinctive by stating that it tries to make the local community a computerized, modern, and learning one. College G states it mission clearly as producing professionals in urgently-needed fields and using its strength in foreign language. College I uniquely focuses on in cultivating "competent talents with skills and ethics for the field of movie, TV, and broadcasting". In contrast, College B, College D, and College E do not have clearly-defined mission, goals, and objectives. Their mission statements contain either politically-correct expressions (such as "being non-profit"), general slogans (such as "centering on students"), languages indoctrinated by the government (such as "contributing to the development through education, science, and technology"), or vague claims (such as "teaching students to learn").

Discussion of Major Findings

First, the above analysis shows that private colleges in China include in their mission statements two key elements: meeting labor market demands and assuring student career success, similar to their counterpart public colleges. Both rational-choice and institutionalism theory can give insight into this conclusion. Rationally, calls on jobs makes sense in a changing market economy with easier access to higher education, more graduates with advanced degrees, and well-publicized graduate unemployment news. Coercive and non-coercive isomorphism may both result in the similarities between private and public colleges in emphasizing jobs. On the coercive side, all of the accredited colleges in China are now obligated to show concern about job prospects and

employment success under the mandates from the Ministry of Education about relating

new program additions and new enrollment quotas in existing programs to graduate

employment rate.[1] Less apparently, colleges, private and public, probably feel more

legitimate if they follow what the Chinese government plans to accomplish through

higher education in its five-year blueprints, of which the recent central theme is to assure

the development of higher education to be in accord with the demands of economic

development. [2] On the non-coercive side, high profile officials and higher education

leaders in China often encourage colleges to copy successful practices in graduate

employment.

However, the analysis of mission statements also suggests that private colleges

are generally more aggressive in meeting labor market demand and assuring graduate

job-seeking success than public colleges are in their claims. As indicated in the

identification of research limitations, the comparison of the differences between the

public and private colleges in this study is done only in spots where that is feasible.

Nevertheless, questions can still be asked when differences are observed. Why are the

private colleges more aggressive in this regard? The reasons may be multiple. One, as

found by the fieldwork, is embedded in the ways how private colleges gain legitimacy.

---

[1] Since 2003, the Ministry of Education has begun to associate new program enrollment with graduate employment. In November 2003, it issued a new policy, briefed as "Eighteen Associations". Its main purpose was to urge the provincial governments and institutions to prioritize graduate employment and to include it in their medium and long-run development plans. It required the local provincial departments of education to relate new programs additions to graduate employment rates and to control bachelor-degree programs offerings in colleges and universities with less than average provincial graduate employment rate in July for three consecutive years (see http://news.xinhuanet.com/newscenter/2003-11/19/content_1187654.htm). In November 2006 the Ministry announced that its national curricula assessment would include graduate employment rate since 2007 (see http://news.sina.com.cn/c/2006-11-22/042810562691s.shtml).
[2] Chinese central government regularly releases its plan on higher education development. For some of the plans, please visit the website of China's Ministry of Education at http://www.moe.edu.cn/. The latest one is *The "Ninth Five" Education Plan and 2010 Developmental Strategic Planning* (Available online at http://www.moe.edu.cn/edoas/website18/info12591.htm).

Unlike public colleges, private colleges in China are only granted limited legitimacy by the government. They have not gained the level of trust that their public counterparts hold from the government. [1] As Levy points out, when private institutions only have minimal state-based legitimacy to operate, they have to gain additional legitimacy from non-state sources to operate successfully (Levy, 2004). In the Chinese case, the dynamic labor market is clearly one most important non-state source. Another is related to how private colleges define their goals. As students choose and enter private colleges with job prospects as one primary goal (Bao, 2005; Wang and Secombe, 2004), private colleges in China have to take related needs seriously and emphasize career success in their mission statements. After all, because of their distinctive nature of being born along with the development of market economy and mostly playing by market rules, private colleges are relatively more flexible and responsive to accommodate market needs, especially labor market needs. They can probably build better relationships with business and industry to improve the relevance of its education delivery to employers' requirement and to bridge graduates to potential jobs, which may often result in good reputation in graduate employment to gain legitimacy, achieve goals, and attract more students.

The analysis also suggests that diversity exists among private colleges in their mission statements, which is consistent with what Levy and Bernasconi find on the inter-institutional pluralism of private institutions in other aspects (Bernasconi, 2004a; Levy, 2004). Similarly, rational choice theory and the new institutionalism suggest plausible explanations. Rational choice theory suggests that organizations have different resources, institutional constraints, and different intentions although they operate in similar

---

[1] Many private higher education leaders I met compared the relationship between private colleges and the government to the relationship between step-son and step-mother.

environments. In the case of private colleges, some may likely have more resources to pursue cultural/human development goals and/or career development further than others and they are able to emphasize their cultural and/or career development roles more in their mission statements. Some may find their unique niche in educational provision and thus draft their unique mission statements. Private colleges that have little or no resource may resort to generic descriptions or just follow the tide in their mission statements. Of course, as the new institutionalism suggests, many may just copy what other colleges, especially the leading ones of their types, state in the mission statements. Emulation is generally apparent in claims about human and cultural development.

In summary, the analysis and discussion of the mission and goal statements of ten private colleges and eight comparable public colleges lead to two conclusions. Notably, all private higher education institutions in China have intentionally underscored meeting labor market demands in their mission statements, as their public counterparts do, but the difference is that they are more aggressive in fulfilling this mission, according to their claims. Also interestingly, private higher education institutions in China are different in what they emphasize in their mission statements and how clearly they state their missions. In sum, private higher education institutions in China do claim that they are intended to and/or do link private higher education to the labor market.

Table 6: Summary of the Analysis of Mission Statements

	Economic	Human/Cultural/Educational
Private Colleges		
Global/International	College C: Four-Year Accredited College F: Non Accredited	College C: Four-Year Accredited College K: Four-Year Accredited College L: Three-Year Accredited
National/General	College C: Four-Year Accredited College D: Four-Year Accredited College F: Non Accredited College K: Four-Year Accredited College L: Three-Year Accredited	College C: Four-Year Accredited College I: Non Accredited College K: Four-Year Accredited College L: Three-Year Accredited
Local/Regional/Individual	College C: Four-Year Accredited College D: Four-Year Accredited College A: Three-Year Accredited College B: Three-Year Accredited College F: Non Accredited College E: Four-Year Accredited College I: Non Accredited College K: Four-Year Accredited College L: Three-Year Accredited	College D: Four-Year Accredited College A: Three-Year Accredited College B: Three-Year Accredited College E: Four-Year Accredited College I: Non Accredited
Public Colleges		
Global/International	Shanghai Second Polytechnic University	Shanghai City College Henan Institute of Science & Technology
National/General	Shanghai Second Polytechnic University Henan Institute of Science & Technology	Henan Institute of Science & Technology Anhui Vocational and Technical College
Local/Regional/Individual	Shanghai Institute of Technology Shanghai Second Polytechnic University Shanghai Xing Jian Polytechnic College Shanghai College of Science & Technology Shanghai City College Xi'an University of Finance & Economics Anhui Vocational and Technical College	Shanghai Institute of Technology Shanghai Second Polytechnic University Shanghai College of Science & Technology Shanghai City College Henan Institute of Science & Technology

Source: See Appendix K.

Where Mission Meets the Labor Market: Fields of Study Provision

As revealed in the previous section, many private colleges in China highlight their efforts in orienting field of study provision to meet labor market demands while declaring their intention to link private higher education to the labor market in their mission statements. A scholar can ask: Are their fields really job-oriented? If so, how have they managed it? Unfortunately, the literature is not as helpful as hoped. Only Levy has given comprehensive and conceptual analyses of field of study provision in the private sector against that in the public beyond any one country (Levy, 1986a, 2003b). One vital type of comparison of program provision in private and public institutions should be at similar levels. What is more, how private colleges have achieved their goals of orienting program provision to the labor market is only sketchily mentioned here and there in literature and seldom well-reported against field of study provision. This section thus pioneers to analyze the fields of study provision in Chinese private colleges against those of their public counterparts, with data about both programs offered inside the fields and enrollment planned for the programs. It also investigates how private colleges in China have executed the mission of meeting labor market demands through program provisions as well as market-oriented program differentiation and adjustments.

Analysis and Discussion of General Program Provision by Field of Study

This study analyzes the programs and fields of study provided by eight private colleges and their eight comparable public colleges in China. [1] The programs analyzed were offered by the colleges in academic year 2006-07, according to obtained Official Admission Plans of Fall 2006. Instead of using international standards for field classification, this analysis abides by the categorization by the Ministry of Education, which classifies disciplines into 11 fields of study, including philosophy, economics, law, education, literature, history, science (including computer science), engineering, agriculture, health sciences/medicine, and administration. [2] The total number of programs provided in each college by field of study is summarized in Appendix L.

---

[1] All of the colleges are from the ten private and eight public colleges analyzed in the previous section on mission statement. College I in Xi'an and one previously-analyzed private college (College G) in Shanghai are excluded because I failed to find comparable public colleges.

[2] Literature includes foreign languages, art, journalism, publishing, social works, communications and mass media, secretary programs, Chinese and other literatures, etc. Administration includes business/public administration, marketing, logistics, transportation, tourism & management, human resources management, financial management/investment, and others. Economics includes trade, finance, and insurance.

In percentage terms, private colleges in China offered considerably more programs and enrolled more students in literature (including arts, foreign languages, humanities, and social sciences), business, and law than their public counterparts did in Fall 2006. 33.9 percent, 21.9 percent, and 10.9 percent of the programs offered in the selected Chinese private colleges were in literature, administration, and economics. The numbers were much higher than those in their public counterparts, which were 8.8 percent, 17.4 percent, and 9.2 percent respectively. Their planned new enrollments reinforce the contrast: proportionally, private colleges in China wound up being permitted to enroll a larger share of their students in literature, administration, and economics than their public counterparts; the shares of new enrollment planned in literature and law in the private colleges were almost twice as much as what were planned in their public counterparts (for complete statistics, see Appendix M). [1] This finding is consistent with the patterns found by Levy and others (Giesecke, 1999a; Levy, 1986a, 2002a). More striking are the differences found inside the fields (Levy, 1986a) and in featured curricula of the same kind of program offerings. Inside literature and in percentage terms, the selected Chinese private colleges offered almost twice as much as their public counterparts did in foreign language programs. They offered job-oriented arts and social sciences, such as decoration and design, automation and graphics, TV editing and performing art, whereas their public counterparts tended to offer more traditional programs, such as art and design, fine arts, Chinese language and literature, apparel and cloth design, and social work. [2] Notably, differences are present in the same types of programs offered by the Chinese private and public colleges investigated, with the former

[1] Only the seven accredited private colleges had planned admission permits.
[2] The private colleges seem trying to avoid such offerings.

clearly highlighting commercial side whereas the latter usually focusing on disciplinary elements. For instance, the privates usually prefix their foreign language programs with "commercial" and include business elements in their curricula, whereas the public counterparts are less likely to include "commercial" in program names and often feature linguistics and literature in curricula.

Most of the eight private colleges studied also had some program provision in engineering and sciences, though the overall scale was smaller than that in their public counterparts. On average, each Chinese private college investigated offered about six such programs, which occupied about one fourth of their program offerings. However, the scales of programs and new enrollment planned in such fields were much smaller than those of their public counterparts, which had half of their programs offered and new enrollment planned in science and engineering. This finding again fits the patterns Levy first discovered (Levy, 1986a) and which, by far, poses the most distinctive difference between the Chinese private and public colleges. The difference is especially apparent in the programs offered and new enrollment planned in engineering. [1]Altogether, the shares of both programs offered and new enrollment planned in engineering by the private colleges were about one third of those in the public colleges. Possibly, the contrasts could diminish a bit as public colleges scamper to get into some of the market-oriented science and engineering fields. But for the most part, private colleges in China seemingly choose their program provision selectively and they do not enter the fields of higher cost where the public sector has traditionally dominated. For example, about half of the programs offered and the new enrollment planned in science and engineering in the private colleges

---

[1] Many engineering programs in China are short-cycle three-year vocational programs, different from its American or German counterparts (Gereffi and Wadhwa, 2005).

were in computer science, whereas, the share was only one fourth in the public colleges

(for details, see Appendix M). As for other sciences, the private higher education sector

had only minimal enrollment, 2.4 percent of total enrollment, and no presence in nature

sciences, whereas the public sector had 9.1 percent in other science programs, mostly

nature sciences.[1]

Private higher education institutions have also begun to venture into health

sciences. The share of such programs offered and the share of new enrollment planned in

health science may be as large as those in their public counterparts, if not more. Two of

the eight private colleges analyzed offered a total of five such programs. In comparison,

only one public college offered two such programs. Private presences in medicine are

also reported in other countries (Levy, 1993). But in China, a significant difference also

exists in what the private and public colleges actually provide inside the field: while the

public institutions limited their offerings to traditional chemical pharmacy and

agricultural animal health, the private covered a range of disciplines, nursing, medical

test and technology, pharmacy, nutrition and hygiene, as well as traditional clinical

medicine. [2]

Avoiding high-cost or public dominated sciences and other programs, privates

have a heavy presence in applied social sciences, foreign languages, economics and

business, law, computer sciences, and even some health sciences by the private higher

education sector in China are by no means unusual, as originally found by Levy in

---

[1] Interestingly, the investigated private colleges and public colleges offered similar share of programs and planned similar share of new enrollments in computer science, around 11%. But the stark difference is: private colleges only have electronics and communications whereas their counterparts have major presence in pure and nature sciences, such as chemistry, biology, mathematics, etc.

[2] The two private colleges were permitted to enroll over 800 new students while the one public college was permitted to enroll only 335 students in Fall 2006 (see Appendix M).

analyzing the cases in several Latin American countries (Levy, 1986a) and then have always been confirmed by others in individual country cases since. [1] More importantly, what is uncovered here regarding the level of contrasts inside the fields and in similar program offerings in the Chinese private sector is stark. Although it confirms what Levy reveals in his studies on the private higher education sector in general, this analysis extends the findings to a mostly non-university and demand-absorbing higher education sector and examines the differences intensively and comprehensively.

The stark private-public differences pose challenges to sound explanations. After all, the substantial presence of those low cost but highly demanded popular fields, such as arts, foreign languages, business, and administration, manifests the cherry-picking nature of private colleges, whether intentionally or unintentionally. Certainly, we do not expect self-criticism or argument about its legitimacy, though some private colleges did mention the convenience and rewards of offering such programs. [2] As in the United States (Kelly, 2001) and elsewhere, criticisms from Chinese public institutions such as "leaving public institutions to provide higher cost but lower demand programs" are common. Nevertheless, other factors may be more relevant, among which practicality is one important factor, as suggested from studies done by (Giesecke, 1999a; Levy, 2003b; Nicolescu, 2001), though it sometimes overlaps with cherry-picking. Beside of being resource-dependent, the distinctive nature of the private higher education sector in meeting the needs of the private, business, and employers can also give good explanation (Levy, 1986a). What is more, the fieldwork of this study finds that this factor is probably

_____

1 On private versus public sector in enrollment, see Slantcheva and Levy (2007), Giesecke (1999a), Nagy-Darvas (1997) and Sharvashidze (2002) for Europe, and Levy (2002a) for South America.
[2] For example, referring to music and performing arts and during the interview of this study, a college president said: "it is nice to see those small but less costly programs attract a good handful of students while bringing dynamic campus life to the university".

a weightier one. As will be revealed later by analyzing the job orientations in both general and niche program provision, Chinese private colleges tend to base their program establishment and adjustment primarily on market job demands, as well as on student program demands, which are in turn influenced by labor market demands.

Job-Orientations in General Program Provision

Exploring how private colleges have established their programs proves to be an effective way to discover not only the intention, but also the action of the private job orientation. As suggested by Levy (1986a: 313-319), private colleges have the freedom to select among alternatives, with their autonomy from state direct control. The author's fieldwork finds that private colleges in China choose from a spectrum of programs in establishing what to provide. More often than not, their choices are derived from a series of scanning and analysis, rather than from an intention to avoid high-cost programs or to shy away from public accountability. Most of the administrators interviewed reported that their fields of study were set up after top-down or bottom-up labor market scanning. [1] In the top-down model, senior administrators (presidents and deans) who have major contacts with business and industry usually take industrial interests and labor forecasts along with targeted programs to committees and departments for further discussion on labor and education demands as well as college capacities. If consensus is built up at the lower levels, new program offerings will then be decided. In the bottom-up model, recommendations on new programs often come from individuals who have knowledge about labor market demands through various contacts. Recommendations are further

---

[1] In the proceedings from Ford Foundation on Private Higher Education in China, Xi'an, China, June 3-5, 2006, published by Peking University, labor market scanning for several programs are reported.

analyzed by institutional committees before being presented to the presidents or deans for final approval. Several private colleges also have intermediate-level labor market scanning through field curriculum committees. Curriculum committees do regular labor market scanning. They survey targeted labor markets and identify popular job demands along with relevant education demands. They recommend new programs to the presidents or deans for final approval after assessing college capacity and getting faculty input. [1] No matter which model the private colleges use, one thing is common: they appeal to the demands of enterprises, employers, as well as students in program establishment.

The appealing does not stop after program establishment. The author's interviews show that almost all of the private colleges investigated adjust admission recruitment plans in fields of study to accommodate labor demand changes in both local and national labor markets. They decreased engineering programs after the manufacturing crisis in the middle and late 1990s, but expanded business programs dramatically following China's entry into World Trade Organization (WTO). On the other hand, private colleges do not just tune aimlessly to student demands in admission. Some of them even try to influence students' educational demand by encouraging students to choose fields with potentially strong job demands. For example, the administrators of one college in Shanghai enhanced engineering program admissions despite the fact that students' educational demand for business was much stronger. In influencing student program choice, the college released current employment information and projected good job prospects for engineering programs during its self-controlled admission processes.

---

[1] Also see description by Zhou (2003) on curriculum committee. For example on general labor market scanning, see "Report of Survey on Recent Urgently-Needed Personnel" by report by Wei Li in a departmental meeting on 12/12/2006 in the Chinese University of Information Systems (online at http://www.ciu.gov.cn/jyzx/jyzx_detail.aspx?id=265, accessed on 3/2/2007).

Probably the most fruitful way for analyzing private job orientation is a parallel examination of fields of study provision and reported labor market demands. It reveals that the current fields of study provision in the examined private colleges are in accordance with forecasted labor market demands. First of all, the heavy private focus on foreign languages, business, and computer sciences is aligned to national labor market demands, according to 2005 China's Human Resource Report. [1] Certainly, the fields of study provided by private colleges are also tuned to local labor market demands, whether the local is the locale where the colleges reside or the locale at which the colleges target. For instance, colleges in Shanghai provide programs that have strong labor demands in Shanghai and Yangtze River Delta. [2] All colleges outside of Shanghai, except one, target at their own local markets as well as local and regional labor markets in other cities with strong labor demands, such as those around Shanghai and/or the whole Yangtze River Delta region as well as around Guangzhou, Shenzhen, and/or the whole Pearl River Delta. [3]

Surprisingly, what fields of study private colleges focus on are what major expansions have recently taken place in China's higher education. Appendix N shows the fields of study composition in China's general higher education from 1997 to 2005. [4] In terms of percentage share, it suggests that economics and administration expanded the most; engineering and education also had major expansions; literature, medicine (health

---

[1] The report deems that fields with greatest potentials in employment and career development are foreign business related accounting, law, financial services, foreign language translation, e-commerce, information science and media, logistics, automation, agriculture technology, environmental technology, biological engineering research and development, international business, production, IT, electronics, etc. (see *2010 College Graduate Employment Forecasting*, online at http://www.job128.com/news.asp?id=14685).
[2] Yangze River Delta includes several satellite provinces around Shanghai.
[3] Guangzhou and Shenzheng are two major cities of Pearl River Delta.
[4] All of the investigated accredited colleges are belonged to general higher education. This figure shows percentage composition by field. For original new enrollment, please refer to Appendix N.

sciences), and law only had slight decreases or increases; and science decreased most. [1]

However, given that the total enrollment in 2005 was more than five times of that in

1997, expansions actually took place in all fields, except history. During 1997 and 2005,

the new enrollment increased seven times in economics and administration

(administration was classified separately from economics since 2001), four times in law

and health science, six times in education, four times in literature and engineering, twice

in agriculture, and once in science. Programs in foreign language, arts, and administration

expanded the most. [2] Given the expansion and scale of expansion in different fields of

study, it seems that both private and public institutions have accommodated the same

demands. Given the dynamic nature of economic development in China during the period

and the expanded institutional program provision profile, labor market demands are the

most likely force driving private program provision choices.

Figure 1: Fields of Study Provision of China's Regular Undergraduate Education: 1997-2005

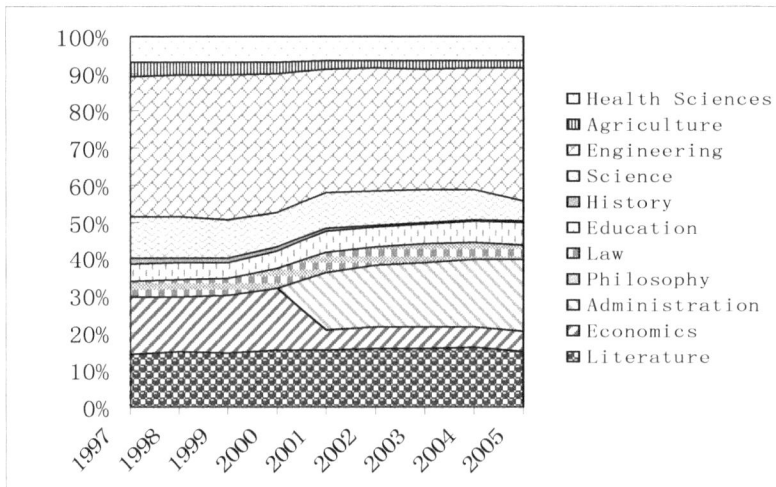

Source: See Appendix N.

---

[1] From 11.0% to 5.4%.
[2] The new enrollment increased from 415,823 to 816,712 in literature during 2001-2005. It increased 38,684 students in foreign language during 2003-2005 and 58,597 in art during 2004-2005.

Job Orientations in Niche Program Provision

The free choices have resulted in distinctive program offerings among Chinese private colleges. Seven of the eight private colleges analyzed have designated some of their programs as niche programs, programs which are usually regarded as being unique, attractive, and strong. [1] Overall, they have designated about one quarter of the programs they offered as niche programs. The most common ones are in English, computer and information sciences, business administration, logistics, accounting, and international economics and trades, [2] though about one quarter of the niche programs are in engineering, science, and health science. Literature programs account for almost half of the niche programs, of which half are related to foreign languages. The likelihood of designating programs in literature and administration as niche programs suggests some extent of intra-institutional homogeneity or isomorphic presence within the private higher education sector. On the other hand, diversity is also manifested and the programs designed by different colleges are quite different from each other. For example, the designated niche programs among the investigated private colleges in Shanghai vary considerably: College A's niche programs are in foreign languages; College B, in journalism, community management, and nutrition; College C, in English and computer sciences; College D, in Arts and Engineering; and College F, in economics and administration. This kind of diversity fits general findings about institutional

---

[1] See Appendix O for a list of college-designed niche programs as reported during the interviews. The administrator of College L did not report its niche program because the original designated niche programs was not well-received by students and employers and the college was still exploring in other programs.
[2] Within commonly designated specific programs, English were designed as niche program by three colleges and all other programs were designated by two colleges. Within all niche fields, economics were designated as niche programs by four colleges, foreign languages and administration by three colleges, arts, computer science, and engineering by two colleges, education, journalism, and health science by one college.

differentiation within the private sector and as a point against isomorphism (Bernasconi, 2004b; Levy, 2002c).

Job orientation permeates the evolution of niche program designation in Chinese private colleges, as this author's fieldwork uncovered, which probably accounts most for the paradoxical phenomenon of having diversity and isomorphism side by side. First, the interviews found that most of the niche programs were designated since college establishment and most founders were said to have been labor market oriented in their designations. At the outset, the founders intended to distinguish their schools from others and prioritized job prospects to attract students through niche program designation. Some of the founders, who were still administrators of the colleges that they had established at the time of my interview, not only claimed that they had set up niche programs in accordance with labor market demands and changed them to accommodate changes in the demands, but also used various exemplary programs to substantiate their claims of prioritizing labor market demands in the process. The choices probably brought in some diversity to the sector, whereas subjection to the same kind of market demands may limit the extent of diversity and then lead to isomorphism.

The claims and examples about job orientations are testified by the ups and downs of many niche programs. Job demands, resulted from the dynamics of the social and economic development, have reinforced the positions of some originally designated niche programs with sustainable job demands, eliminated some with weak job demands or attractions, let some with low and unstable demands scramble, and permitted others to reemerge with renewed demands. Supply Chain Management and Journalism are good examples of those fortunate programs that have extraordinary internal and external job demands in the globalization of Chinese market economy. Failure has been the fate of some other programs that were originally designated as niche programs. For instance, Gardening Arts was initially a niche program by one college in 1990s, but it was soon found to have difficulty both in recruiting new students and in securing jobs for graduates. The engineering programs are still struggling in two colleges analyzed because major layoffs happened to manufacturing at the end of 1990s and the traditional lookdown on manual jobs in China. Still, others languished for several years, but recently came back. For example, the nutrition and food health program in one college was initiated at the early stage of college establishment, yet soon was neglected because of anticipated low job demands. Fortunately, in 2006, it was finally established with increased labor demands as well as governmental funding. Nevertheless, the ebb and flow of niche programs is consistent with Levy's analysis of private institutions in competitive market, where success is not assured and failure can happen (Levy, 2006b). Ultimately, the market forces lead to some convergence in what programs to be designated as niche ones by the private institutions.

The job orientations are apparent when private colleges later introduced new niche programs; some are now considering adding more niche programs to meet labor market demand changes. Most of the newly introduced programs are foreign languages, such as German, Korean, Spanish, and Arabic. The development of the global economy and the booming position of the big cities in China were clearly the reason. The fundamental reasons for establishing niche programs are the presence in Shanghai of big and small German manufacturing companies, such as Siemens, and Korean companies, such as Hyundai and Samsung, and the closer business and general relationship with

Latin American and Arabian countries. A variety of art programs are also on the newly-introduced list, which ranges from interior arts and design, jewelry arts and appraisal, to movie and animation, human beauty and image design, gardening art, and music and piano education. As one president put it, the underlined factors are surely related to the booming economy, which result in better living conditions and increased demand for professionals to satisfy psychological as well as physical needs, which in turn demands increases in professional education. Also importantly, new niche programs are now under consideration because of perceived increase in labor market demands. In general, different colleges are interested in different programs for niche designation, which largely depend on institutional choice and capacity, though some still tend to follow suit.

Twisting traditional programs toward vocationally specific jobs and then designating them as niche programs to meet special demands from certain enterprises in local, regional, or national market are probably equally important to demonstrate the job orientations of private efforts. For example, physical education is a traditional program in many colleges and universities, but a niche one in College K, which incorporates both Chinese Gongfu training and cultural elements, a call from Gongfu Training schools. By doing so, the college fills a void, because most college graduates from physical education programs have limited Chinese Gongfu training and those graduates from secondary schools have lots of Chinese Gongfu training but little theoretical and cultural knowledge. Needless to say, College K's graduates are sought by employers for being equipped to disseminate Chinese culture while performing Gongfu Training. In most of the colleges investigated, majors such as electronics, automation, and engineering often became niche programs after incorporating important practical training and job placement elements, prominently "Education by Order".

Discussion of Major Findings

Elaborately, the above analysis has laid out the institutional efforts managed to meet labor market demands through field of study provision in the Chinese private colleges investigated. T o a high degree, the analysis reveals not only "what" programs are provided, as existing private higher education publications have done , but also important information about "how much" the colleges do as well as "how" they do it. By in large, all the elements regarding "what", "how much", and "how" demonstrate that provision for fields of study has been an anchor where the private colleges investigated in China manage their efforts at enhancing the relevance of private higher education to work (Brennan, Kogan, and Teichler, 1996: 2). The scattered but ample examples also lead to two important generalizations: on the one hand, the private higher education institutions investigated have made major efforts to link private higher education to the labor market through job-oriented program provisions. On the other hand, while job prospects in the labor market are vital in determining what general and niche programs will be offered, in any particular college institutional awareness, choices, resources, and relationship with employers are often the decisive factors in what programs are picked up for provision and then singled out for "niche" designation. The generalized conclusions add another explanation to the paradoxical side-by-side existence of both institutional isomorphism (Levy, 1999) and diversity (Bernasconi, 2004a; Bernasconi, 2004b; Levy, 2004) within the private higher education sector: very likely, the consistent presence of job orientations across private colleges leads to institutional isomorphism in one way or another, such as in field of study provision. Nonetheless, different resources and strategies among institutions keep ample diversity afloat in Chinese private higher education.

How Mission Meets the Labor Market: Educational Delivery and Career Services

How do private colleges meet labor market demands after fields of study have been set up and updated? Besides field of study provision, literature on higher education and graduate employment suggests (Little, 2001: 123-125) that higher education institutions enhance the relevance of higher education to the job market by emphasizing job-related knowledge, skills, and abilities through their educational delivery, and strengthen the linkage between higher education and work through various career services. Have the private colleges in China done things like what the literature says? Other than field of study provision, how have they actively or proactively managed the relationship between higher education and the labor market in order to improve graduate employability and bridge graduates to employers.

<u>**Patterns of Private Efforts in Educational Delivery**</u>

This author's interviews and fieldwork were especially interested in management efforts relevant to educational delivery. The author asked the interviewees to describe their institutions' practices in curriculum setup, curricula changes, faculty hiring and qualifications, course teaching, relevant structures and policies, and networking and partnerships. The author then sought evidence to support what was described. Efforts managed by the private colleges investigated show major patterns in educational delivery.

First, in their curriculum design and delivery, the private colleges have emphasized certain market demands such as foreign languages, computer competency, and professional and practical skills. In this era of globalization and information technology, almost all colleges have made some types of efforts to improve students' language and computer skills, though the efforts vary across colleges and fields of study. Some efforts are extraordinary, comparatively speaking. For instance, College C defines its distinguishing features to be "always committed to quality education and emphasizing the importance of enabling students to have a solid command of English and be good at computer skills". [1] And in English, it has introduced foreign curricula, foreign teaching materials, and foreign teachers. It has also tried to deliver advanced major courses in English and sent over a dozen of its own faculty abroad to be educated. Still, students in some colleges complain about poor quality English teaching and minimal computer access.

Nevertheless, most of the private colleges investigated put major efforts into practical training, though they adopt different strategies to provide the training. Some do it through improving the practicality of regular courses, as will be illustrated in Case Two and Case Three, while one college engages practitioners from industry in core course teaching and one performing art college enables students to perform and produce in their art courses. Some establish special practical training courses. As will be illustrated in Case One, one college facilitates training courses for almost all majors on campus. Still others seek partnerships with employers, build external training bases, and set aside time for students to be trained in training bases, as will be illustrated in Case Four. The efforts can be enormous. Not only are they managed entrepreneurially, sometimes they are even

---

[1] From the college mission.

creative. As will be illustrated in Case Three, students in one performing art course were led to observe people's acts on the street, and then they were asked to perform on street, as different professionals, homeless beggars, disabled, and even as people with mental problems. [1]

Private colleges also adjust and update their curricula to accommodate new labor market demands. The reported adjustments range from constantly immersing new elements into existing courses, adding one or more courses to existing curricula, to swapping curriculum structures. In adding courses, for example, one college had its teacher trained by outsiders and then added an Auto CAD course to a graduation cohort to meet newly-developed labor market demand in the last semester, after the graduating students found they were short of the knowledge in Auto CAD, newly developed skills for several majors, to be employed by many employers. Some colleges use unique curriculum structures to accommodate new labor market demands that are not predictable at the time curricula are designed. College E, for instance, has different adjustment strategies for specialized programs, such as insurance and supply chain management, and for general programs, such as English and economics. In specialized programs, the fourth-year curriculum is set to teach courses incorporated with new market needs, other than those general requirements of the special fields. If job demands from certain companies make it necessary, courses are specially designed and taught to accommodate corporate requirements. In the general programs, the college adopts the strategy of adding popular or distinguishing elements to its regular curricular, such as "English programs + IBM software certificate". Apparently, curriculum changes have many advantages. First and foremost, compared to field of study changes, curriculum changes can be adopted

---

[1] This was reported by a local newspaper.

quickly and thus less dramatically. Certainly, in an ever-changing economy, curriculum changes are relatively less costly, but more important and sometimes more crucial to graduate employment, especially short-term employment.

Because of organizational flexibility, private colleges can and do make efforts to secure specially qualified faculty in order to make changes and adjustments happen. For example, almost all of the colleges with engineering programs hire advanced technicians; College I, a movie and media college, hires many actors, hosts, and directors to teach their programs in acting, directing, and hosting. Private colleges also give special preference to teachers who have corporate backgrounds, and they sometimes seek CEOs, CIOs, CFOs, and corporate directors as adjunct or part-time instructors. In addition, private colleges select young faculty to be trained in companies or be part-time in corporate positions that are relevant to what they teach. Finally, the flexibility of private colleges has one major advantage in that their teachers are usually contracted for relative short periods, three to five years. This gives private college flexibility to drop fields without involving the usual legal issues once the education or labor market for a field evaporates.

Most importantly, partnerships are presented in management efforts to link educational delivery to the labor market. All of the colleges investigated have undertaken college-industry cooperation to associate learning and research with producing and practices to enhance the linkage, especially for practical training purposes. For example, College C has signed cooperation contracts with two dozen corporations, hotels, business centers, and IT bases for establishing "practical training bases"; College D has even more such corporate partners for its practical trainings, as illustrated in the following Case One;

College A utilizes its funding company's personnel in different business areas for teaching different courses; College I partners with the film industry to various courses, as to be described in Case Three; and College L has major advertising firms and production company participation in teaching its advertising courses, as to be illustrated in Case Two. Although most partnerships are with industry, there are also agreements and cooperation with governmental agencies, professional associations, foreign universities, public colleges and universities, and even, sometimes, with other private higher education institutions.

In their efforts to link education delivery to labor market demands, the private colleges investigated have institutionalized the management processes through established structures and policies. To assure successful implementation of various emphases and necessary changes, they have set up structures and made policies, along with human and financial commitment. Most of them have feedback-based curriculum adjustment structures to review curriculum and to discuss curriculum adjustment according to teacher observation, alumni feedback, industrial consultations, employer responses, and institutional analysis. For practical training, not only have they established organizational structures and made relevant policies, but they also set up major facilities, such as on-campus training centers, as will be illustrated in Case One, and off-campus training bases with various industry sectors.

Patterns of Private Efforts in Career Services

The author's interviews and fieldwork also paid attention to private management efforts in career services. The author observed several major patterns in the private effort.

First, in almost all of the Chinese private colleges investigated, career services are institutionalized. Established organizational structures with associated policies and employed advisers are common and the most important features. All of the private colleges investigated have special offices staffed with employment advisors, of which two thirds are exclusively for career services. The other third also have admissions functions. These offices usually employ a number of professional employment advisers, ranging from one to a dozen. While most advisers are recent college graduates, leading advisors often have substantial experiences in dealing either with graduate employment at public colleges or in managing human resource departments for firms and companies. As will be described in Case Five, one of so many examples that are truly laudatory and worthwhile to describe is College E, which has a team of professional advisors, forming an internal network for career instructions and building an external network with employers for job placement. Recently, website support has become the other important tool for institutionalizing career services. Almost all colleges investigated use the internet to disseminate information regarding graduate employment, such as career planning and job hunting articles, lists of graduates seeking jobs, lists of employers seeking graduates, as well as graduate employment policies. For these purposes, half of them only have one or two web-pages to list information, whereas the other half have separate websites, providing personalized log-ins for graduates to search employer databases and for employers to search possible hires. One even sets up an independent and business-like domain, primarily for its graduate employment purposes.

The private colleges investigated provide a variety of career services, though they are different in what services they provide and when as well as how to provide them.

Most of the colleges engage in a series of events and activities from November or earlier, prior to students' graduation the following June. For example, in College A, the events for 2007 graduating students were featured with its president's presentation on entrepreneurship and self-employment, speeches by the editor-in-chief of a famous magazine on careers and employment, lessons by local labor intermediary officials about psychological adjustment during job-hunting, as well as presentations and recruiting by a group of employers. [1] Three colleges also provide structured career services throughout each year of student college presence. Often started by career planning and series of course offerings during the first year of student enrollment, such services are either structured internally by the college, or cooperatively by several local colleges, or even mandated by the provincial department of education. Still, as criticized, graduating students of one college complained that it provided almost no graduate employment services, other than one or two campus-wide warm-up meetings and a couple of superficial class sessions on job-hunting.

Of the services provided, practical training and job placement are the two most emphasized. All of the private colleges investigated said that they had undertaken major efforts in securing opportunities for their students to do practical training. Their claims are bolstered by recognized efforts and by corroborating statements from students, employers, other colleges, and scholars. For example, it is well-known that College E spent a major sum annually to secure practical training for its students and to locate jobs for its graduates. Besides encouraging graduates to participate in various job fairs and training, half of the private colleges investigated even go so far as to promise career arrangement and formal job placement. In two colleges with relative small sizes, it is said

---

[1] Information comes from college newsletter.

that each student can get two to three job recommendations. Moreover, a couple of colleges also promise that their alumni can come back for further job services for free, if they are not satisfied with their jobs.

One way or another, the majority of the private colleges investigated seek to get alumni feedback. The author observed that College K uses one computer program to track its graduates; College L abides by the graduate employment feedback survey of its provincial department of education; College A asks its class supervisors to track their graduates; College D surveys their graduates each year during August and October by questionnaire and by visits to its alumni; College E has an alumni visit team, headed by its president and having visited its alumni across the country. Several of the colleges have also set up alumni associations. More importantly, they utilize their alumni network, by inviting them to give employment feedback, to serve on curriculum committees, to encourage entering students, to present to graduating students on their job-hunting experiences, as well as to recruit them.

Networking with different entities, the private colleges build partnerships to provide adequate practical training, keep their promises of job placement, and bridge between graduates and employers. External partnerships are the most apparent. Most private colleges partner with industry and employers to conduct practical training and perform job placement services, which is also commonly practiced in many public colleges. Many of the private colleges investigated also partner with governmental, nonprofit private, and even prominent commercial labor intermediaries and human resource recruiting companies, which is seldom heard in the public sector. For example, College K is the only known college in China that has solicited, financed, and moved the local Labor and Talent Exchange Center to reside on campus. College E even partnered with China Human Resource (www.chinahr.com), a company listed on New York Stock Exchange, for its job fairs. Perhaps the most unique is the private colleges' partnership, unheard of in the public sector, with parents for the purpose of graduate employment. Three of the colleges investigated informed students' parents about the current situation of graduation employment and instructed them on how to help their children to secure positions. In the private sector, internal networking is also undertaken, for purposes of both career advices and job placement. For instance, several private colleges formally ask their faculty and staff to utilize relatives and friends in employing their graduates. Such practices are also unheard of in the public sector.

Cases Illustrating the Private Efforts in Educational Delivery and Career Services

Overall, scattered evidence suggests that private efforts at enhancing graduate employability and bridging students to employers are ample, though strategies vary across colleges. The following five cases, four dealing with course delivery as well as practical training and one on career services, illustrate how private colleges have linked their education delivery to the labor market and built the linkage between higher education and work through different types of partnerships, along with relevant structures and policies. The five cases take place in different colleges, two in recently accredited four-year colleges, two in an accredited three-year college, and one in an unaccredited college.

Case One: *On-Campus Practical Training with an Entrepreneur Advising Board.*

[1] In facilitating its mission to meet the "needs for advanced applied professionals in science and technology", College D, an accredited four-year college, has built an on-campus practical training center to carry out various vocational/technical trainings. The center is well financed and equipped, with almost four million dollars' (¥30 million RMB) worth of facilities, for trainings in different fields. Moreover, its different practical trainings are guided by clear policies on how the facilities should be managed, how the trainings should be carried out, how the teachers should be selected, how the outcomes should be documented and assessed, and how the needs of adjustment should be executed. The management involves a well-defined team, with one president leading and participation of different administrative staff as well as regular faculties. Lastly, but most importantly, the college has secured and signed mutual agreements with 100 or so companies in a variety of enterprises to support its practical trainings. The college asks the companies to train and employ its students, to participate in its curriculum and teaching material development, and to send their high-level executives and technicians to teach its courses on campus. It even cooperates with two hotels and one electronics product company to educate student cohort classes according to their designs, usually with the prerequisites that the hotels and the company participate in the training processes and hire some of its students later on. Of course, while possible, the college also helps the companies in personnel training, marketing efforts, and relevant research. The efforts seem to pay off. The college is now recognized and rewarded by the city with an award and grant for practical training; its graduate employment rate has been over 90 percent for several consecutive years.

---
[1] Information comes from the college website specifically for practical training and from the field trip.

Case Two*: "Education by Order" for Individual Companies.* [1] To produce the right advertising professionals that corporations demand, College L, an accredited three-year college, established an Advertising Program Curriculum Committee, with the help of local advertising association and participation of 25 corporations and advertising firms in 2000. By mutual agreement and relevant policies and with practical training bases in three local production companies and two local advertising firms, it has set up a distinctive educational delivery model. [2] Cohorts of students are trained through curricula composed of regular courses and special practical training courses. Students take their regular classes Monday through Friday, mostly on-campus, and take their special practical training classes on Saturday and Sunday, mostly in training bases. A group, including professors of the college, executives, division managers, experts from well-known local product companies, and leading professionals from local advertisement companies, makes joint efforts for teaching and training. Students and faculty of the college engage in real advertising tasks for corporations. Arrangements are made for graduating students to temporarily take relevant positions for one to three months while having the instruction and supervision of the workers of the positions. The "education by order" model was praised by employers and education officials as "the right way to link

---

[1] The information for this section mostly comes from news and documents, some from my interviews.
[2] An exemplary course, Enterprise Brand and Image Design, can show the features. It was co-taught by three professors from the college, one advanced advertisement professional from an advertisement firm and one economic analyst from a chemical production company. Based on the actual branding needs of a real company, the teaching engaged students in market survey, brand marketing plan, package design, advertisement, conference announcement, etc. During the processes, students learned about the product in its production, were informed the marketing requirements by the product company, were instructed on marketing survey goals and tasks by an advertisement firm, did a survey plan, were organized to execute the plans, and then finally compiled their final reports and presented to the advertisement firm and the product company.

college students to corporations" and "accurately helped corporations to find the right people they needed".

Case Three*: "Learning by Practicing and Producing" in College and Corporation Co-owned Business.* [1] As with John Dewey's "learning by doing", students in College I, an unaccredited three-year movie and mass media college, are asked to practice and produce during courses, such as producing movies and dramas .The college has a TV station and a co-owned film and TV show production crew for practicing and producing. Students run the station. They practice what they learn for courses in the station, and they learn while running the station. Except for the director position, students take up all positions of the TV station as well as Film and TV show crew. Students of performing arts often participate in real professional shooting of and acting in video films and TV dramas. Students of hosting preside over regular college events and the college TV channel, as well as host a variety of social shows and events. Photography students engage in creative photography by themselves and in shooting movies; choreographer students help others to dress up for movies and events; students of directing direct films, TV dramas, and other programs. All these are guided by professors, who are themselves practitioners of their professions. Consequently, the college has issued and received approvals for five television dramas and one movie since 1999. One drama was popularly broadcasted nationwide while the author visited the college. Therefore, upon graduation and unlike graduates from many public colleges, its graduates not only have already had practiced what are supposed to do for real jobs, but also have their own product to demonstrate their performance. As a result, most of them are usually hired far before

---

[1] Information comes from the college website, my interview, and local newspaper.

graduation. Some of their graduates are well-recognized in their careers, especially

television hosting.

   Case Four: *"Comprehensive Practical Training for Graduating Students through Partnership"*. In College A, practical training occupies a major chunk of most program curricula, sometimes as high as 40 percent of total program course hours. With a full-time specially designed position, practical training officer, the college provides four types of practical training: observations, practical training through specific courses, program practical training, and comprehensive practical training for graduating students. [1] Among the four, the required comprehensive practical training for graduating student classes is the most emphasized and best managed. Often running from February through April, its goal is to improve student understanding of the country and their fields, utilize learned skills and knowledge through practice, enhance problem-solving abilities, and improve social skills. It is coherently managed with dozens of different policies and well structured with key personnel from major offices, such as academic affairs, student affairs, and career services, as well as deans, department chairs, practical training instructors, and class supervisors. As with many other private colleges, having training bases is one of the most important features of the comprehensive practical training. The president reported that the college had signed formal training partnership agreements with over 50 companies in summer 2006. The practical training officer was said to engage in contact with companies in different fields regularly. The training base companies often participate in curriculum design and select their best employees to provide practical training. Additionally, its mother-company, with well-established

---

[1] Office of Academic Affairs, 2005. Temporary Management Methods for Practical Training in College A. Institutional document, released on 10/28/2005.

business in technology, finance and investment, manufacturing, pharmacy, and real estate, also serves as reliable base for various training purposes.

Case Five*: Building Internal and External Networks with a Team of Professionals.* [1] Of many impressive examples in career service, what College E has done is the most commendable, despite disclosed malpractice in its reported graduate employment rates. [2] As shown in

Figure 2, the college sets up both internal and external networks, adopts marketing strategies, and proactively makes major efforts in its services. Relying on a coherent team of a dozen professional career service advisors, its well-organized internal networks are established to instruct and support students for employment. On the team, one vice-president is primarily responsible for career services and graduate job placement. Under the Center for Career Services, the professional advisors perform key functions. They conduct career counseling, teach career planning courses, arrange career-related presentations, perform job placement, write recommendations, handle employment information, document graduate employment profiles, make contact with employers, visit and survey employers, and even provide human resource management suggestions to employers. Each advisor is also responsible for career service activities for one or two specific schools, their departments and student cohorts. At the class and individual level, class supervisors help career service professionals to provide services to individual students in their classes. The team working on internal student career counseling and planning service is also responsible for its external networks in marketing

---

[1] Information comes from the interview and a published book of the vice-president of the college.
[2] In 2006, a news report suggested that some employment rates reported by the college might be not authentic. I also found that someone changed the answers in a dozen or so questionnaires from one program, which then were discarded.

119

students to employers, by adopting business-like practices. In its geographical market differentiation, the team first surveys students and employers before coming up with a national job recommendation and placement plan, based on student family province origins, fields of study structure, and student preferences for employment regions. It then undertakes further market differentiation. Under regions, they differentiate the labor market in terms of provinces, cities, corporations, positions, and occupations. While its presidents and deans focus on contacts at the regional and province level, individual professional advisors work more at province, city, and local corporation level. [1] The college also adopts different strategies to connect graduates with employers, such as so-called supermarket strategy, auction strategy, promotion strategy, general supply strategy, education by order strategy, training base strategy, part-time strategy, apprenticeship strategy, and indirect intermediary strategy. [2] The team regularly visits employers and inquires about the possibilities of hiring their students. It also recommends students to potential employers. As the first of its kind to initiate "education by order" strategy in 2002, the college still uses the strategy in some programs. [3] Additionally, it has over 63 external practical training bases across China. Its graduates are often employed by the base companies after practical training. The college utilizes its own resources to provide on-campus practices. For example, most on-campus services, stores, logistic team, and dining rooms are partially managed by its own students.

---

[1] Information comes from the interview.
[2] All of the strategies closely resemble to what take place in commercial companies. For the length and purposes of this case, only the terms are introduced here.
[3] Changwan Ke, 2002, Education by Order Silently Went into Private Colleges. 2/12/2002. *China Education Daily.* Page 1. Available online at http://www.jyb.com.cn/gb/jybzt/2002zt/mbjy/19.htm.

Figure 2 The Internal and External Networks for Career Services in College E

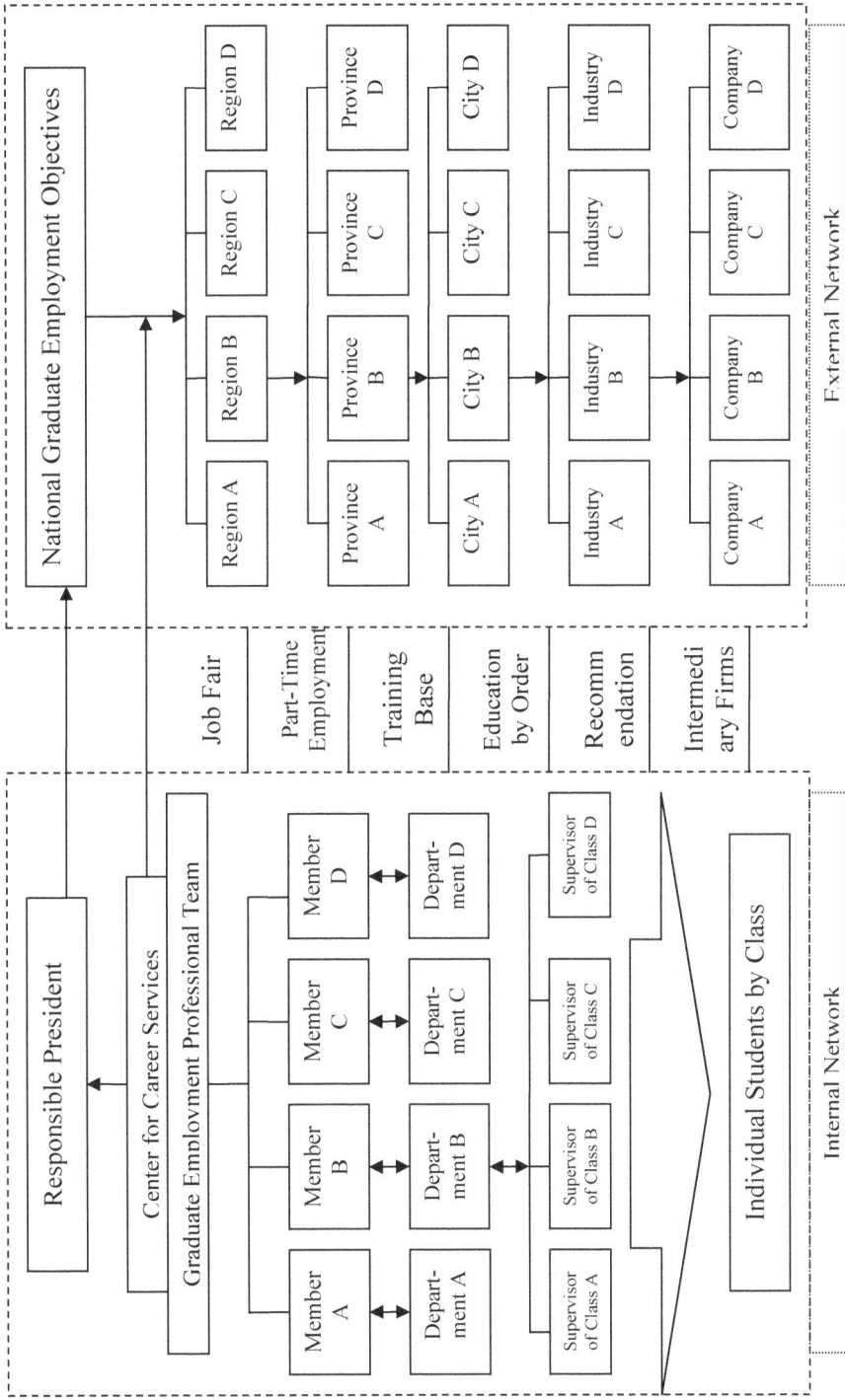

Source: Interviews, documents, and a book on private education (the author is kept anonymous).

Discussion of Major Findings

The patterns observed and the cases described suggest two seemingly paradoxical findings about educational delivery and career services in the private colleges investigated: on one hand, the colleges are similar to each other in making efforts to link private higher education to the labor market. First, they emphasize several common elements, especially practical skills and training, to meet labor market demands. They then establish structures and policies to institutionalize their efforts. Lastly, they network with various internal or external entities to carry out their efforts. On the other hand, they are also different from each other in how much effort they have made and precisely *how* they have managed their efforts.

The literature on private higher education and on higher education and the labor market would give reasonable explanation for the paradoxical findings. First, what the private colleges have done to meet labor market demands fits well with literature on how higher education institutions generally approach the relationships between higher education and work (Brennan, 2004; Brennan, Johnston, Little, Shah, and Woodley, 2001; Brennan, Kogan, and Teichler, 1996; Little, 2001; Paul, Teichler, and Van Der Velden, 2000; Teichler, 1989, 1994, 1995, 1996, 2002, 2003). Consistent with the literature, the private colleges investigated have approached the relationship from its two dimensions. Their emphasis on certain elements that are appreciated by the labor market in educational delivery is clearly to improve the employability of their graduates, along the dimension on the relevance of higher education to work (Brennan, Kogan, and Teichler, 1996: 2; Business/Higher Education Round, 2002). Their networking efforts serve as fundamental linkages between higher education and work in the sense of

122

bridging graduates to employers through career services (de la Fuente, 1995). The networking efforts also sometimes function to improve the relevance of higher education to work when they are directed towards curricula delivery and practical training (Rosenbaum, Kariya, Settersten, and Maier, 1990; Villar, Juan, Corominas, and Capell, 2000). Moreover, as discussed previously on the job orientation in program provisions, the distinctiveness of the new private higher education explains why the private colleges investigated seek to meet labor market demands (Levy, 1986a, 1986b, 1987, 1991, 1992). Again, private higher education literature would use the concepts and theories on institutional isomorphism (Levy, 1999) and institutional diversity (Bernasconi, 2004b; Levy, 2002c) to interpret the similarities in job-orientated efforts and the differences in types and levels of efforts. The consistent seeking of legitimacy through meeting job demands colleges may result in the similarities across private colleges, whereas different resources and rational choices contribute diversity among them.

Nevertheless, the generalized findings pose a major question: how commonly do the demand-absorbing private colleges actually do what the colleges selected in this study do? First, it must be stated clearly that the colleges selected for case study were the result both of selection and self-selection. Bias might have resulted from self-selection even though the selection was neutrally managed. Additionally, half of the private colleges investigated are well-known in China and thought of as quite good, serious, enterprising colleges. Although they are typical among the accredited colleges, they may also be somewhat atypical of the whole private higher education sector, because the majority of private institutions are not accredited. If we categorize the private colleges investigated as demand-absorbing and non-elite, they are nonetheless in the upper echelon of that category. Colleges such as College E, College K, and College C could even qualify as semi-elite. From the perspective of career services, that is the case especially for College E, whose effort level is almost unmatched in either the private or the public sector. Nevertheless, though not every private college investigated engages in practical training at the same level as the four colleges described in the first four cases, the main practices described in these cases are rather typical of efforts in the Chinese private higher education sector in general.

Another question arises here: how novel and immense are the private efforts, compared to what public colleges do? Of course, not having surveyed public colleges makes any conclusions difficult. Nevertheless, the author's general knowledge about the public colleges, a review of the websites of the public colleges analyzed, and some publications on public college graduate employment suggest that private-public differences are notable, especially in practical training and institutional networking. In general, private colleges give more emphasis to meeting labor market demands in educational delivery and career services than their public counterparts, particularly through practical training. They also make more effort in networking with employers for education and service purposes. However, as major parts of Chinese public higher education prioritize the job market and entrepreneurial activity, most public higher education institutions in China also seriously engage in various efforts to facilitate graduate employment, at a magnitude that we can speculate might be higher than their counterparts in many other countries, including the Untied States.

Summary of the Chapter

In its endeavor to answer the research question on how and how well private higher education institutions have made efforts to link private higher education to the labor market, this study focuses on "how" in this chapter. It examines how private higher education institutions in China have made efforts to link private higher education to the labor market by analyzing their mission statements, fields of study, educational delivery, career services, as well as relevant networking efforts. It finds that private colleges have committed their efforts in structures, policies, and activities to incorporate labor producing for market demands in their mission; to provide fields of study and programs in accordance with market needs; to enhance graduate employability through special curriculum elements, curriculum changes, education delivery, and institutional networking; and to bridge graduates and jobs through various career services and institutional networking.

Beyond the above general summary of relevant findings, differences among the private colleges investigated, in both practices and intentions, are mentioned throughout this chapter. Moreover, those serious though commercial private colleges are different from others in major ways. Recapped along the eight criteria set up in Chapter One to distinguish serious private colleges from mere demand-absorbing ones, the major differences are shown in Table 1 and as explained below.

Accreditation and Aspiration for Accreditation: Except three, all of the ten private colleges investigated are accredited. Among the unaccredited colleges, only one of them seriously pursued accreditation, with a brand new campus for expansion and various facilities for student learning to meet key criteria for accreditation.

Program Provision: As all of the interviewees described about how their programs had been established and changed along with market economy development and changes, it seems that all private colleges have established their programs in accordance with market demands. Except one, all of the private colleges investigated also have one or more designated niche programs.

Curriculum Provision: Market-appreciated special elements, such as English competency, computer skills, and practical skills are emphasized by almost all of the private colleges investigated, in their curriculum establishment and course delivery. The interviewees of several colleges also mentioned their feedback-based curriculum changes and related organizational structures.

Faculty Composition and Qualification: All of the private colleges investigated have a core of qualified full-time faculty for their education delivery. Several colleges also give special preferences to faculty with market-recognized reputations and qualifications, such as oversea education, advanced degrees, faculty with major research and publications, as well as faculty with both academia and business experiences.

Administration: Several private colleges have appropriate structures, well-established policies, and smooth coordination in their efforts, while some can barely demonstrate what they have done for graduate employment.

Job Concern: As mentioned before, almost all of the private colleges investigated are concerned with job prospects and about graduate employment rates.

Employer Feedback: Except one, all of the private colleges investigated have some type of partnership with employers, either for education delivery or for graduate employment. Half of them also have institutionalized structures to pursue regular networking with business and industry.

Alumni Feedback: All of the colleges have some networking efforts with alumni. Less than half of the private colleges investigated have structures to follow up with their graduates and most of them do so through recently established alumni associations.

Table 7: Comparing the Management Efforts of Private Colleges

Criteria	Specific Efforts	College										
		A	B	C	D	E	F	G	I	J	K	L
Accreditation	Being Accredited? Aspiring for Accreditation by Trying to Meet Accreditation Standards?	Y	Y	Y	Y	Y	N/N	N/N	N/Y	N	Y	Y
Program Provision	Market-Oriented? One or More Niche/Brand Fields?	Y	Y	Y	Y	Y	Y	Y	Y	N	Y	Y/N
Curriculum Provision	Job-Oriented Element? Feedback-Based Changes?	Y	Y/N	Y/N	Y	Y	Y	Y/N	Y	N	Y	Y
Faculty Composition and Qualification	A Core of Qualified Full-Time Faculty for the Programs? Major Efforts or at least Concern to Hire Reputable and Qualified Faculty?	Y	Y	Y	Y	Y	N	N	Y	N	Y	Y
Administration	Coherent Administrative Structure & Policy?	Y	N	Y	Y	Y	N	N	N	N	Y	Y
Job Concern	Labor Market Scanning and Concern about Labor Market Demand?	Y	Y	Y	Y	Y	Y	Y	Y	N	Y	Y
Employer Contact	Various Networking Efforts with Employers? Follow-Up Structure?	Y	Y/N	Y/N	Y	Y	Y	N	Y/N	N	Y	Y/N
Alumni Feedback	Various Networking Efforts with Graduates? Follow-Up Structure?	Y/N	Y/N	Y/N	Y	Y	Y/N	Y	Y/N	N	Y	Y/N

* An interviewed private college affiliated to a public university.
Note: *"Y" means "Yes", which indicates a college has done things mentioned in the "content"; "N" means "No", which indicates a college has not done things mentioned in the "content" for a particular criteria.*
Source: *Interviews, websites, publications, newspaper, and fieldwork.*

CHAPTER FIVE: QUANTITATIVE DATA ANALYSIS ON INITIAL

GRADUATE EMPLOYMENT OUTCOMES

Using the data collected through the graduate student survey introduced in

Chapter Three, this chapter approaches the "how well" part of the research question. It

analyzes initial graduate employment outcomes and graduate feedback on institutional

efforts linked to graduate employment. The four major employment outcomes identified

by the literature review presented in Chapter Two are analyzed: employment status,

earnings, job and education match, and job satisfaction. This chapter also examines the

associations between the measured outcomes and two efforts related to graduate

employment, niche field and career service office, as identified in Chapter Four.

Employment Status

Given the criticism of its value in the labor market (Goodman, 2003), finding out

whether private college graduates in China are well hired in the labor market is crucial.

Fortunately, our graduate survey provides ample data. The findings on college

employment performance are reassuring. The majority of the private college graduates

surveyed were employed shortly before or soon after graduation. Of the 458 private

college graduates who responded to the question on employment status within four-

week period around graduation on July 1, 2006, 58.9 percent indicated either that "I had

a job offer or one job" or "I was self-employed". 28.4 percent reported "I had no job

offer or job, and was still searching". The rest reported either "I had no job

offer/unemployed, but was not searching", "I haven't graduated or I was preparing for examinations", or "I was preparing for or was in further education" (see Figure 3 for details). In summary, of the private college graduates who were actively seeking employment in 2006, two thirds (67.5%) found jobs and, thus, could be categorized as "being employed".

Private v. Public

Compared to reports by public officials and other publications, the initial employment rates of private college graduates in China are comparable to those of their public counterpart. The 67.5 percent initial employment rate of the private college graduates is comparable to that of official reports about general college graduates, most of whom are from public colleges, which was 71.8 percent in 2006. [1] Although the initial rate is much higher than the 32.9 percent rate reported by (Wu, 2003) for private colleges, it is close to her report for public colleges, 66.9 percent. This finding on the comparability of the employment rate of private college graduates to public ones is consistent with other studies (Cao, 2000; Zhou, 2003).

The employment rates by education level found by this study are comparable to those of general college graduate employment at the associate degree level, but better at the bachelor degree level. The employment rates for the private college graduates surveyed were 66.5 percent at associate degree level and 93.3 percent at bachelor degree level, which are both higher than that of general college graduate cohorts, mostly public college graduates, which respectively are 62.1 percent and 81.7 percent (Bao, 2006b).

---

[1] The Minister of Education in China reported the rates at National Work Conference on College Graduate Employment (see the news for 2006 rate at http://job.pzhu.cn/show_article.asp?id=349 about 2006). The rates were combined rates of both graduate and undergraduate students.

The finding about employment rates by education level still holds even if only the colleges in Shanghai are considered. [1] According to the Shanghai Municipal Department of Education, the college graduate employment rate in Shanghai was 89.1 percent at associate degree level and 91.6 percent at bachelor degree level in October 2006. [2] Apparently, at the bachelor degree level, the employment rate of private college graduates, 93.3 percent in July 2006, was higher than the general college graduates three to four months later. Although at associate degree level, the employment rate of private college graduates was 26.1 percent lower in late June and early July 2006 than general graduates in October 2006, such a gap could possibly be caught up to within a period of three to four months. For example, the employment rate of graduates from College D, a three-year private college, was 73.6 percent in early July 2006 and jumped to 99.4 percent in early December of the same year. [3]

Figure 3: Graduate Employment Status/Rate in Surveyed Private Colleges

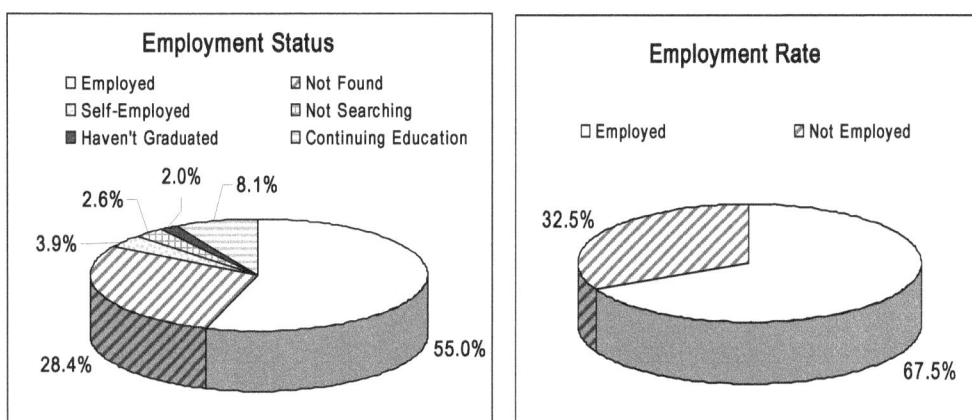

---

[1] The employment rate of the one college outside of Shanghai is 83.3%, higher than that in Shanghai
[2] Chinese College Graduate Employment Information Net. "Shanghai College Graduate Employment is 91.38%", see news at http://job.chsi.com.cn/jyzd/jyxx/200612/20061230/733217.html (accessed 4/20/2007).
[3] The report on December employment rate was from the college newsletter.

Associations of Initial Employment Status with Other Factors

While the majority of the graduates of the new private sector find jobs around graduation, this study finds that the private institutions investigated are significantly different from each other in this regard (Chi-square = 95.535, coefficient = .415, df =25, p < 0.001), even though all of them were established recently and have similar years of operation. College A, College C, College D, and College E had a much higher percentage of employed graduates than College B and College F (see Table 8). The employment rates in all of the first four colleges were over 70 percent, whereas it was only 39.2 percent in College F, the only unaccredited private college, and 51.2 percent in College B, an accredited three year college in Shanghai.

What factors may contribute to the significant institutional differences in graduate employment rate? Although most research on higher education and the labor market does not examine institutional effects, as if where graduates went to college does not matter, many studies suggest that certain educational, background, and labor market characteristics make differences in employment outcomes. Educational level and fields of study are two major factors, as mentioned in the literature review of Chapter Two. In the Chinese case and for the new private higher education sector, accreditation status could be crucial. Other factors identified include student demographic and family background characteristics, such as gender, ethnicity, social-economic status, parents' educational level, student grades, student personality and preferences. [1]

---

[1] See the findings of series of studies on "The National Graduates Survey in Canada" (online at www.statcan.ca/english/sdds/5012.htm), "Higher Education and Graduate Employment in Europe and Japan" (online at http://www.uni-kassel.de/wz1/TSEREGS/publi_e.htm), and Recent College Graduate Survey of National Center for Educational Statistics. Min, Ding, Wen, and Yue (2005) is a good empirical

Consistent with others, this study finds that several factors likely contribute to the significant differences in initial graduate employment rates among the new Chinese private institutions, including field of study, educational level, college GPA, high school origin, college entrance score, and accreditation status (see Table 8). In terms of accreditation status, the overall employment rate of graduates from the accredited private colleges was 71.5 percent, which is 32.3 percent higher than the 39.2 percent employment rate of the unaccredited private college graduates. Understandably, other things may go along with accreditation, presumably better student background, better quality instruction, established networks, and higher public trust. Nevertheless, since only one unaccredited college participated in the survey, the finding here can be of random effect.

Institutional differences may also be results by different fields of study, since this study finds that employment rate likely varies by fields of study (Chi-square = 9.915, Coefficient = 0.156, N=400, df =4, $p < 0.05$), as suggested by many (Finnie, 1999a, 1999c; OECD, 1992; Teichler, 1989). Administration had the lowest employment rate, only 57.1 percent, much lower than that in other fields, all of which are over 70 percent. While the demand for graduates in administration may play a role, the supply side may give a better explanation. For example, planned enrollment for fall 2006 in administration was 18.9 percent, higher than any other field except literature, which includes three different types of programs: languages, arts, and other humanities and social sciences (see Appendix M). Additionally, while not being representative in sampling, the total number of graduates in administration in the sample is almost twice as many as that of other fields.

study on Chinese graduate employment.

Found likely to be related to initial employment rate, educational level (Chi-Square = 4.741, Coefficient = 0.108, N =400, df = 1, p < 0.05), student college GPA (R = 0.193, p <0.01), and college entrance score (R = 0.242, p < 0.01, N =164) are also factors possibly contributing to the institutional diversity. Graduates with bachelor degrees had over a 93 percent chance to be employed, 30 percent higher than those with an associate degree. Overall, the higher the college grades, [1] the higher the employment rate will be. [2] As observed and informed by teachers of the new private institutions, this study finds that students with higher college entrance scores (N= 194, mean = 322.3, min = 122, max = 600, SE = 7.081, SD = 98.6) are more likely to perform better [3] and then are often more sought after by employers. Graduates with college entrance scores of 250 or lower had only a 55.8 percent chance of being employed around graduation. Those with scores between 251 and 400 had a 73.4 percent chance and those with scores above 400 had a chance of over 90.9 percent. Of course, as labor economics would explain, the three factors can serve as signals for employers or associate with productivity.

Different profiles in student high school origin may also lead to institutional diversity in employment status. As suggested by other studies (Bao, 2006a; Sapatoru, Nicolescu, and Slantcheva, 2003), this study finds that private college graduates from academic high schools are significantly more likely to be employed than those of vocational high school origins (Chi-Square = 12.525, Coefficient = 0.183, N =362, df =

---

[1] GPA is originally on 100 scale, mean = 74.1, min = 60, max = 96, SE = .544, SD = 8.1; then recoded to 8 scales, starting at 60 and each scale added 5 points.
[2] College GPA has an interestingly inconsistent relationship to employment rate: those with grades between 70 and 80 have a lower employment rate than those with grades between 60 and 70. Possibly, although the employers still consider the signed productivity associated with degree and grades in their hiring, those with grades between 60 and 70 may have attractive traits, as some teachers and administrators suggest, or they are not as choosy about accepting jobs.
[3] It correlation with college GPA is 0.160, p<0.05.

1, p= 0.001). The employment rate of private college graduates surveyed who graduated from academic high schools was 72.3 percent, 21.6 percent higher than those from vocational high schools. The labor market may reward certain academic characteristics of graduates from academic high schools (Cappellari, 2004). For example, the graduates surveyed from academic high schools had a significantly higher average GPA than those from vocational high schools (68.7 v. 75.4, t=5.138, df =214, p < 0.001).

In summary, several variables related to productivity, either signaling or of human capital, are somehow related to graduate employment status, which in turn might have contributed to institutional differences in graduate employment rate. However, this research fails to confirm the relationships between employment status and many other variables that are found by many (Fitzgerald and Burns, 2000; Min, Ding, Wen, and Yue, 2005), including gender, father's educational level, mother's educational level, family's province origin, family's urbanity, and work experience. The reason is unknown, though the special attributes of Chinese private colleges or their unique labor markets might be one (Bao, 2006a 614) and the small sample size can be another.

Examining Institutional Effects on Employment Status Using Regression

The above analysis reveals that significant institutional differences in initial graduate employment status exist. These differences may be influenced by factors that are valued by the labor market and directly or indirectly relevant to institutional characteristics (e.g., accreditation status), higher education experiences (educational level, field of study, college GPA), as well as graduates' academic background characteristics (e.g., high school type, college entrance scores), as categorized by Fitzgerald and Burns (2000).

Can the associated factors explain the significant institutional differences in employment status? With Fitzgerald's classification, logistic regression analysis (see Table 9) reveals interesting findings. First, it shows that "specific institution", which indicates where graduates went for college, explains more (Model 1B) about employment status than college accreditation status (Model 1A), though the latter has a very strong relationship to employment status (BCI = 12.98). [1] As shown in Model 1B, both College F and College B have significant negative relationships to employment rate. Presumably, College F could be due to its non-accreditation status, in that employers are less likely to trust the quality of the graduates from unaccredited colleges. However, the reason for College B, an accredit college, is unknown. Second, when the higher education experience related factors is controlled (see Model 2), the significant negative relationship between employment status and College F, an unaccredited college, disappears, whereas the significant negative relationship between College B and employment status stays the same. Third, the negative and significant relationship between College B and employment status is strengthened (see Model 3), the only significant factor shown in the logistic regression modeling, after controlling variables of both background characteristics and higher education experiences. To sum up, regression analysis consistently shows that where graduates went to college matters and institutional characteristics may matter the most although employment status is

----

[1] BCI (Bayes Information Criterion = Wald-logarithm N) was proposed by Raftery in 1995 as a way of assessing the independent variables in a logistic regression equation. BIC of 0-2 is weak, 2 - 6 is moderate, 6 - 10 is strong, and over 10 is very strong (see http://www2.chass.ncsu.edu/garson/PA765/logistic.htm).

contingent upon a variety of other factors that are related to higher education experiences, background, and labor market characteristics.

It makes sense that where graduates went to college matters for employment status. First, accredited status should be crucial in bringing trust from employers for the new private higher education sector in China. Other associated institutional factors, such as academic ranking nature (Min and others, 2005) and college selectivity (Fitzgerald and Burns, 2000), may also work. Nevertheless, existing publications and the above regression analysis cannot give satisfactory explanations on why a specific institution matters so significantly within the new private sector, particularly in the case of College B, a college similar to the other private institutions investigated from major perspectives.

The findings from the qualitative analysis on diverse institutional management efforts in Chapter Four give some further clues. For instance, two major efforts, niche field and the existence of a separate office for career services, are both found to be related to employment status. Majoring in a field of study designated as "niche field" seems to lower the possibility of getting employed around graduation (Chi-square = 7.809, df =1, $p < 0.01$, contingency coefficient = 0.138). 61.2 percent graduates of the niche-fields were employed shortly before or soon after graduation, whereas 74.3 percent of regular fields were employed then. In contrast, a separate office for career services is helpful (Chi-square = 39.611, df =1, $p < 0.001$, contingency coefficient = 0.300) for employment status. Those graduated from private colleges with separate offices for career services have an initial employment rate of 77.9 percent, which is 31.3 percent higher than those who graduated from colleges without such offices. Logistic regression (see Table 10) further suggests that the relationship between a separate career office and employment status is strong and a separate career office probably accounts for most of the institutional differences in initial employment status. For example, College C, College D, and College E had significant different employment rates from the combined employment rate (58.6%) of College A and College F, [1] holding other things constant (see Model 1). However, once the existence of career service office is controlled, the differences are no longer significant, while surprisingly, the relationship between the existence of a separate career service office and employment status is still strong (Wald statistics = 15.076, N=400, BCI=9.085). The odds of being employed upon graduation for graduates from private colleges with separate offices for career services are almost six times of that for graduates from colleges without such offices. This finding suggests that the existence of a separate career service office is likely critical for graduate employment status

---

[1] Because of small sample, the existence of career service is related to College B and College F (career service = 1 - College B – College F). Thus, the regression model has to combine sample of College A and College F.

Table 8: Associations of Initial Employment Status with Other Variables

	Employment Status (N)		Unemployment Rate (Percent)	Employment Rate (Percent)
	Unemployed	Employed		
Specific Institution (Chi-Square = 43.988***, Coefficient = 0.315***, N =400, df = 5)				
College A	10	38	20.8	79.2
College B	40	42	48.8	51.2
College C	4	20	16.7	83.3
College D	34	95	26.4	73.6
College E	11	55	16.7	83.3
College F	31	20	60.8	39.2
Total	130	270	32.5	67.5
Field of Study (Chi-Square = 9.915*, Coefficient = 0.156*, N =400, df = 4)				
Administration	54	72	42.9	57.1
Applied Economics	17	56	23.3	76.7
Computer Science	22	52	29.7	70.3
Engineering	16	40	28.6	71.4
Literature	21	50	29.6	70.4
Total	130	270	32.5	67.5
Accreditation Status (Chi-Square = 19.699***, Coefficient = 0.217***, N =400, df = 4)				
UnAccredit College	31	20	60.8	39.2
Accredited College	99	250	28.5	71.5
Total	130	270	32.5	67.5
Educational Level (Chi-Square = 4.741*, Coefficient = 0.108*, N =400, df = 1)				
Associate Degree Level	129	256	33.5	66.5
Bachelor Degree Level	1	14	6.7	93.3
Total	130	270	32.5	67.5
High School Type (Chi-Square = 12.525***, Coefficient = 0.183***, N =362, df = 1)				
Academic High School	80	209	27.7	72.3
Vocational High School	36	37	49.3	50.7
Total	116	246	32.0	68.0
By Range of GPA				
60-64.99	7	15	31.8	68.2
65-69.99	3	10	23.1	76.9
70-74.99	31	30	50.8	49.2
75-79.99	7	12	36.8	63.2
80-84.99	11	42	20.8	79.2
85-89.99	2	15	11.8	88.2
90-94.99	0	2	0.0	100.0
95 and Above	0	1	0.0	100.0
Total	61	127	32.4	67.6

Source: The graduate survey of this study.

Table 9: Regression Analyses of Employment Status and Related Variables

Model	(1A)		(1B)		2		3	
Model R^2 (Nagelkerke)	0.060^c		0.165^c		0.276^c		0.344^c	
Percentage Predicted Correctly	67.7		70.4		72.8		74.5	
N	409		409		195		161	
	B	EXP(B)	B	EXP(B)	B	EXP(B)	B	EXP(B)
Constant	-0.575	0.563	1.019	2.769	-1.757	0.173	-1.421	0.242
Institutional Characteristics								
Accreditation Status (Reference: Unaccredited College)	1.315^c	3.724	×	×	×	×	×	×
Specific Institution (Reference: College A)								
College B	×	×	-1.306^b	0.271	-1.897^c	0.150	-2.139^c	0.118
College C	×	×	0.591	1.806	-1.689	0.185	-1.901	0.149
College D*	×	×	-0.069	0.933	×	×	×	×
College E	×	×	0.403	1.496	0.040	1.040	-0.713	0.490
College F	×	×	-1.625^c	0.197	-1.203	0.300	-0.643	0.526
Higher Education Experiences								
Field of Study (Reference: Literature)								
Administration	×	×	×	×	-0.361	0.697	-0.072	0.930
Economics	×	×	×	×	-0.101	0.904	-0.162	0.850
Science	×	×	×	×	-0.086	0.917	0.057	1.058
Engineering	×	×	×	×	0.286	1.331	37.904	--
Educational Level (Reference: Associate Degree Level)	×	×	×	×	2.493	12.098	2.154	8.620
College GPA	×	×	×	×	0.044	1.045	0.024	1.024
Background Characteristics								
High School Type (Reference: Academic High School)	×	×	×	×	×	×	-0.362	0.696
College Entrance Score	×	×	×	×	×	×	0.004	1.004

Note:

1. "a" indicates the coefficient is significant at 0.05 level, "b" at 0.01 level, and "c" at 0.001 level.

2. The dependent variable in four models is the same: employment status. The Independent Variables (IV) in the following models are:

- *Model 1A: accreditation status;*
- *Model 1B: specific institution;*
- *Model 2: specific institution, field of study, educational level, and college GPA;*
- *Model 3: specific institution, field of study, educational level, college GPA, high school type, and college entrance score.*

* The survey did not ask college GPA and entrance score in College D.

Source: *The graduate survey of this study.*

Table 10: Regression Analysis of the Relationship between Employment Status and the Existence of Career Service Office

Model	1		2	
Model R2 (Nagelkerke)	0.090***		0.144***	
Percentage Predicted Correctly	67.5		70.3	
N	400		400	
	B	EXP(B)	B	EXP(B)
Constant	.347	1.415	-.438	.645
Institutional Characteristics				
Specific Institution (Reference: College A and F)				
College B	-.298	.742	.487	1.628
College C	1.263*	3.534	.274	1.316
College D	.681*	1.975	-.307	.735
College E	1.263**	3.534	.274	1.316
Career Service (Reference: Yes)			1.773***	5.890

Source: The graduate survey of this study.

Starting Salary

Private college graduates are employed well, as reflected by their starting salaries. Of the 270 employed private college graduate respondents, 80.4 percent reported that their starting salary and their average monthly starting salary was ¥1255.0 (roughly $152), ¥1173.2 (roughly $147) at the associate degree level and ¥2600 ($325, N=11) at the bachelor degree level. In Shanghai, private college graduates at the associate degree level earned about ¥1308.9 (roughly $164) at start, which is ¥550 higher than that of their counterparts from the one college outside of Shanghai.

Private v. Public

Compared to published earnings of comparable graduate cohorts, private college graduates in Shanghai may earn a higher starting salary than their public counterparts at the bachelor degree level, and as much as their public counterparts at the associate degree level, although this may not be so for graduates from private colleges outside of Shanghai. According to the Shanghai Labor Bureau, the average salary for 2005 Shanghai college graduates at the bachelor-degree and the associate degree level were ¥2,262 and ¥1760 respectively in February 2006. [1] Clearly, the starting salary of private college graduates with bachelor degrees in this study was much higher than their public counterparts who had worked for about six months. Although at the associate degree level, private college graduates of this study earned about ¥400 ($50) less around graduation than their counterpart college graduate cohort earned six months later, they could probably have made a ¥400 increase in monthly salary after a half year. Nevertheless, in 2006, the starting salary of the associate degree level graduates sampled from the one private colleges outside of Shanghai were considerably less (¥758.3) than their public counterparts that made ¥1333 (Min, Ding, Wen, and Yue, 2005). A further exploration of the sample of the college outside of Shanghai suggests a likely explanation. Although the college indicates that a considerable number of its graduates were employed in high-income provinces, less than 10 percent (4 of 43) of the respondents were employed so. Instead, about 85 percent of the respondents were employed in the same low-income province where the college is located.

Associations of Starting Salary with Other Factors

Similar to employment status, significant institutional differences of the new private sector also exist in graduate starting salary (Kruskal Wallis Test, Chi-square = 88.299, df =5, p = 0.000). For example, the average starting salary of graduates from

1 Shanghai Municipal Labor and Social Security Bureau, 2006 Graduate Salary Analysis and Instruction. Available online at http://www.12333.gov.cn/gzba/biyetongji.html.

College C, a four-year college, was about ¥1000 higher than that of graduates from the other colleges. The starting salary of graduates from College E, a three-year college outside of Shanghai, was about ¥500 less than the overall average (see Table 11).

Further analysis suggests that the institutional differences in graduate starting salary may be contributed by many factors. Graduate starting salary is not only likely to be related to education level (Kruskal Wallis Test, Chi-square = 26.683, df =1, p < 0.001), as attested by many studies (Brennan, 2000; Smyth, Gangl, Raffe, Hannan, and McCoy, 200 ; Silver, Lavallée, and Pereboom, 1999) and revealed above, but also to be related to many other factors of institutional characteristics, higher education experiences, as well as, prominently, background and labor market characteristics, though it is not likely related to gender, age, father's educational level, GPA in college, high school type, college entrance score, college's accreditation status, and pre-college work experiences.

First, the differences in starting salary among graduates from different fields of study in the new Chinese private higher education sector are significant (Kruskal Wallis Test, Chi-square = 21.545, df =4, p < 0.001, see Table 11), consistent with many studies (OECD, 1992; Paul and Murdoch, 2000; Schomburg, 2007; UNESCO, 1998). The average starting salaries of graduates in "literature" was ¥1698.8, which is considerably higher than the average ¥1243.9.

Second, possibly because the labor market rewards work experience (three months or more) after entering college, the average starting monthly salary for those who had some experiences after entering college earned a average of ¥1,317.1, which is significantly (¥179.6, about $20) more than those who did not have such experiences (Chi-square = 5.705, df =1, p <0.05).

Interestingly, starting salary is somewhat related to mother's educational level, but not father's educational level. Graduates whose mothers had an educational level "below high school" earned significantly less (¥240.1, about $30) than their counterparts whose mothers at least had high school. The difference is statistically significant (Kruskal Wallis Test, Chi-square = 6.967, df =1, p < 0.01), confirming the findings of many studies. [1]

Given the existence of earning differences among occupations in different regions of China and Shanghai is the city where the majority of the graduates surveyed had resided, studied, and worked, not surprisingly, this research finds the starting salary of private college graduates is somewhat related to both family and employment province. [2] Graduates whose families were located in high income province (N=163) had ¥550 (about $75) higher starting salary than that of those whose families were located in middle-income province (14 graduates) or low-income province (32 graduates). [3] The average starting salary of graduates (N=116) employed in high income province were ¥715.9 and ¥605.9 respectively higher than the graduates employed in middle-income province (the sample is small, N=3) and low-income province (N=44). See Table 11.

---

[1] For example, Griffin and Ganderton (1996) has reviewed relevant studies and findings on parental education and children employment. It finds that mother's education has significant effect on black graduates' earnings; for all groups, it has significant relationship with children education, which in turn affects children's earnings.
[2] Most of the respondents are resident in Shanghai and went to college in Shanghai; and their family province and employment province is highly related (Chi-square = 222.569, df =1, p = 0.000, coefficient = 0.701).
[3] The classification of province region is based on Appendix A.

Finally, this research finds that starting salary is somehow related to family location regarding urbanity (Kruskal Wallis Test, Chi-square = 18.052, df =2, p <0.001), but not to employment urbanity location as suggested by Min, Ding, Wen, and Yue (2005). Graduates from urban areas had the highest average starting salary, ¥1357.6, which is ¥223.9 higher than that of graduates from suburban areas, and ¥510.5 more than that of graduates from rural areas. While other assumptions can be made about this interesting finding, it is possible that the salary differences are not significant in different locations of the same city region, given most respondents are employed in the region of two big cities. Also probable is that those graduates have grown up in urban areas may have more access to better jobs and better paid jobs.

In brief, the above analysis suggests that starting salary of private college graduates is related to a variety of variables. Some of the variables are relevant to productivity, such as educational level and work experiences after entering college. Some are related to employment industry and geography, such as field of study and employment province. Still, others are family related, such as mother's educational level and family location urbanity.

Examining Institutional Effects on Starting Salary Using Regression

Can the related factors explain the institutional differences in graduate starting salary for the new private higher education? To answer this question, multiple regression analysis is used (see Table 12). First, the analysis finds that which private college graduates went to matters substantially for their starting salaries in China, after associated labor market characteristics are taken into consideration. It accounts for about an extra of 13.4 percent of the variance in graduate starting salary (see R^2 changes from 23.3% in Model 1 to 36.8% in Model 2). Graduates of College C earned significant more (57.0% more) than graduates of College A, whereas graduates of College E and College F earned significantly less, about 41.0 percent and 29.2 percent less respectively.

Second, graduates from College F, a college without accreditation, still earned significant less (28.4% less) than their counterparts in College A, even after the associated higher education experiences and background characteristics are both controlled (see Model 4). Graduates of College B, which resides in the same city as College A, earned similarly at start to the graduates of College A.

Third, while unaccredited status may be assumed to be related to the significant lower starting salary of the graduates from College F, institutional effort in niche field designation explains better. This study finds that whether graduates majored in a designated niche field likely has some relationship with starting salary (Spearman R =0.221, N=222, p < 0.01). After niche field designation is introduced into the regression modeling, the significant difference in graduates starting salary between College F and College A disappears (see Model 5 of Table 12). Niche field designation likely has a negative relationship with starting salary, once the differences in salaries among different fields of study are taken into consideration, although the average salary of graduates in niche-fields is ¥268.5 (¥1395.7 v. 1117.2) more than that in regular fields.

Table 11: Association of Starting Salary with Other Variables

	N	Minimum	Maximum	Mean	S.E.	STD
By Institution (Chi-square = 88.299, df =5, p = 0.000)						
College A	29	300	2,500	1,417.2	99.9	537.9
College B	26	600	2,100	1,167.3	83.3	425.0
College C	16	1,800	3,600	2,412.5	152.7	610.9
College D	86	420	3,000	1,308.8	53.6	496.8
College E	52	400	1,500	758.3	35.3	254.8
College F	13	400	2,400	1,084.6	164.4	592.8
By Field of Study (Chi-square = 21.545, df =4, p = 0.000)						
Administration	55	300	3,000	1,146.4	71.7	531.8
Applied Economics	42	400	3,400	1,261.4	91.5	592.8
Computer Science	48	420	2,200	1,113.8	61.3	424.6
Engineering	37	400	2,500	1,045.9	84.6	514.6
Literature	40	600	3,600	1,698.8	123.5	781.1
By Degree Level (Overall) (Chi-square = 26.683, df =1, p = 0.000)						
Associate Degree Level	211	300	3,000	1,173.2	35.8	520.6
Bachelor Degree Level	11	1,800	3,600	2,600.0	199.1	660.3
By Work Experience after Entering College (Chi-square = 5.705*, df =1, p =0.017)						
work experience < 3 Month	81	300	3,400	1,137.5	65.8	592.0
work experience <=3 Month	111	400	3,400	1,317.1	57.4	605.2
By Mother's Education Level (Chi-square = 6.967, df =1, p = 0.008)						
Under High School	58	300	3,400	1,064.1	69.7	530.8
High School or Above	146	400	3,600	1,304.2	51.7	624.9
By Family Province Region (Chi-square = 45.338, df =2, p = 0.000)						
High Income Province	163	300	3,600	1,376.7	48.1	614.5
Middle Income Province	14	500	1,800	814.3	101.6	380.0
Low Income Province	32	400	1,500	779.1	52.3	296.0
By Family Location (Chi-square = 18.052, df =2, p = 0.000)						
Urban	132	300	3600	1357.6	54.9	631.2
Suburban	52	400	3400	1133.7	78.6	566.6
Rural	21	400	1,800	847.1	77.7	356.0
By Employment Province Region (Chi-square = 57.092, df =1, p = 0.000)						
High Income Province	171	400	3,400	1,349.2	43.2	565.5
Middle Income Province	3	600	700	633.3	33.3	57.7
Low Income Province	44	400	1,500	739.3	33.5	222.5
OVERALL	**222**	**300**	**3600**	**1243.9**	**41.0**	**611.2**

Source: The graduate survey of this study.

Table 12: Regression Analysis of Institutional Effects on Starting Salary*

Model	1		2		3		4		5	
Model R^2	0.233^d		0.368^d		0.378^d		0.396^d		0.397	
R^2 Change			0.134^d		0.010		0.018		0.001	
N	178		178		178		178		178	
	B	SE-B	B	SE-B	B	SE-B	B	SE-B	B	SE-B
Constant	6.521^d	0.076	6.937^d	0.224	6.987^d	0.231	6.784^d	0.252	6.842^d	0.254
Institutional Characteristics										
Specific Institution (Reference: College A)										
College B	×	×	-0.149	0.120	-0.122	0.123	-0.159	0.129	-.140	.135
College C	×	×	0.570^a	0.147	0.475	0.298	0.413	0.297	.403	.298
College D	×	×	-0.041	0.092	0.019	0.100	0.003	0.102	.004	.102
College E	×	×	-0.410^a	0.211	-0.353	0.216	-0.284	0.219	-.301	.222
College F	×	×	-0.292^a	0.143	-0.287^a	0.153	-0.284^a	0.153	-.256	.164
Niche Field									-.043	.087
Higher Education Experiences										
Educational Level (Reference: Associate Degree Level)	×	×	×	×	0.117	0.320	0.194	0.320	.220	.324
Field of Study (Reference: Literature)										
Administration	×	×	×	×	-0.041	0.102	-0.005	0.104	-.014	.106
Economics	×	×	×	×	-0.099	0.102	-0.077	0.103	-.089	.107
Science	×	×	×	×	-0.144	0.103	-0.099	0.105	-.085	.109
Engineering	×	×	×	×	-0.138	0.113	-0.134	0.116	-.125	.118
Background Characteristics										
Mother's Educational Level (Reference: < High School)	×	×	×	×	×	×	0.109	0.066	.101	.070
Family Location (Reference: Rural)										
Urban	×	×	×	×	×	×	0.108	0.074	.062	.107
Suburban	×	×	×	×	×	×	0.048	0.114	-.045	.115
Labor Market Characteristics										
Work Experience (Reference: < 3 Months)	0.128^b	0.063	0.116^b	0.060	0.102^a	0.061	0.089	0.063	.094	.064
Employment Province										
High Income Province	0.508^d	0.078	0.135	0.206	0.137	0.207	0.187	0.209	.188	.209
Middle Income Province	-0.111	0.306	-0.111	0.283	-0.121	0.286	-0.127	0.285	-.126	.285

Note: * The natural log of starting salary is used in the analysis. "a" indicates the coefficient is significant at 0.10 level; "b" indicates the coefficient is significant at 0.05 level; "c" indicates the coefficient is significant at 0.01 level; "d" indicates the coefficient is significant at 0.001 level.

Source: *The graduate survey of this study.*

Job and Education Match

Private college graduates are well hired as also shown by their job and education match status. This research finds that while significant differences exist among graduates from different private colleges in job and education match, most Chinese private collage graduates can find jobs related to their fields of study, using their knowledge and skills acquired from courses, and corresponding to their education level.

Job and Education Level Match

Job and education level match is one well-studied aspect of job and education match (Allen and De Weert, 2007; Allen and Velden, 2001; Di Pietro and Urwin, 2006). In responding to the survey question "What was the minimum education you think appropriate for your first job", [1] a little less than two thirds (62.6%) of the employed private college graduates (N=235) reported that their jobs matched their education level, which is probably similar or better than their counterpart public college graduates. Specifically, 62.2 percent graduates at the associate degree level and 69.2 percent (N=13) at the bachelor degree level were employed in jobs matching their education level. The comparative numbers were 16.2 percent and 3.3 percent less respectively for their public counterparts (Yue and Yang, 2006).

As in employment status and starting salary, institutional diversity of the new private higher education sector is present in graduates' job and educational level match. The differences in match status among the six Chinese private colleges surveyed were

---

[1] According to Allen and Velden (2001), asking graduates to report the necessary minimum education is more accurate for assessing the mismatch between education level and job than asking the degree requirement of the first job.

significant (Chi-square = 15.463, df =1, p = 0.009, Coefficient = 0.248. See Table 13).

Specifically, College F had the highest graduate job and education level match (81.2%),

followed by College C (73.7%) and College A (71.9%). In contrast, only about one third

of the employed graduates in College B found jobs that matched their education level.

Moreover, while the association of job and education level match with the above-

mentioned variables are examined, this research fails to identify any other significant

relationship, even with college entrance score and educational level, as Yue and Yang,

(2006) suggests.

While so many factors are not related to job and education level match, what

then contributes to the significant institutional differences of the new private sector?

Wolbers's (2003) suggestion on the association of apprenticeship-type and vocational

education with job and education match status points out a direction, especially relevant

to the vocational nature of private colleges in China. Could the often vocation-oriented

niche fields or the practice-concentrated separate career offices give some explanation?

Interestingly, the existence of a separate career office has a significant relationship with

job and education level match (Chi-square = 8.018, df=1, p < 0.01) as with employment

status, though "niche field" does not. 80.0 percent of the employed graduates from

colleges with separate offices for career services were hired in jobs matching their

education level, whereas only 60.0 percent from colleges without such offices were so.

Clearly, career service offices play important roles in facilitating students to get jobs

matching their education level, possibly due to their services in practical training or

something.

Job and Field Match

A second perspective to look at job and education match is to examine to what extent the jobs graduates have gotten are related to their fields of study. In characterizing the relationship of their fields of study with their first jobs on a four-point Likert scale, 65.5 percent graduates reported that their jobs were "related" (47.6%) or "closely related" (17.9%) to their fields of study and the rest reported either "somewhat related" (26.0%) or "not related at all" (8.5%). Compared roughly to reports about general college graduates saying that 17 percent of them are "closely related" and 24 percent are "not related at all", [1] private college graduates seem to have higher levels of job and field match. Their higher level of job and field match level can also be confirmed by Wu's (2003) study, which reports that 58.1 percent public college graduates are employed in jobs matching their fields of study. [2]

Institutional diversity of the new private higher education is also present in job and field match. Significant differences exist in graduates' job and education match among different colleges (Chi-square =35.188 and p = 0.002, see Table 13). Of their employed graduates, 89.5 percent in College C and 79.3 percent in College E (see Table 13) were employed in area matching their fields of study, whereas only 50 percent or less achieved so in College A (48.5%), College B (46.7%), and College F (50.1%). Field of study (Chi-square =26.331, N=246, df=12, p=0.010), education level (Chi-square =4.932, df =1, p < 0.05, N =246), and college GPA (R = 0.354, p < 0.01, N = 67) are possible contributors for their relationships with job and field match. Engineering

---

[1] Zhi Lian Zhao Pin. 2006. Survey on "Are What You Studied Useful?" 17% graduates in 2006 reported that their jobs were completely related to their fields, 34% "related to a high extent", 25% "only a little bit related", and 24% "not related at all" (see http://jobseeker.zhaopin.com/channel/Publish/Company/Public/2006_5_12/D008.htm, accessed 5/1/2007).
[2] Interestingly, her report about private college graduates job and education level match is lower, 32.4%.

graduates had very high level of job and field match, 94.7 percent. In contrast, only about two thirds (66.7 percent) graduates in literature, three fifths in computer sciences and in administration and a half (52.1%) graduates in applied economics were employed in jobs related to their fields. 63.8 percent of the graduates at associate-degree level and 92.9 percent of the graduates at bachelor degree level were employed in jobs related to their fields of study. Finally, the higher the grades are, the more likely the graduates can find jobs related to their fields. Possibly, the labor market hires graduates in accordance with perceived or actual factors that are related to productivity, such as grades and degree level. The number of job demands in different fields is presumably different and thus becomes another factor on job and field relevance. On the other hand, the supply side can also be factor. For instance, the enrollment in computer science and administration are relatively higher than other program (see Table 4 and Appendix M).

Can the above associated variables explain all the institutional differences in job and field match among different colleges? Regression modeling (Table 14) suggests that graduates from College C and College E were significantly more likely to be employed in jobs matching their fields than graduates from College A (see Model 1), when holding all other factors constant. When controlling the effect of field of study, educational level, and College GPA, graduates from College E still had significant higher chance to be employed with job and field match (see Model 2). Also, college GPA had a strong positive relationship with job and field match.

Again, institutional efforts in niche field designation and career service office structure seem to explain some of the significant institutional differences otherwise unexplained by the other factors. Both niche field (Chi-square = 12.388, df =3, p < 0.01,

Coefficient = 0.219) and career service office (Chi-square = 18.465, df=3, p < 0.001, Coefficient = 0.264) are likely related to job and field match status. Graduates seem to benefit from the existence of a separate office for career services in this regard. The respondents had a 69.5 percent chance to find jobs matching their fields of study if their Alma Master has such an office; otherwise, their chances were only around 21.7 percent. In contrast, niche field designation seemingly has adverse effect on the chance: 59.1 percent of the graduates who majored in niche fields were employed in areas match their fields, whereas as high as 71.0 percent of those in regular fields were employed so. More importantly, regression analysis (see Table 14) finds that the significant associations of College E and economics with job-field match (see Model 3) disappear after controlling the effects of niche field and career service office (see Model 4).

Job and Skills/Knowledge Match

A third perspective of job and education match that looks at the utilization of skills and knowledge acquired in college also suggests that graduates of the new private sector are employed well. About two thirds (67.5% of 246) of the private college graduates investigated reported that their jobs utilized the skills and knowledge they had learned at college "to a very high extent" (19.9%) or "to some extent" (47.6%). The rest of graduates reported that their jobs did not use their skills and knowledge or use them "to a low extent". Study on job and skills/knowledge match regarding college graduates in China is lacking. Statistics on European college graduates in Allen and De Weert (2007) suggests that the respondents are comparable to their European counterparts, whose job and skill match level is 3.48 on a five-point scale (Allen and De Weert, 2007), equivalent to 69.6 percent.

As with the other two aspects of job and education match, institutional diversity is present in job and skills/knowledge match (Chi-square = 35.549, df =15, p = 0.002). College C (94.7%, the only college with bachelor-degree graduates) and College E (81.1%) had significantly higher job-kills/knowledge match than the other colleges. In contrast, only half of the graduates of College A (51.5%) and College B (48.4%) were employed in jobs that utilize their skills and knowledge. While other measured factors are not likely related to the differences, education level may be (Spearman R = -.176, N =246, p = 0.002). All graduates (N=14) with bachelor degrees were employed in jobs that utilize their skills and knowledge, whereas only 65.5 percent of the graduates at associate degree level were so.

Nevertheless, "niche field" and "separate career service office" may again be related to the institutional diversity of the new private higher education as they have similar relationships with job and skills/knowledge match, to with job and field match. The existence of a separate career service office (Chi-square =15.083, df = 3, p < 0.01, Coefficient = 0.240) helps job and skills/knowledge match for private college graduates. Employed graduates from colleges with separate career service offices generally had a 71.4 percent chance to be employed in jobs utilizing their learned skills and knowledge, about 20.3 percent higher than those from colleges without such offices. On the contrary, niche field may slightly lower the chance (Chi-square =8.151, df=3, p < 0.05, Contingent Coefficient = 0.179, N=246). Those employed graduates of niche field had a 65.2 percent chance to be employed in jobs using their skills and knowledge, whereas those of regular fields had more than 70 percent chance.

Table 13: Job-Education Match Status and Job Satisfaction of Respondents by College

	College A	College B	College C	College D	College E	College F	Total
Job and Education Level Match (Chi-square =15.463, df =5, p = 0.009)							
Mismatch (under-educated)*	28.1% (15.6%)	65.5% (13.8%)	26.3% (10.5%)	34.1% (11.4%)	43.1% (21.6%)	18.8% (0%)	37.4% (13.6%)
Match	71.9%	34.5%	73.7%	65.9%	56.9%	81.2%	62.6%
(Total N)	32	29	19	88	51	16	235
Job and Field Match (Chi-square = 35.188, df =15, p = 0.002)							
Closely related	9.1%	10.0%	26.3%	20.0%	20.8%	18.8%	17.9%
Related	39.4%	36.7%	63.2%	47.4%	58.5%	31.3%	47.6%
A little bit related	45.5%	30.0%	10.5%	28.4%	13.2%	25.0%	26.0%
Not related at all	6.1%	23.3%	0.0%	4.2%	7.5%	25.0%	8.5%
(Total N)	33	30	19	95	53	16	246
Job and Skills/Knowledge Match (Chi-square = 35.549, df =15, p = 0.002)							
To a very high extent	12.1%	9.7%	36.8%	16.0%	28.3%	31.3%	19.9%
To some extent	39.4%	38.7%	57.9%	52.1%	52.8%	25.0%	47.6%
To a low extent	36.4%	29.0%	5.3%	27.7%	15.1%	25.0%	24.4%
Not at all	12.1%	22.6%	0.0%	4.3%	3.8%	18.8%	8.1%
(Total N)	33	31	19	94	53	16	246
Job Satisfaction (Chi-square = 35.300, df =15, p = 0.002)							
Very satisfied	6.1%	0.0%	15.8%	9.1%	0.0%	6.3%	5.9%
Satisfied	84.8%	53.3%	73.7%	71.6%	66.7%	81.3%	70.9%
Dissatisfied	6.1%	40.0%	10.5%	19.3%	33.3%	12.5%	21.9%
Very dissatisfied	3.0%	6.7%	0.0%	0.0%	0.0%	0.0%	1.3%
(Total N)	33	30	19	88	51	16	237

* Both under-education and over-education are considered as job and educational level "mismatch". The graduates listed as "under-educated" include those graduates whose educational levels are lower than the minimum educational levels that they reported to be appropriate to their jobs.
Source: The graduate survey of this study.

Table 14: Examining Institutional Effects on Job and Field Match Using Logistic Regression

Model	1		2		3		4	
Model R² (Nagelkerke)	0.112 [c]		0.394 [c]		0.216[c]		0.228[c]	
Percentage Predicted Correctly	66.7		72.3		69.9		69.1	
N	246		112		246		246	
	B	**EXP(B)**	**B**	**EXP(B)**	**B**	**EXP(B)**	**B**	**EXP(B)**
Constant	-.061	.941	-1.769[a]	.171	-1.524*	.809	.284	1.328
Institutional Characteristics								
Specific Institution	(Re: College A)		(Re: College A)		(Re: Coll. A & F)		(Re: Coll. A & F)	
College B	-.073	.930	-.772	.462	.148	1.160	.281	1.324
College C	2.201[b]	9.031	.403	1.496	2.095*	8.123	1.866	6.464
College D	.786	2.194	×	×	.721*	2.056	.623	1.864
College E	1.400[b]	4.057	1.280 *	3.597	1.168*	3.217	.805	2.237
College F	.061	1.063	.668	1.950				
Career Service Office							.066	1.069
Niche Field							-.569	.566
Higher Education Experiences								
Field of Study (Reference: Literature)								
Administration	×	×	-.387	.679	.140	.753	.066	1.068
Economics	×	×	-1.127	.324	-.654	.175	-.830	.436
Science	×	×	-.012	.988	-.301	.531	-.196	.822
Engineering	×	×	1.645	5.179	2.105	.011	2.173	8.786
College GPA	×	×	.499 [b]	6.091				
Educational Level (Re: Associate Degree)			1.807	1.647	.698	2.010	.979	2.661

*Note: "a" indicates the coefficient is significant at 0.05 level; "b" indicates the coefficient is significant at 0.01 level; "c" indicates the coefficient is significant at 0.001 level; * indicates the coefficient is significant at 0.10 level. Model 4 uses College A and College F as reference group because otherwise, College F and Career Service Office has perfect relationship with College B. Model 4 also does not include GPA in calculation because the survey failed to get GPA data from College D because of negligence. If College D is dropped, college sample is too small for analyzing variances of career service office.*
Source: The graduate survey of this study.

Job Satisfaction

Self-reported job satisfaction also suggests that the responding private college graduates were pleased with the new private sector employment. This research finds that the majority of them (76.8%) were satisfied with their jobs obtained around graduation, including 5.9 percent being "very satisfied". Only slightly over one fifth indicated that

155

they were "dissatisfied" (21.9%) or "very dissatisfied" (1.3%, see Table 13). Roughly compared to the general college graduate cohorts, mostly of public colleges and of whom, 4.6 percent being "very satisfied", 32.8 percent "satisfied", 50 percent "so so", 10.3 percent "dissatisfied", and 2.9 percent "very dissatisfied" (Min, Ding, Wen, and Yue, 2005: 7), private college graduates are very likely either similar to their public counterparts in job satisfaction or are more satisfied.

Similar to the findings on other initial employment outcomes, the institutional differences in job satisfaction among different colleges are also significant (Chi-square =35.300 and p = 0.002). Over 80 percent graduates in College A (91.0%), College C (89.5%), College F (87.6%), and College D (80.7%) were satisfied or very satisfied with their jobs. In contrast, only about half of the graduates of College B and two thirds of College E were satisfied (see Table 13). Moreover, specific institution, which indicates where graduates went to college, is the only measured factor likely related to job satisfaction.

Not surprisingly, job satisfaction is associated with other aspects of employment outcomes, though not with educational and background characteristics. It is positively related to starting salary (Pearson R = 0.183, N=201, p = 0.009), job and education level match (Spearman R = 0.142, N = 220, p = 0.035), and job and skills/knowledge match (Spearman R = 0.217, N =221, p = 0.001). Additionally, job satisfaction is also somehow related to employment sector (Chi-square = 15.411, df =6, p= 0.017). Graduates worked in the public sector reported the highest level of job satisfaction. 88.2 percent of those employed in the public sector were satisfied with their jobs.

Comparatively, 79.7 percent of those employed in the foreign-related companies and 69.7 percent of those in private sector were satisfied.

But surprisingly, while career office and niche field are examined against graduate job satisfaction, the existence of a separate career office is found to be likely related to graduate job satisfaction (Chi-square = 7.744, df =1, p < 0.01, Coefficient = 0.200), though niche field designation is not. 65.2 percent employed graduates from colleges without separated career services office were satisfied with their jobs, whereas 84.3 percent from college with the offices were satisfied.

Graduate Feedback on Institutional Worthiness and Management Efforts

To gauge how well private colleges in China have made their efforts to link private higher education to the labor market, this study also looks at graduate feedback on the value of the private higher education and on institutional efforts in field of study provision, curricula educational delivery, career services, and institutional networking.

Feedback on Overall Institutional Worthiness

Overall, almost two thirds (63.5%) of the graduates surveyed (N=460) regarded their education at the surveyed Chinese private colleges as being "valuable" (58.9%) or "highly valuable" (4.6%), and significant differences exist among graduates of different colleges (Chi-square =99.554, df =15, p =0.000). Only 7.0 percent of them regarded it as "not valuable at all" and 29.6 percent regarded it as "a little bit valuable". Graduates from College D value private higher education the highest and 83.9 percent of them regarded it as "valuable" or "highly valuable", followed by College E (72.2%), College

C (70.5%), and College F (66.7%). College B was valued the least and only 31.3 percent of its graduates thought its education "valuable" or "highly valuable". College A was also valued low and 47.4 percent of its graduates regarded its education "valuable" or "highly valuable". Another way to look at the value of private higher education is to examine whether its graduates would have chosen the same or similar nature institution again if they were given a second chance. Interestingly, almost the same percentage of graduates (63.61%, N=426) reported that they would have "likely" (49.06%) or "very likely" (14.55%) chosen the same or similar nature private institution. [1]

Since the value of higher education is reflected by the return from jobs, not surprisingly, graduate feedback has relationships with some of the above-analyzed employment outcomes. Specifically, this research finds that it is likely related to job and field match (Spearman R = 0.235, p < 0.001) as well as to job and skills/knowledge match (Spearman R = 0.274, p <0.001), but not to employment status, starting salary, job and education level match, and job satisfaction. Additionally, it is also likely related to field of study (Chi-square =35.998, p <0.001). Engineering graduates valued private higher education the most and 88.3 percent regarded it as being "valuable" or "highly valuable", followed by computer science graduates (70.4%). Literature (54.8%) and administration (55.6%) graduates valued private higher education the least, and only a little over half of them deemed it as "valuable" or "highly valuable".

---

[1] Not surprisingly, most of those who choose "less likely" or "not likely" would have chosen to go back to an extra year of high school and take the college entrance examination again (12.6% chose "very likely" and "24.7% "likely"). Interestingly, about 14% of all respondents said they would not have considered continuing education after their high school at all. Among the six colleges, College F has the highest percentage of graduates (23.0%) and College C has the lowest percentage of graduates (4.5%) indicated that they would have chosen not to continue study at all (Chi-square =26.679*, df=15, p = 0.031).

Feedback on Institutional Management Efforts

All graduates were asked about their satisfaction level with their college experiences in ten matters around educational provisions and career services. Included in educational provision matters are fields of study, curriculum, interactions with other students, and qualifications of faculty. Included in career service matters are information and opportunity provision around internship, practicum, co-op experiences, information provision about general employment, opportunity provision for graduates to participate in career planning, job recommendation and job placement, and job-hunting advices (see A9 of Appendix H). [1] More than half of the private college graduates surveyed reported that they were "satisfied" or "very satisfied" with their experiences in these matters, though less satisfied with institutional efforts in career services than with those efforts in educational provision. Specifically, often about 70 percent or more were satisfied with educational provisions, only about 60 percent or less were satisfied with career services (see Table 15). [2]

Consistent with the findings on institutional diversity in management efforts in Chapter 4, significant institutional differences are also present in graduates' satisfaction with the ten surveyed aspects of institutional management efforts (see

Table 16). Graduates from College D were consistently far more satisfied with all of the ten institutional managed efforts than the rest, whereas those from College A and College B were considerably less satisfied, especially the latter.

---

[1] The ten questions were originally asked by the Higher Education and Graduate Employment in Europe project. A factor analysis, not shown in this dissertation, indicates that the ten questions are of the two factors, educational provision (Cronbach Alpha = 0.740) and career services (Cronbach Alpha = 0.937).
[2] No significant difference is found in the satisfaction level with any of the items by graduates who were employed and those who were not employed.

Table 15: Graduate Feedback on Ten Institutional Management Efforts

I am satisfied with	Strongly Agree (%)	Agree (%)	Disagree (%)	Strongly Disagree (%)	Not Provided (%)	Total N
1.... the field of study I chose.	12.6	67.1	17.4	3.0	0.0	438
2.... the courses I took.	11.1	61.3	22.5	5.1	0.0	432
3.... the interaction with other students.	15.6	69.2	12.4	2.8	0.0	429
4.... the qualifications of faculty in my department.	12.6	65.7	19.3	2.3	0.0	429
5... information provided about internship, practicum, co-op experiences.	6.0	55.7	28.6	9.7	0.0	433
6... information provided about general employment (i.e. job vacancies).	8.8	52.9	28.8	9.5	0.0	431
7.. opportunities to participate in internship, practicum, co-op experiences.	7.5	52.8	29.9	9.8	0.0	428
8.... opportunities to be recommended or provided for job placement.	7.5	51.1	29.2	12.2	0.0	425
9... opportunities to receive advice about planning my career.	5.8	55.8	27.1	10.5	0.7	428
10... opportunities to receive advice about obtaining a job.	8.4	52.1	30.1	8.9	0.5	428

Source: The graduate survey of this study.

Table 16: Percentage of Graduates Satisfied or Very Satisfied with Institutional Management Efforts by College

I am satisfied with	College A	College B	College C	College D	College E	College F	Overall
1.... the field of study I chose.	78.6	62.6	88.5	89.6	75.3	86.8	79.7**
2.... the courses I took.	61.1	56.0	88.5	90.8	74.0	75.9	72.5***
3.... the interaction with other students.	81.5	71.9	72.0	85.0	88.3	88.7	84.8**
4.... the qualifications of faculty in my department.	68.5	64.0	66.7	84.0	77.9	79.2	78.3***
5... information provided about internship, practicum, co-op experiences.	57.4	30.3	62.5	82.5	51.3	70.4	61.7***
6... information provided about general employment (i.e. job vacancies).	57.4	28.1	70.8	84.4	61.0	62.3	61.7***
7... opportunities to participate in internship, practicum, co-op experiences.	51.9	31.5	96.0	81.7	50.6	69.8	60.3***
8.... opportunities to be recommended or provided for job placement.	51.9	25.0	92.0	89.3	53.9	64.2	58.6***
9... opportunities to receive advice about planning my career.	50.0	31.1	70.8	84.3	60.3	81.1	62.1***
10... opportunities to receive advice about obtaining a job.	55.6	28.1	70.8	82.3	50.0	69.8	60.8***

Note: * Chi-Square Test is significant at 0.05 level; ** Chi-Square Test is significant at 0.01 level; *** Chi-Square Test is significant at 0.001 level.
Source: The graduate survey of this study.

As shown in Table 17, private college graduate satisfaction with institutional management efforts are associated with all of the investigated employment outcomes in one way or another, except starting salary. Institutional management efforts might have affected initial graduate employment outcomes, or vice versa. Nevertheless, employment status is likely related to graduate satisfaction with job placement service, though the relationship is weak; job and educational level match is related to career planning and job-hunting advice opportunities, employment information dissemination, job recommendation and placement, as well as information and opportunities for participating in internships, practices, co-op experiences. Job and field match level (original 4-scale data is used) is related to fields studied, course taken, teacher qualification, as well as job placement. Job and skills/knowledge match level (original 4-scale data is used) has relative strong relationship to fields studied, courses taken, teacher qualifications, job placement, career planning, and somewhat also to job-hunting advices and information dissemination on internship, practicum, co-op experiences. Job satisfaction also has a relatively strong relationship with many career services, including career planning, job-hunting advices, information on practical training and internships, as well as job placement.

Discussion of Major Findings

How well have private higher education institutions in China managed their efforts in linking private higher education to the labor market? Different from what (Goodman, 2003) pictures, the analysis of this chapter shows that the private colleges investigated have done well from two perspectives: initial graduate employment outcomes and graduate feedback on institutional worthiness and management efforts.

The descriptions of initial employment outcomes show that the graduates of the new

private sector are well-accepted by the labor market. Two thirds of their graduates were

employed around graduation, a comparable or better performance than their public

counterparts. They are also treated fairly well as seen in their starting salaries. The

favorable situation of graduates in job and education level match, job-field match, and

job-skills/knowledge indicates that the educational provisions of new private higher

education in level, fields of study, skills and knowledge has also equipped graduates

with

Table 17: Correlation of Graduate-Reported Satisfaction with Institutional Management Efforts and Initial Employment Outcomes

I am satisfied with	Employ-ment Status	Starting Salary	Education Level Match	Field Match Level	Skill/Kn owledge Match Level	Job Satis-faction Level
1.... *the field of study I chose.*	-.051	-.098	-.027	.197(**)	.275(**)	.112
2.... *the courses I took.*	-.024	-.001	-.042	.183(**)	.264(**)	.085
3.... *the interaction with other students.*	.032	.023	-.050	.006	.080	-.044
4.... *the qualifications of faculty in my department.*	-.058	-.029	-.034	.190(**)	.264(**)	.116
5... *information provided about intern-ship, practicum, co-op experiences.*	-.040	-.087	-.109	.124	.148(*)	.204(**)
6... *information provided about general employment (i.e. job vacancies).*	-.100	.014	-.137(*)	.129	.127	.112
7... *opportunities to participate in intern-ship, practicum, co-op experiences.*	-.052	-.091	-.069	.115	.118	.100
8.... *opportunities to be recommended or provided for job placement.*	-.123(*)	-.005	-.195(*)	.149(*)	.242(**)	.219(**)
9... *opportunities to receive advice about planning my career.*	-.066	-.026	-.144(*)	.121	.196(**)	.200(**)
10... *opportunities to receive advice about obtaining a job.*	-.038	-.076	-.140(*)	.025	.167(*)	.201(**)

* Spearman R is significant at 0.05 level; ** Spearman R is significant at 0.01level; *** Spearman R is significant at 0.001 level.
Note: *"Very Satisfied" is coded as 1, "Satisfied" as 2, "Dissatisfied" as 3, and "Very Dissatisfied" as 4. Similar coding is used for "field match level", "skill/knowledge match level", and "job satisfaction level". "Employed" is code as "1" and "not employed" as "0"; "job and education level" matched is coded as 1, and mismatch as 0.*
Source: *The graduate survey of this study.*

the right qualifications, which are taken immediately on board in jobs that match their education well. Their graduates are likely to be more satisfied with their employment than their public counterparts. The reports on graduate feedback demonstrate that the new private higher education is also well-accepted by its direct customers- students. The majority of the graduates thought that private higher education was valuable, and also were satisfied with the performance of private management efforts in various aspects around field of study, curriculum, faculty, other students, career planning, practical training, and job placement. Thematically, the sample of private higher education institutions in this research produces results at odds with one major less flattering study in China (Wu, 2003), but more similar to international and other Chinese works on private higher education and the labor market (McMahon and Wagner, 1981; Sapatoru, Nicolescu, and Slantcheva, 2003; Zhou, 2003).

Nonetheless, as Bernasconi (2004b) and Levy (2004) have found about general private higher education, diversity is evident in institutional performance of the Chinese new private higher education sector with regard to graduate employment. Institutional differences are embedded in the rosy pictures of initial graduate employment outcomes and graduate feedback. On initial graduate employment outcomes, College C was considerably better than the average, whereas College B was much worse than the average in all the examined aspects. Though not as much as College C did, College D also performed well. The other three colleges had around average performance (see Table 18). Surprisingly, similar patterns are observed in graduate feedback on institutional worthiness and management efforts, though College D distinguished itself from the rest and College A performed worse than the average in all but two of the eleven items. College C still received favorable feedback from its graduates on institutional worthiness and all but two aspects of the ten institutional management efforts, whereas College B still received unfavorable feedback from its graduates on all the aspects of institutional worthiness and management efforts. College E and College F still had a close to average performance.

Table 18: Summary of Initial Employment Outcomes and Graduate Feedback by College *

	College A	College B	College C	College D	College E	College F
Graduates' Self-Reported Initial Employment Outcomes						
Employment Status	Y	N	Y	Y/N	Y	N
Starting Salary	Y/N	Y/N	Y	Y/N	N	Y/N
Job-Education Level Match	Y	N	Y	Y/N	N	Y
Job-Field Match	N	N	Y	Y	Y	N
Job-Skill/Knowledge Match	N	N	Y	Y/N	Y	N
Job Satisfaction	Y	N	Y	Y	N	Y
Graduate Feedback on Institutional Worthiness and Management Efforts						
Institutional Worthiness	N	N	Y	Y	Y	Y
Management Efforts						
1… *field of study*	Y/N	N	Y	Y	Y/N	Y
2… *courses*	N	N	Y	Y	Y/N	Y/N
3…. *student interactions.*	Y	N	N	Y	Y	Y
4…. *faculty qualifications*	N	N	N	Y	Y	Y
5… *practice information*	N	N	N/Y	Y	N	Y
6… *employment information*	N	N	Y	Y	Y/N	Y/N
7… *practice opportunities*	N	N	Y	Y	N	Y/N
8…*job recommendations*	N	N	Y	Y	N	Y/N
9…*career planning*	N	N	Y	Y	Y/N	Y
10… *job-hunting advice*	N	N	Y	Y	N	Y

* *"Y" represents results considerably better than the average; "N" represents results considerable worse than the average; "Y/N" indicates results close to the average.*
Source: *The graduate survey of this study.*

164

Questions can be asked on the general findings about comparable performance of the new private higher education sector to the public sector in linking higher education to the labor market as well as on the diversity within the new private sector in this regard, while more so for the surprisingly similar patterns across institutions in both initial graduate employment outcomes and graduate feedback. What factors may relate to the good performance of the new private sector? What could have contributed its institutional diversity? Are graduate employment outcomes associated with institutional management efforts? The exploration of the factors related to initial employment outcomes and the association of the outcomes with institutional management efforts reveals interesting findings about the role of the new private higher education sector in link higher education to the labor market.

Examining the relationships between initial employment outcomes and factors of institutional characteristics, higher education experiences, as well as background and labor market characteristics, this study finds that many factors are somehow related to initial employment outcomes and they are possibly contributors to institutional diversity, whereas others are not. For employment status, institutional accreditation, field of study, educational level, college GPA, high school origin, and college entrance score are related, whereas gender, father's educational level, mother's educational level, family's province origin, family's urbanity, and work experiences are not. For starting salary, education level, field of study, labor market rewards work experience (three months or more) after entering college, mother's educational level, family location, and employment province are related, whereas gender, age, father's educational level, GPA in college, high school type, college entrance score, college's accreditation status, and pre-college work experiences are not. For job and education level match, education level is the only factor. For job and field match, field of study, education level, and college GPA are possible contributors. From the labor market perspective on graduate job placement, one could read the related factors into a fairly strong tilt towards program provision, student specific skills training, and labor market, as opposed to general capacities and personal connections. And, for these graduates and for the new private higher education, it is important. Compared to public college graduates, the graduates of the new private higher education come from lower family background, and personnel connections are probably not an advantage to them. [1] Compared to public colleges, not only do the institutions of the new private sector have less experience and resources to build up student general capacities, their students also have less aptitude and probably less desire as well for improving their general capacities, given their academic background. On the other hand, potentially, the institutions of the new private sector have tremendous room to improve in program provision, skills training, as well as employer networking, because of their commercialized management and structural flexibility as well as the ever-changing labor market.

Albeit different in the types and levels of efforts that the institutions of the new private higher education sector have made, as Chapter Four concludes, they have probably taken advantage of the tremendous room and played important roles in linking its education to the labor market, through program provision, skills building, and labor market targeting and employer networking. A major finding of this study that supports such a hypothesis is: "Specific institution", which indicates where graduates went to

---

[1] An ongoing project in the Higher Education Institute of Xiamen University (China) reveals that their parents are less educated, earn less, and are often of farming or small business career.

college is found to be not only related to all the aspects of the examined initial employment outcomes, but sometimes also is the solo related factor, as with job-skills/knowledge match and job satisfaction. The finding on the importance of institutional effects on starting salary in this research is aligned to that of a few studies (Bosker, Velden, and Loo, 2001; Fitzgerald and Burns, 2000; Min, Ding, Wen, and Yue, 2005). For example, college prestige and selectivity (Min, Ding, Wen, and Yue, 2005), college location/region, college total enrollment, college nature (e.g. liberal art college) (Fitzgerald and Burns, 2000) and department level participation in facilitating graduate employment (Bosker, Velden, and Loo, 2001) are identified as useful. Apparently, the strong relationships of "specific institution" with initial employment outcomes suggest: while the graduate survey instrument examines some of the factors in educational provision, skills building, and labor market, many are not examined, but probably nevertheless are managed by the institutions and also related to initial employment outcomes.

The introduction of two major institutional management efforts, niche-field designation and the existence of a separate office for career services, into the quantitative analysis of initial employment outcomes and the exploration of their relationship with initial employment outcomes further confirm the hypothesis as well as the suggestion. Despite the difficulty and trickiness to explain how the two types of efforts might have worked, due to possible interactions among the considered variables, the regression analyses are especially helpful in showing how strongly institutional management efforts may influence initial employment outcomes. The existence of a separate office for career services has consistent positive relationships with all the aspects of initial employment outcomes, except starting salary, whereas niche-field designation likely has negative relationships with all the aspects of initial employment outcomes, except job-education level match and job satisfaction. As mentioned before and particularly in accordance with the commercial and vocation nature of the new private higher education, the separate offices for career service have probably engaged in a variety of activities to network with employers that are directly good for graduate job placement as well as to improve apprenticeship and skills training opportunities that are indirectly good for graduate job placement (Wolbers, 2003). The negative effect of niche-field designation reveals a paradoxical, but disturbing role that the new private higher education plays, because of its commercial and demand-absorbing nature: On one hand, its institutions have selected and provided the most popular and even rewarding fields for their students in its efforts to link to the labor market. On the other hand, their motivation to reduce costs by enrolling considerable more students in their niche fields, in effect, hinders their graduate employment in the short run.

CHAPTER SIX: CONCLUSIONS AND IMPLICATIONS

The proliferation of demand-absorbing and commercial private higher education institutions is one of the most extraordinary developments reshaping the landscape in worldwide higher education in the latest decades. With the growth, however, has come considerable debate and skepticism. One key area of controversy involves institutional management efforts and performance regarding graduate employment. This is often the key to whether these institutions are serious demand-absorbing institutions or just low-quality demand-absorbers (even fraudulent).

China, by the suddenness of emergence, dramatic growth, and potential enormity of these institutions, is a major case epitomizing the international trends. Nevertheless, most controversial criticisms and debates about the new private higher education in efforts and performance are based on impression and ad hoc reports, in and outside of China, and especially for graduate employment. Serious studies on institutional management efforts and graduate employment in the sector exist, but only a few and rarely relating efforts to performance. On the other hand, arguably, employment is the foremost concern of college students in economic-booming China nowadays. Thus, for practical and scholarship needs, this dissertation examines how and how well private higher education institutions have made efforts to link private higher education to the labor market.

This study does not exhaustively analyze all institutional efforts or assess the quality of various efforts directly. Nor does it rely on one or two overarching theories.

Instead, it identifies and describes spectra of managed practices and graduate employment performance, in both objective labor market outcomes and subjective graduate feedback, from major aspects, while employing concepts and theories from literature on private higher education and on higher education and the labor market. As a result, this research pioneered a systematic study on the employment of the private sector that had not been done before. Additionally, based on its analysis, this chapter can now contribute to build a conceptual model to distinguish those serious and even semi-elite demand-absorbing private institutions from those mere demand-absorbing ones, along eight criteria on "effort" dimension and seven criteria on "outcome" dimension.

This concluding chapter first synthesizes the data analysis and builds the conceptual model, after revisiting the research question, literature, and research methodology. It then reviews major contextual limitations and suggests how conclusions could be generalized to broader contexts. Third, it draws relevant practical implications from this research. Lastly, it points out directions for future research.

Synthesis of the Analysis and Findings

Chapter One states the research question and reveals the practical needs of this research. It describes the paradoxical and intriguing phenomena of the tremendous expansion of the new demand-absorbing and commercial private higher education sector (Altbach, 1999; Levy, 1999, 2005; UNESCO, 2003) on one side, and the criticisms and even condemnation about its low quality and profiteering in its institutions on the other

(Bollag, 2003; Castro and Navarro, 1999; Giesecke, 2006; Kruss, 2004), in China and around the world, particularly concerning graduate employment efforts and outcomes.

The literature review in Chapter Two provides guidance for the research design and data analysis of this research. On one hand, the literature on private higher education suggests why private higher education may make efforts to link private higher education to the labor market, because of its distinctiveness in mission and field of study provision (Levy, 1986b, 1987) as well as its special role of picking up differentiated and excess labor demand (Bollag, 1999; Cao and Levy, 2005; Levy, 2006a; Wolff and Castro, 2001). It also documents what efforts they may have managed to meet labor market demands, through field of study provision, course delivery, career services, and networking. On the other hand, the literature on higher education and the labor market not only identifies major initial employment outcome indicators to reflect how well the institutions have made efforts to link private higher education to the labor market (Brennan, 2000; HEFCE, 2001; Koskinen, 2005), but it also lays out how they may approach the relationship between the two (Teichler, 1996, 2002, 2003). The intersection between the two literatures is small, but sharp and vital. The review gives special attention to those rare studies of overlap and reveals the need of pursuing this research from a scholarship perspective.

A mixed methods research design was adopted to approach the research question, as described in Chapter Three. Qualitative data about how institutional efforts were collected through interviews, fieldwork observations, and document seeking. Altogether, the author interviewed a dozen administrators of ten private colleges, each around one to two and a half hours, and did some fieldwork there within two months.

Publications, official and unofficial reports, newspaper and campus newsletters, and other documents were also collected. Quantitative data about initial graduate employment outcomes and graduate feedback on institutional worthiness and management efforts were gathered through graduate questionnaire surveys in five private colleges, which resulted in 463 valid samples. Fundamentally, different data sources and research methods serve as triangulations to enhance the reliability of this research (Denzin, 2006; Patton, 2002).

The heart of the data analysis are reported in two chapters, which produces the main findings on how and how well private higher education institutions have made efforts to link private higher education to the labor market. Overall, the analysis reveals a picture about institutional management efforts and initial graduate employment outcomes of the private higher education sector that differs from what critics charge. More importantly, as shown in this synthesis, theory about the relationship between higher education and the labor market can be used to delineate how the private institutions have managed their efforts and several indicators about graduate employment outcomes can be useful to reflect how well the efforts are made. The "distinctiveness" concept in private higher education literature is prominently utilized to further explore why the private institutions have made the efforts and what association exists between efforts and outcomes.

First, mostly different from what critics charge (Goodman, 2003), the data analysis in this research finds that nearly all of the private colleges investigated have seriously made major efforts to link private higher education to the labor market, along the two dimensions identified by the literature on higher education and the labor market:

the relevance of higher education to work and the linkage between higher education and work (Brennan, 2004; Brennan, Johnston, Little, Shah, and Woodley, 2001; Little, 2001; Paul, Teichler, and Van Der Velden, 2000; Teichler, 1996, 2002, 2003). The private colleges investigated have managed to build student employability through field of study provision and educational delivery, with networking efforts for both, and to bridge graduates to employers through career services and their relevant networking efforts. In field of study provision, as in many other countries, the Chinese private colleges have offered most of their programs in several soft sciences (Altbach, 1999; Giesecke, 1999a; Hopper, 1998; Sharvashidze, 2002), dominantly in arts, foreign languages, economics and business, and computer sciences. In educational delivery, consistent with most studies on skills for employment (Brennan, 2000; Clanchy and Ballard, 1995; HEFCE, 2000; Mason, 2002), the colleges pay special attention to certain elements that are deemed important for graduates to get jobs, including foreign language competency and computer skills. But differently, rather than generic skills, they have paid major attention to practical skills and abilities. To boost student practical skills, most of them have committed major resources, by attracting teachers with practical backgrounds, networking with industry for program design and course delivery, setting up their relevant facilities, and cooperating with relevant business. In providing career services, all have set up offices with professional staffing to perform career service functions; career services often include career planning, resume and interview instructions, career counseling, and courses on jobs hunting and careers, job/internship placement, alumni feedback, and outreach, as many reported (Chesler, 1995; McGrath, 2002). But differently, the private colleges investigated have especially emphasized practical

173

trainings and job placements, while networking with employer, industry, business, and even governmental agencies and labor intermediaries.

Essentially, the private institutions' efforts for linking private higher education to the labor market and their uniqueness are embedded in the distinctive nature of private higher education, as literature on private higher education suggests. First of all, meeting labor market demands and making relevant efforts are integral parts of the privates' key mission. The data analysis showed that a substantial chunk of the privates' mission is to produce the right labor for economic development and to prepare students for jobs and careers. All of the Chinese private colleges investigated emphasize the economic and labor development side much more strongly and aim at job preparation goals, albeit non-elite and sometime even low status, although most also frame their education delivery and services as for social development and human concerns. Their emphases on job preparation and linkages to labor market demands stand out in their mission statements. Compared to the public counterparts, they give more attention to market demands when mentioning establishing their fields, programs, and curriculum. They also include more elements about their partnerships with industry and business in their mission statements. These findings appear to be consistent with what Levy finds (Levy, 1986a): private higher education tends to be more attuned towards the privates, business, and labor market. Furthermore, the Chinese private colleges investigated do not just seriously say it, they also seriously do it. Their efforts, reported in this study, confirm private higher education literature on specialized and focused fields of study provision (Levy, 1986a, 2003b, 2006a). Mostly, these colleges focus on a limited number of specialized programs and tune to several fields that are highly demanded.

The private higher education literature on the particular clienteles of the private institutions and their flexibility in governance also shed light on educational delivery, career services, and networking. As in other countries (Levy, 2002a, 2002b, 2003a, 2003b, 2004, 2006a), individual Chinese private higher education institutions are oriented towards special groups of constituents, students, employers, or others of the labor market and higher education market, rather than the general public. In educational delivery, students of the Chinese private colleges are academically less prepared and less likely to be interested in the generic skills and general academic fields. Practical skills, along with popular computer and language skills, mainly fit with their students' higher education goals and interests, though probably also being those of many employers at the same time. So are career services, particularly job placement. Additionally, the entrepreneurial governance and flexible structure not only encourages institutions to seek private business and other partnerships, but also are attractive to employers with specialized human resource training needs, or of special labor market (Bao, 2006a). Many such employers, e.g. small and medium business, business in suburban areas, business in not well-developed regions, business of fast-growing, business with strong practical skill needs, may not have the resources to build relationships with the public colleges or have the kind of jobs attracting the public college graduates. The public colleges may not have the ability or willingness to accommodate their needs in a timely fashion, either.

What is more, not only are the findings of this research different from what critics charge about the lack of efforts on the side of private institutions, the analysis of quantitative data finds that the management efforts of the private colleges are relatively well accepted by both their direct customers, graduates, and their indirect customers, employers in the labor market. Overall, the Chinese private college graduates appear to be as well received by the labor market as their counterpart college graduate cohorts, as reflected by several major employment outcomes. Two thirds of the graduates found jobs shortly before or soon after graduation. Among those who were employed, two thirds found jobs that match the education level they possessed, the fields of study they had pursued, or the skills and knowledge they had acquired. Three fourths were satisfied with their jobs. Such findings are thematically consistent with several studies (McMahon and Wagner, 1981; Sapatoru, Nicolescu, and Slantcheva, 2003; Zhou, 2003), though not with less flattering ones such as Wu (2003). Moreover, the outcomes seem surprisingly consistent with graduates' feedback. Again, about two thirds of all graduates rated the private higher education they had received as "valuable" or "highly valuable" and similar number of graduates reported that they were satisfied with various institutional management efforts. The analysis, with qualitative data about management efforts from the interviews, documents, publications, as well as quantitative data from graduate surveys about employment outcomes and feedback on management efforts, thus actually forms (Figure 4) a triangulation. Consistent findings from different data sources and different collecting methods reinforce the reliability of the picture described by this research on management efforts of the new private higher education sector.

Figure 4: Triangulation in the Data Analysis on Management Efforts

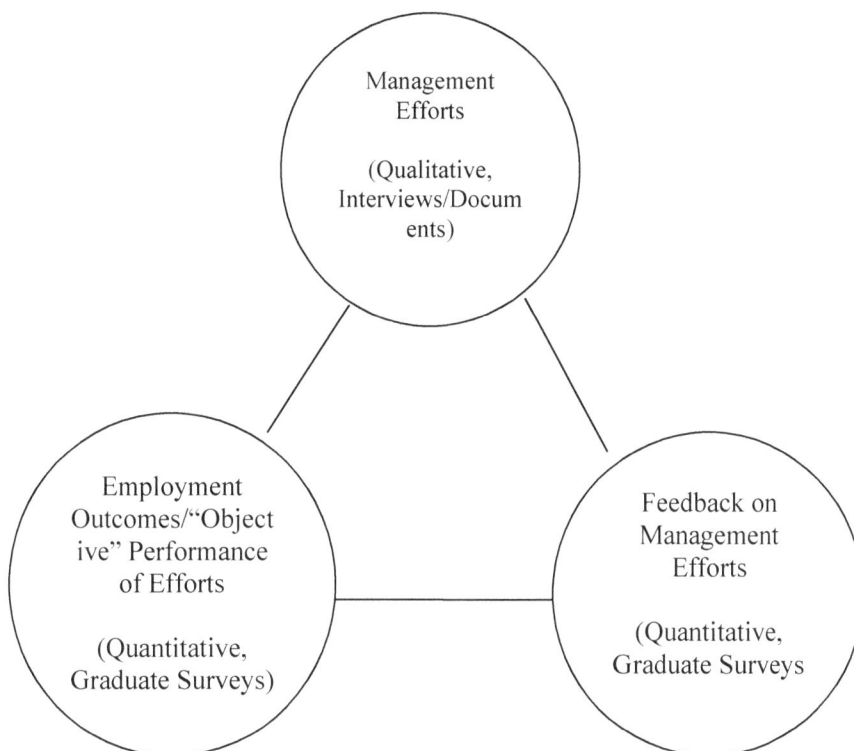

An important line of inquiry examines attributes and sources of variations in graduate employment outcomes. On the key relationships between institutional management efforts and initial graduate employment outcomes, two main findings emerge. A separate office for career services is positively associated with initial outcomes, whereas niche-field designation is negatively associated with initial employment outcomes. A separate office for career services is found to benefit employment status, job and education level match, job and field match, job and skills/knowledge match, and job satisfaction. On the contrary, niche-field designation is found to be adversely related to employment status, starting salary, job and field match, and job and skills/knowledge match. As for separate offices for career services, this study suggest that somehow such offices often involve in other management efforts: engaging in career advice, providing vocational and practical training opportunities, networking with employers and industry, seeking graduate feedback, and other relevant activities. The positive relationship of separate offices for career services is probably related to their vocational and job-oriented nature. Such efforts might have benefited employment outcomes in one way or another, as international literature on career services for graduate employment often describes (Chesler, 1995; McGrath, 2002). Again, private higher education literature offers good explanations. The distinctiveness of the private institutions in catering the privates, business, and the labor market can still be used to explain institutional involvement in various career services and educational delivery.

What may have caused the adverse effect of the niche field designation on initial employment outcomes? Detailed analysis of graduates and college planned enrollment by field of study gives some clue. Likely not the niche programs, which have slightly better employment outcomes if we look at the fields of the niche programs, but the high enrollments in the niche programs are probably more responsible for the negative relationships between niche-field designation and employment outcomes. Here, private higher education literature on the demand-absorbing and commercial nature of the new private higher education best explains this paradoxical phenomenon of niche program designation. For one thing, the institutions place much emphasis on being responsive to labor market demands in their educational delivery and often concentrate on several popular programs that the labor market demands, especially the less costly ones (Levy,

2003b, 2006a). For the other, they commercially provide programs (Banya, 2001;

Hopper, 1998; Levy, 2003b, 2005; Stetar and Berezkina, 2002) on an economic scale

and maximize the possibility of labor market demands, which then probably results in

their decisions to enroll more students in those niche programs where the institutions

have invested some resources and are of some quality. Moreover, the labor market

probably demands the graduates of the niche programs. For instance, the labor market

yields higher average salaries to graduates of niche programs seemingly confirms such a

hypothesis on demand, although graduates of niche programs are not employed

immediately after graduation and less likely to be employed in fields matching their

education. Given that most Chinese private colleges report employment rates of more

than 90 percent within six months after graduation, probably the Chinese private

colleges just neglect those short-term negative effects of niche program designation,

which is, nevertheless, driven by minimizing costs and maximizing "products".

On the other hand, what critics charge is not baseless, because while it is

generalized to conclude that the private colleges investigated in China have made efforts

to link the new private higher education to the labor market and that their graduates

have performed as well as their counterpart college graduate cohorts in the labor market,

wide effort and outcome variations exist among them, not just between accredited and

unaccredited private colleges. Qualitative analysis of institutional management efforts

suggests that the private colleges are different in the level of commitment they have

made in their efforts and the strategies they have adopted to link private higher

education to the labor market. Even though some unaccredited private colleges are

unusually good, such as College I of Case #3, they are generally not so concerned about jobs, at least much less so than attracting paying students for particular educational provisions they have. They are less likely to contact their alumni for feedback and also less likely to secure a network of industry and business for educational delivery or career services. It was very difficult to get unaccredited colleges' input and agreement to my research fieldwork, partially for lack of such resources, but mostly because they had not done relevant work. Such differences also apply to accredited colleges. Some colleges make tremendous commitments, such as College E, with two dozen professionals and a one million yuan budget, while others make minimum efforts in career services, employer feedback, and partnership-building. In terms of initial employment outcomes, significant differences consistently appear among the five colleges examined in all of the four indicators as well as in graduates' evaluation of the worthiness of various colleges' private higher educational provision, even after considering other variables that are somehow related to the indicators in one way or another. Moreover, the colleges have significant lower performance in initial graduate employment outcomes and graduate evaluations are also the ones with less visible commitment to establishing the linkages between private higher education and the labor market because the associations of efforts with outcomes. Therefore, rather than being homogeneous, the private higher education sector is internally permeated with diversity in effort type and quality.

Figure 5: Analytical Model to Differentiate Private Institutions by Measured Management Efforts and Labor Market Outcomes

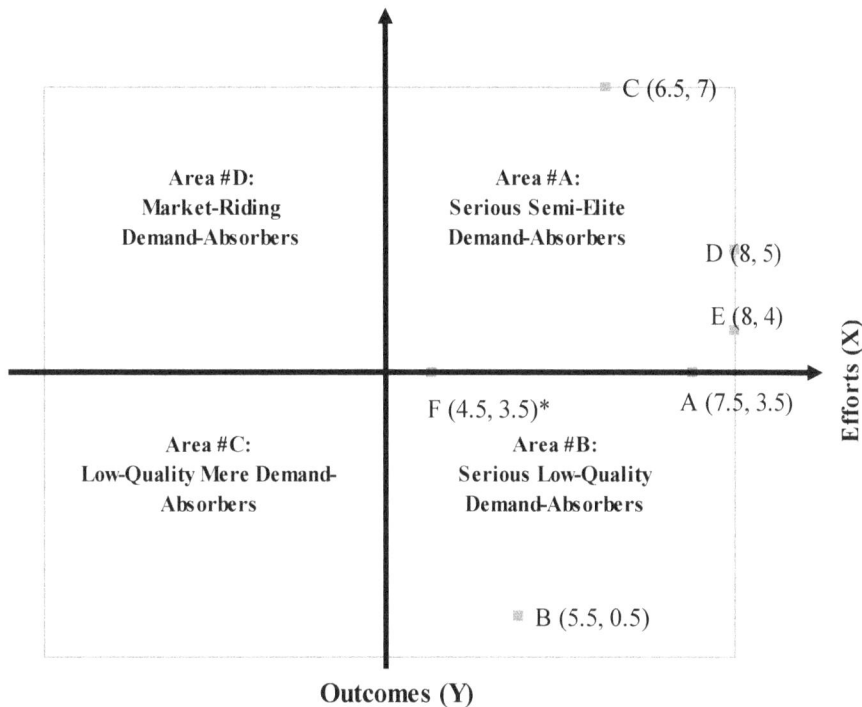

* Unaccredited private institutions.

Note: a). A – F represent different colleges and the numbers in the followed parentheses represent their scores on the efforts (Y) dimension and the outcomes dimension (Y). For example, "A (7.5, 3.5)" should be interpreted as: College A has made efforts in seven aspects and some efforts in an eighth aspect; it has achieved above average outcomes in three of the six indicators and its achievement is close to average.

b). Dimension X: Efforts is based on the eight criteria introduced in Chapter One. They include accreditation, program provision, curriculum provision, faculty composition and qualification, administration, job concern, employer contact, and alumni feedback. Value for each college on Dimension X is based on the summary Table 7 of Chapter Four.

c). Dimension Y: Outcomes, is based on six employment indicators analyzed in Chapter Five (employment status, starting salary, job and education level match, job and field match, job and skills/knowledge mach, job satisfaction) and one overall graduate feedback on institutional worthiness. Value for each college on Dimension Y is based on the summary Table 18 of Chapter Five.

d). If the answer is "Y" for a criterion, then the college is valued as 1 for that criterion, "N" as 0, and "Y/N" or "N/Y" as 0.5. The sum of values on effort-related criteria in one college becomes the value of that college on dimension effort; the sum of values on outcome-related criteria becomes the value on dimension outcomes.

e).Although this figure aggregates the results of the criteria, arguably some criteria have more weight than others. For example, employment status and salary may reveal more about outcomes than the three job-education match criteria.

f). Dimension X and Dimension Y cross at their mid-points.

Contextual Limitations and General Conclusions

Beside the limitations presented in Chapter One and Chapter Three, contextual caveats pose further limitations to generalize the conclusions of this study to broader contexts: the new private higher education in China and around the world.

First, the sampled colleges and graduates are not representative of the new private higher education sector. For qualitative analysis on institutional management efforts, six of the ten private colleges investigated are in one city, Shanghai. Preference was given to accredited colleges, though purposefully, and only three unaccredited private colleges were selected. Even if the one college investigated with bachelor degree graduates may represent what serious private institutions can do in making efforts towards graduate employment, given the total number of such institutions in China is small (25), the other colleges are probably more representative for the accredited colleges, especially those in Shanghai. For quantitative analysis on initial employment outcomes and the associations of management efforts with outcomes, most of the responding graduates (82.9%) of the six private colleges surveyed were from five colleges in Shanghai; the one dozen graduates with bachelor degrees were also from one college in Shanghai; the graduates at the associate degree level but without degrees were also one unaccredited college in Shanghai.

Despite that the samples and conclusions are more representative of the new private higher education in Shanghai, especially for the accredited institutions, this research fails to reveal any consistent differences in both management efforts and outcomes for the private colleges investigated in and outside of Shanghai. On management efforts and as partially reflected by Table 7 of Chapter 4, this research finds that almost every college has engaged in some efforts; those serious and even semi-elite demand-absorbing colleges outside of Shanghai have made similar level of efforts as those in Shanghai; Outside of Shanghai, though the one unaccredited college has made slight fewer efforts than the one accredited college, just as what happened to the colleges in Shanghai, it has not necessarily made significantly fewer or more efforts than all of the unaccredited colleges in Shanghai. Thus, the conclusions of this research on management efforts are also possibly applicable to the accredited colleges in Shanghai and also that in the rest of the country.

On initial graduate employment outcomes, Shanghai is certainly one of the most developed places in China and it presumably has more jobs in terms of geographical intensity and even probably better jobs and jobs paying considerably higher salaries. All these might affect initial employment for graduates who seek jobs in Shanghai. Accreditation status somehow affects employment outcomes, such as starting salary. However, this research also fails to find systematic institutional differences between the one college outside Shanghai and the other colleges in Shanghai and between those accredited colleges and the one unaccredited college, as shown by Table 18. As seen from the survey, the college outside Shanghai had better or comparable outcomes in all examined aspects of initial graduate employment, except graduate starting salary, which is very likely related to where graduates work. It had the highest employment rate upon graduation; its job and field match as well as job and skills/knowledge match were the second best; its job satisfaction and job and education level match were slight lower than those of the overall survey, but better than one accredited college in Shanghai. For the one unaccredited college in Shanghai, although the starting salary and employment status were significantly lower, the latter being likely related to lower student academic background, its job and education level match was the highest of all colleges. Its job and field match level, job and skills/knowledge match, and job satisfaction level were close to the average. Thus, the conclusions of this research on initial employment outcomes are also possibly applicable to the whole new private higher education sector in Shanghai—and perhaps even to the new private higher education institutions in much of the rest of the country.

Internationally, the Chinese case is stark and China is in the midst of one of the world's most extraordinary economic growth spurts and higher education expansion, which may present some uniqueness in the institutional management efforts of the new private higher education sector and its graduate employment. High labor market demands could have been a major factor in good employment outcomes. Nevertheless, the management efforts in the new private higher education sector in China are by no means unique or new. Our findings on graduate employment outcomes are consistent with several studies. In countries with comparatively stable economic and higher education development such as the United States, the private two-year colleges are said to have engaged in more relationship-building with employers and industry than the community colleges (Deil-Amen and Rosenbaum, 2004; Person and Rosenbaum, 2006). Japanese private higher education is similar in such relationship-building (Yoshimoto and Yonezawa, 1994). In countries with enormous higher education expansion, such as Mexico, most of the new private technological universities offer programs oriented to the regional or local labor market demands and engage in the participation of business and industry in field of study provision , educational delivery, and practical training

(Brunner, Santiago, Guadilla, Gerlach, and Velho, 2006: 54), just as the Chinese private colleges investigated have done. The findings on private college graduates' comparable employment outcomes to their public counterparts in major aspects are similar to what has found by other studies (McMahon and Wagner, 1981; Sapatoru, Nicolescu, and Slantcheva, 2003).

In sum, this research generally concludes that private higher education institutions in China have made serious efforts in linking private higher education to the labor market and their efforts are well-accepted by the labor market and their graduates. However, due to the small and unrepresentative college and graduate samples as well as unique Chinese contexts, especially regarding the Shanghai locus, generalizing conclusions to the whole private higher education sector in China are not nearly conclusive.

Policy Implications of This Study

Despite its limitations, some policy implications can be drawn from this research.

First of all, the findings on institutional management efforts can be also used by the direct constituents of private higher education in particular and higher education in general, namely institutions and their students. With the knowledge about what efforts other colleges have made, those who have not made the efforts may review and rejuvenate their practices in linking higher education to the labor market, while being cautious about their practices in niche field designation, admissions, and educational provisions. Certainly, armed with the knowledge about the relationships between institutional efforts and employment outcomes, students may seek more information

185

about relevant practices in their interested institutions and fields of study before they make enrollment commitment, while colleges can attract the right types of students they cater for.

The findings on how and how well private higher education institutions have made efforts to link the new private higher education to the labor market can also provide guidance for policy-makers. The existence of major institutional efforts and good initial employment outcomes in the new private higher education sector deserves corresponding treatment in general higher education policy-making. Given the low and lower student academic background of the new private sector, the achievement of comparable graduate employment outcomes in the private sector to that of the public sector is especially plausible and well worth even perhaps some policy support. On the other hand, the diversity in institutional efforts and graduate employment outcomes warrants differential treatment in private higher education policy-making. In establishing policies to hold the private institutions accountable, the serious demand-absorbing or even semi-elite institutions deserve more flexibility and favorable treatment, while instructions and supervisions is needed side by side for those with minimum efforts and/or below average graduate employment performance. More importantly, since serious institutional management efforts and good initial graduate employment outcomes have earned the acceptance of the perhaps most important constituents of higher education, both employers and students, in some of the unaccredited private colleges, they should also deserve prominent attention from policy-makers in establishing various accreditation and assessment processes for those institutions.

For countries with increasing college graduate population and/or unemployment problems, such as China, this study suggests that attention can be given to the supply side to diminish the impact of relevant problems. For instance, in China and many other countries, it is generally agreed that job supply is plenty, but the supply of the jobs that graduates can find and would like to take and have the ability to take is not. While the results of the problem are multi-faceted and reflected in employment rates, starting salary, job and education match, job satisfaction, etc., the causes of the problem are many, as suggested by the literature on higher education and the labor market (Allen, Boezerooy, de Weert, and van der Velden, 2000; Brennan, 2000; Teichler, 2000; UNESCO, 1998). On the side of higher education institutions, several major factors appear important. What fields of study are provided with how many students per field, are important to educational provision. In educational delivery, the important factor is what skills and knowledge to be emphasized; in career planning, it is how students are taught to follow the labor market demands as well as personal interest; in networking, it is how institutions to bridge employers and their graduates. To approach the problem from both results and causes, policy can be made to achieve more transparency and better practices. Not only can information about graduate employment rate be required to be disclosed to governmental agencies, as the Chinese government currently requires, other aspects of initial employment outcomes, along with employment rate, are also important to be public to widely inform the public, especially the current and future students in selecting programs and institutions. While holding institutions accountable by releasing information about employment outcomes, best practices in institutional efforts are desirable to be identified.

Directions for Future Research

Issues arise in this research, which point to directions for future research. Roughly, the directions can be classified into three groups/dimensions: depth, breadth, and length.

On depth, more detailed qualitative analysis of institutional management efforts by pattern type, especially with the help of more focused fieldwork on management processes, is desirable to identify the essential elements embedded in various practices. In analyzing the qualitative data for Chapter Four on institutional management efforts, the author wished having had the resources for longer fieldwork to observe how major managed efforts had been implemented. Although triangulation, through college report, graduate feedback, third-part publications and some of my observation, seems to confirm the validity of what are described and reported in this study, doubts sustain in some findings that the author chose not to report. Because of the short fieldwork, reported details on the implementation process, the structures, the activities, and the policies are far from optimal. Without such details, essential elements cannot be identified and replications are thus hindered. For example, this study finds that a separate office for career services is beneficial to employment outcomes, but it fails to identify what is missing in those career service offices with other functions.

On breadth, more college cases and graduate samples for quantitative data analysis, ideally using a multi-level modeling and including comparable public colleges within one country as well as colleges across countries, are important to improve the accuracy of statistical findings, particularly those on institutional effects. In this study, small college cases and graduate samples limit the quantitative data analysis, especially better and advanced analysis. For example, this study has only one unaccredited college, one college outside of Shanghai, one college with bachelor degree graduates. Ideally, with adequate college and graduate sample size, multi-level analysis, fits best the needs of recognizing the relationships of graduate employment outcomes with other factors, especially institutional effects.

Another issue came up repeatedly in assessing how and how well private colleges have made efforts in linking higher education to the labor market is: what to compare. While this study has good reason not to include Chinese public colleges in the fieldwork and graduate survey and has made relevant comparisons when possible, the accuracy and quality of the comparison accuracy is limited because of lack of some data element in one way or the other and lack of comparable data. For example, four-point scale data on the private colleges investigated are compared to five-point scaled data on public colleges; data in July 2006 on the private colleges investigated are compared to data in other year or in different month of the same year; data in Shanghai are compared to data in somewhere else. Occasionally, this study used data from other countries for comparison. However, given China is in a unique economic and educational growth period, it is unknown whether what works in China and in the Chinese new private higher education sector can work in other countries. Moreover, if employers' input is also investigated, the comparison can be even richer. Thus, research design with considerable samples of Chinese public colleges and colleges in other countries, along with input from employers, can probably produce better comparison and reveal accurate findings on institutional management efforts of the private higher education in China and around the world.

On length, longitudinal research design is critical to examine graduate employment outcomes and institutional effect in both short-term, as this study does, and in long-term, that this study does not do. In China, though there is no empirical study to sustain, scholars and practitioners suspect that those efforts made for boosting short-term graduate employment outcomes by private institutions, such as practical skills and work experiences, may not have long-term effect. Therefore, while a few existing works indicate that short-term graduate employment outcomes stay consistently in long-term (Silver, Lavallée, and Pereboom, 1999), it is unknown whether they stay mostly the same in the Chinese new private higher education. Study is thus needed to confirm or refute the suspicion for the benefit of scholarship and practice.

Nevertheless, for a full picture and scientific findings on institutional efforts, graduate employment outcomes, and the associations of efforts with outcomes regarding linking private higher education to the labor market, the pursuit of the above-mentioned three directions should be complementary. Cooperation, among higher education institutions, employers, students and parents, scholars, and policy makers, within a country or across different countries, with or without international organizations, such as OECD, UNESCO, and the World Bank, are necessary. The efforts, such as the recent undertaking by OECD on *The Labour Market Orientation of Tertiary Education in France and in OECD Countries: Assessment and Prospects* (OECD, 2007), are especially useful. The concluding hope is that the findings and shortcomings of this research may offer insights to inspire and facilitate relevant initiatives.

APPENDICES

Appendix A: Distribution of Private Higher Education Institutions in China

	Province	Accredited 2-Year Colleges[1]	Accredited 4-Year Universities[2]	Total Private Institutions[3]
High Income Provinces	Shanghai	14 (14)	1	187
	Beijing	9 (9)	1	87
	Tianjin	1(1)		69
	Jiangsu	14 (3)	1	55
	Guangdong	20 (10)		53
	Liaoning	6 (4)		40
	Zhejiang	7 (3)	1	35
	Fujian	14 (6)	1	6
Middle Income Provinces	Hebei	12 (9)		118
	Shandong	15 (2)		94
	Henan	8 (6)	1	83
	Heilong Jiang	4 (1)	1	57
	Inner Mogolia	1 (1)		45
	Hunan	6 (3)		37
	Jilin	3 (3)		24
	Chongqing	5 (5)		11
	Hainan	1 (1)		7
	Hubei	10 (9)		6
	Xinjiang	2		3
Low Income Provinces	Shaanxi	14 (13)	1	96
	Shanxi	3 (1)		55
	Jiangxi	8 (3)	1	33
	Sichuan	6 (3)		32
	Gansu	1 (1)		23
	Anhui	8 (5)		7
	Guangxi	6 (1)		6
	Guizhou	1		3
	Yunnan	3 (2)		3
	Ningxia	2 (1)		2
Total		205	9	1277

* Source 1 and 2: see the listing of the 214 accredited private institutions as of 6/24/2004 at http://www.cer.net/article/20030331/3081104.shtml . The parentheses have the number of accredited institutions in capital cities. Except for the rural location of Yang'en University of Fujian, all other four-year universities are in capital cities. Source 3: 1999 data (Yan & et. al, 2003).

Appendix B: Institutional Consent Form

Project and Researcher Information: My name is Yingxia Cao. I graduated from Institute of Higher Education at Xiamen University and now pursue my Ph.D. at the State University of New York at Albany. You may contact me by yisacao@hotmail.com or call 0563-4037981, or send letter to: Liangmaoxiang #13, Ningguo, Anhui 242300. My academic advisor is Dr. Daniel Levy, SUNY's Distinguished Professor and Director of the world's major center on the study of pr h ed, funded by the Ford Foundation. You may contact him by call 001.518.4425177 or email dlevy@uamail.albany.edu. I am working on my dissertation, "Private Higher Education and the Labor Market in China: Institutional Management Efforts and Initial Employment Outcomes" and now ask for your precious help.

Purpose of the Interview: This project tries to discover how and how well institutions have managed to meet labor market demand. As someone who has the experiences and knowledge about this institution, you are in a special position to provide relevant information. Your institution is selected from the over one thousand private institutions in China. The information you provided will be very important. During the interview, questions about your institution's field of study provision, career services, and networking efforts will be asked. The whole interview will be short of an hour. Your candid responses that identify institutional shortcomings (including those at other institutions) are especially welcome.

Risk and Benefit: I don't anticipate any risk in your participation other than you may feel uncomfortable answering some questions asked. The benefit to your institution of this interview will be my dissertation report and a specific report about your institution with some recommendations.

Confidentiality: The interview content will be stored in my personal computer with password. I will not identify your institution's name or your individual name in any publication or public statement for information obtained by this study unless your institution or you prefer me to identify. I will use Alphabet such as ABC when mention an institution and a pseudo name when mention a person. All information obtained by this study is confidential unless disclosure is required by law. In addition, the Institutional Review Board and the University at Albany responsible for monitoring the study may inspect these records.

Voluntary Participation and Consent: Your participation in this project is voluntary. Even after you agree to participate in the research or sign the informed consent document, you may decide to leave the study at any time without penalty or loss of benefits to which you may otherwise have been entitled. If you have any questions concerning your rights as a research participant that have not been answered by the investigator or if you wish to report any concerns about the study, you may contact the Office of Research Compliance at 001.518.437.4569 or orc@uamail.albany.edu. Please sign the consent form below. One copy of this document will be kept together with the research records of this study. Also, please keep a copy of consent form for your record.

Name _____   Position _____

Signature _____   Date _____

I have read, or been informed of, the information about this study. By signing my name, I hereby represent my institution _____to consent the participation in this study.

Appendix C: Institutional Consent Form in Chinese

学校调查意向书

中国民办高等教育与劳动力市场：高校经营管理与毕业生初期就业状况的视角

课题及研究者概况。我名叫曹迎霞，毕业于厦门大学高教所，现为纽约州立奥尔伯尼大学（University at Albany）博士候选人和加州私立拉文大学（University of La Verne）研究员。在纽约州立大学杰出教授及福特基金资助的世界私立高等教育研究中心主任Daniel C. Levy导师的指导下，我现在正在为题为"中国民办高等教育与劳动力市场：高校经营管理与毕业生初期就业状况的视角"的博士论文收集材料，特此诚请您的帮助和指教。若有兴趣，您可以和我或我导师联系。我的联系方式为：电邮ycao@ulv.edu，电话0563-4037981，邮寄地址"安徽省宁国市粮贸巷13号"。我导师的电邮为dlevy@uamail.albany.edu，电话001-5184425177。

调查的目的。我的毕业论文试图弄清中国民办高校是如何满足劳动力市场需求的。本研究从一百多所民办高校中精选您校代表中国民办高等教育现状，其调查分为两个部分：访谈和问卷调查。访谈致力于访问对您或其他对校毕业生就业有很了解的人，希望通过大约一小时的访谈，了解您校课程与专业设置、毕业生就业指导、就业网络建立方面的情况。问卷试图通过2006届毕业生对27个问题个有关他们所学专业、工作和就业、家庭和个人背景的情况的回答，得到他们对您校课程与专业设置、毕业生就业指导、就业网络建立方面的反馈。

访谈对您校的利弊。除了被调查对象可能会对有些问题的问法感到不舒服之外（他们可以不回答其中任何问题），我不认为调查会对您校有坏处。不仅如此，本研究结论可能能够对您校的毕业生就业问题提出一些有用的建议和意见（若您觉得有必要，本研究论文结束之后，我可以就您校情况进行具体分析）。

调查的保密性。访谈和问卷调查的资料将锁在中国并在毕业论文答辩后销毁。调查的内容内容将输入个人计算机并加上密码。除非您代表您校更愿意使用实名，本研究的所有公开报告在提及本研究所获信息时将一律采用虚名。除非法律上需要、奥尔伯尼大学及其学校监管会的检查和我论文导师的指点，其他任何人不得以查看本调查的录音带和原始调查回卷内容。

调查的自愿性。参加本调查是完全自愿的。若您愿意代表您校参加此调查，请在下面签名。即使在签名之后，您有权停止调查而不受任何惩罚。若您对作为调查对象的权利在我的解释之后还有所疑问，您可以与我校研究监管处联系(电话001.518.4374569，电邮为orc@uamail.albany.edu)。我将与访谈、问卷的材料一起保存和销毁您的签名(请自我保存一份此签名作为您个人记录)。

姓名＿＿＿＿＿＿＿＿＿＿＿＿＿＿ ，职务＿＿＿＿＿＿＿＿＿＿＿＿＿＿

签名＿＿＿＿＿＿＿＿＿＿＿＿＿＿ ，日期＿＿＿＿＿＿＿＿＿＿＿＿＿＿

我已被告知此研究信息，特此代表＿＿＿＿＿＿＿＿＿＿＿＿（高校名）签名让我校接受调查。

Appendix D: Interview Consent Form [1]

Project and Researcher Information: My name is Yingxia Cao. I graduated from Institute of Higher Education at Xiamen University and now pursue my Ph.D. at the State University of New York at Albany. You may contact me by yisacao@hotmail.com or call 0563-3290925, or send letter to: Liangmaoxiang #13, Ningguo, Anhui 242300. My academic advisor is Dr. Daniel Levy, SUNY's Distinguished Professor and Director of the world's major center on the study of pr h ed, funded by the Ford Foundation. You may contact him by call 001.518.4425177 or email dlevy@uamail.albany.edu. I am working on my dissertation, "Private Higher Education and the Labor Market in China: Institutional Management Efforts and Initial Employment Outcomes" and now ask for your precious help.

Purpose of the Interview: This project tries to discover how and how well institutions have managed to meet labor market demand. As someone who has the experiences and knowledge about this institution, you are in a special position to provide relevant information. Your institution is selected from the over one thousand private institutions in China. The information you provided will be very important. During the interview, questions about your institution's field of study provision, career services, and networking efforts will be asked. The whole interview will be short of an hour. Your candid responses that identify institutional shortcomings (including those at other institutions) are especially welcome.

Risk and Benefit: I don't anticipate any risk in your participation other than you may feel uncomfortable answering some questions asked. The benefit to your institution of this interview will be my dissertation report and a specific report about your institution with some recommendations.

Using of Tape Recorder: I would like to record what you say so that I do not miss or misinterpret what you will say. If at any time during the interview you would like to turn the tape record off, all you have to do is press the "Off" button on the recorder. Please sign below if you are willing to have this interview audio recorded. You may still participate in this study even if you are not willing to have interview recorded.

Signature _____   Date _____

Confidentiality: The interview content will be stored in my personal computer with password. I will not identify your institution's name or your individual name in any publication or public statement for information obtained by this study unless your institution or you prefer me to identify. I will use Alphabet such as ABC when mention an institution and a pseudo name when mention a person. All information obtained by this study is confidential unless disclosure is required by law. In addition, the Institutional Review Board and the University at Albany responsible for monitoring the study may inspect these records.

Voluntary Participation and Consent: Your participation in this project is voluntary. Even after you agree to participate in the research or sign the informed consent document, you may decide to leave the study at any time without penalty or loss of benefits to which you may otherwise have been entitled. If you have any questions concerning your rights as a research participant that have not been answered by the investigator or if you wish to report any concerns about the study, you may contact the Office of Research Compliance at 001.518.437.4569 or orc@uamail.albany.edu. Please sign the consent form below. One copy of this document will be kept together with the research records of this study. Also, please keep a copy of consent form for your record.

Signature _____   Date _____

   I, _____ (Print Your Name), have read, or been informed of, the information about
      this study. By signing my name, I hereby consent to participate in this study.

---

[1] This consent form has adopted the format and required text of *Informed Consent*, Office of Research Compliance, University at Albany.

Appendix E: Interview Consent Form in Chinese

访谈意向书

中国民办高等教育与劳动力市场：高校经营管理与毕业生初期就业状况的视角

课题及研究者概况。 我名叫曹迎霞，毕业于厦门大学高教所，现为纽约州立奥尔伯尼大学（SUNY at Albany）博士候选人和加州私立拉文大学（University of La Verne）研究员。在纽约州立大学杰出教授及福特基金资助的世界私立高等教育研究中心主任Daniel C. Levy导师的指导下，我正为题为"中国民办高等教育与劳动力市场：高校经营管理与毕业生初期就业状况的视角"的博士论文收集材料，特此诚请您的帮助和指教。若有兴趣，您可以和我或我导师联系。我的联系方式为：电邮ycao@ulv.edu，电话0563-4037981，邮寄地址"安徽省宁国市粮贸巷13号"。我导师的电邮为dlevy@uamail.albany.edu，电话001-5184425177。

访谈的目的。 我的毕业论文试图弄清中国民办高校是如何满足劳动力市场需求的。本研究从很多学校中精选您校代表中国民办高等教育现状。鉴于您对您校及毕业生就业的了解和经验，我真心希望通过大约一小时的访谈，得以了解您校课程与专业设置、毕业生就业指导、就业网络建立方面的情况。同时尤其希望听到您对中国民办高校毕业生就业问题方面的不足的指点。

访谈对您的利弊。 除了您可能会对有些问题的问法感到不舒服之外，我不认为访谈会对您有坏处。不仅如此.本研究可能能够对您校的毕业生就业问题提出一些有用的建议和意见。

访谈的录音。 为了确保访谈内容的完整性，本访谈拟采用录音。若您同意录音，请在此签名。若您不同意录音，我只用笔录。在您同意录音并签名之后觉得有些内容不适合录音的，您只要关上录音键即可。

签名＿＿＿＿＿＿＿＿＿＿＿＿＿＿＿，日期＿＿＿＿＿＿＿＿＿＿

访谈的保密性。 访谈的录音带和意向书将锁在中国并在毕业论文答辩后销毁。访谈的内容将输入个人计算机并加上密码。除非您或者您校更愿意使用实名，本研究的所有公开报告在提及本研究所获信息时将一律采用虚名。除非法律上需要、奥尔伯尼大学及其学校监管会的检查和我论文导师的指点，其他任何人不得以查看本访谈的录音带和原始内容。

访谈的自愿性。 参加本访谈完全是自愿的。若您愿意参加此访谈，请在下面签名。即使在签名之后，您有权停止访谈而不受任何惩罚。若您对作为访谈对象的权利在我的解释之后还有所疑问，您可以与我校研究监管处联系(电话为001.518.4374569，电邮为orc@uamail.albany.edu)。我将与录音带一起保存和销毁您的签名(请自我保存一份此签名作为您个人记录)。

签名＿＿＿＿＿＿＿＿＿＿＿＿＿＿＿，日期＿＿＿＿＿＿＿＿＿＿

我＿＿＿＿＿＿＿＿＿＿＿(楷书您的姓名)，已被告知本研究信息，特此签名以示接受访谈。

Appendix F: Interview Guide with Open-Ended Questions [1]

As noted above, the interview is for my dissertation's data collection. You have signed the consent form, which indicates your consent to my interview. Do you have any questions to ask before the interview starts?

Section I. Management Mechanism in Field of Study Provision
First, I'm interested in knowing the programs and courses provided by your institution.

1. What programs have been provided by your institution? Any niche programs? How the decisions about program provision have been made?
2. Based on your experiences, what would you say about the institution's programs and how they endeavor to meet labor market demand? At local, regional, and national labor market? What about niche programs?
3. How does your institution accommodate faculty employment to program changes? What special employment preference does your institution have in faculty qualifications, if any? What is your faculty composition in terms of type of contract?
4. What would you say about the courses provided in your institution in preparing students for employment? In terms of skills? Knowledge? How have your institution kept curriculum provision meeting employers' needs? Has your institution gotten feedback from graduate employment? From employers? If so, how?
5. What do you think your peer private institutions have done about program provision? Program and labor market fit? Faculty employment and development? And what about your peer public institutions in program provision? In program and labor market fit? And in faculty employment and development?

Section II: Management Efforts in Career Services
It is very helpful to get your description about how your institutions have accommodated program and course changes as well as faculty employment to meet labor market demand. I have wondered about that for some time. I am also interested in gathering information about the various career services in your institution.

6. What kind of career development services does your institution provide for students? How are such services provided? When? Any special structure or personnel handle such services?
7. Does your institution provide graduate job placement services? If so, what kinds? By which institutional unit or units? Do you know the percentages of your graduates getting their jobs through your institutions' job placement services? Does your institution have a considerable number of graduates go to the same employers each year or in consecutive years? If so, please elaborate?

---

[1] Many of the questions asked in this interview guide have been adapted from the Alumni Outcome Assessment, Office of Institutional Research, University at Albany. The transitional paragraphs at the beginning of the first three sections have imitated (Patton, 2002: 375)

8. Does you institution also provide job placement services to your alumni? What about career development? And how do you think your alumni are satisfied with the overall career services (both career development and job placement services) they received at school?
9. What do you think your peer private institutions have done in career development services? In job placement services? What about your peer public institutions?

Section III. Institutional Networking
We are more than halfway through our interview now. It's going well. You have provided important information. I greatly appreciate that. How is it going for you? Another general topic that I would like to concerns your institution's connections with other organizations for graduate employment.

10. Does your institution have special arrangements with outside organizations (e.g. government agencies, industry/business, other higher education institutions, and nonprofit organizations) regarding field of study provision and career services? If so, what are they? Would you please describe each arrangement? With whom? About what? How it started? How it goes? What do you think is the future of such arrangements?
11. What do you think the employers know about your programs and graduates? How do they know that? And roughly how many percentages of employers have prior experience with graduates from here?
12. Have your institution contacted with your alumni in the past one year? If so, for what reason? How it worked out? Does your institution have alumni association? If so, what's the role of your institution in alumni association's activities?
13. Does you institution have systematic assessment of graduate employment? If so, what mechanism (method, channel, and time) has been used? How the resulted data have been utilized? What kind of data does you institution have? Can your institution provide me the data for my research?
14. What information does you institution have about graduates and current students? How is such information updated? How can I get the mailing address for your 2005 alumni's current mailing addresses?

Section IV. Other
15. Before we end this interview, are there any other thoughts or information about graduate employment you would like to share with me? Or anything about other management practices not mentioned?

Appendix G: Interview Guide with Open-Ended Questions in Chinese

访谈问题

如前所述，此次访谈意在为毕业论文收集材料。您已经同意访谈。请问在访谈之前您还有什么问题要问吗？

第一部分：学科设置及管理机制

首先，我对您校的专业和课程设置很感兴趣。

1．您校有哪些专业？有没有核心专业？一般专业和核心专业是怎样确定的？

2．凭借您多年的经验，您对您校专业设置及其在满足劳动力市场需求上的做法有何看法？这些专业在满足全国、地区和地方劳动力市场的情况如何？能否就您校核心专业具体谈谈？

3．您校是如何在教师聘任方面使教师聘任与专业设置的变更相一致？对所聘任的教师的资格有特殊要求和考虑吗？若有，怎样达到一致的？

4．您对您校课程设置在为毕业生就业的准备方面有何看法？在知识准备方面呢?在技能准备方面呢？能否谈谈您校是如何确保课程设置与用人单位的要求一致的？您校有从毕业生和用人单位获得相关的反馈信息吗？若有，怎样获得的？

5．就您所知，其他兄弟民办高校专业和课程设置工作是怎样进行的？专业和市场需求方面的工作做得如何？他们在教师聘任和提高上有何相关做法？其他兄弟共公办院校呢？

第二部分：就业指导及其经营管理

您对你校如何在课程和专业设置及其变更、教职员的聘任方面如何满足劳动力市场需求的介绍对我很有启发。同时，我也希望了解您校的就业指导工作。

6．您校提供哪些就业指导服务？这些服务是如何进行的？在何时进行的？有特别办公室或人员负责吗？

7．您校为毕业生安排工作吗？若有，是什么样的工作安排方式？哪个机构进行安排？您知道平均每年大概有多少比例的毕业生是通过学校安排就业的？您校有相当多的毕业生在同一年或连续几年到同一单位工作吗？同否具体介绍一下？

8. 您校为已经毕业的毕业生提供就业指导和工作安排吗？您认为您校毕业生们对他们在校时所接受的就业服务（指导和工作安排）的满意情况如何？

9. 就您所知，能够谈谈其他兄弟民办高校是如何提供毕业生就业指导工作的？工作安排呢？其他兄弟公办高校呢？

第三部分：高校毕业生就业网络

我们的访谈已经过半，其进展非常好，我非常感谢你提供的宝贵信息。您的感觉如何？我还希望了解您校如何与其他机构联系并建立毕业生就业网络的。

10. 在专业设置和就业服务方面，您校有无建立与其他机构（政府、企业、其他学校和非营利性组织）的合作关系？若有，是哪些？请具体谈谈合作的性质、单位、内容、过程和现状。您认为这些合作的将来如何？

11. 您认为用人单位对您校毕业生的专业设置和毕业生的了解的程度如何？今年的用人单位中有多少比例已签有过用您校毕业生的经验？

12. 您校过去一年有联系过已经毕业的毕业生吗？若有，原因是什么？结果如何？您校有校友会吗？若有，学校在校友会中扮演什么样的角色？

13. 您校对毕业生的就业有系统的评估吗？若有，是什么样的评估机制？结果如何利用的？您校有什么样的数据？可以为我的研究提供相关的数据吗？

14. 您校有已经毕业的毕业生和在校生的何种数据？这些数据是如何更新的？我怎样才能获得2005届毕业生现在的邮寄地址呢？

第四部分：其它

15. 在结束我们的访谈之前，您还有什么需要补充的吗？您认为我在毕业生就业问题上有什么遗漏的吗？或您还有什么相关信息愿意与我交流的吗？

Private Higher Education and the Labor Market in China:
Institutional Management Efforts and Initial Employment Outcomes

Graduate Questionnaire Survey

Dear Graduates:

My name is Yingxia Cao, doctoral student at the State University of New York at Albany. I come from a remote rural area in Anhui and had no access even to high school because of poverty. Fortunately, I caught a slim chance to university after graduating from secondary vocational education. With higher education, precious help, and personal perseverance, I am now working on my Ph.D. dissertation. I earnestly need your precious help to fill in the questionnaire for my dissertation project to finish my six-year doctoral study in the US.

In this project, I want to know how private higher education can provide not only higher education access, which you have taken, but assure its graduates a good job. Based on your report, this study will make recommendations to your Alma Mater, on how to improve her graduate employment management –for both current students and alumni. It thus potentially benefits you and your alumni. In the questionnaire, you will be asked questions on the field and college you studied, your employment situation, job search, and background. It may take you about 10 minutes. You are selected to represent thousands of your alumni and your response is very important for both my dissertation and my recommendation to your Alma Mater.

Your participation is voluntary and your response is confidential and anonymous. The information you provided in the questionnaire will be entered my computer with password upon receipt. Except me, nobody is supposed to review the information you provided unless disclosure is required by law and the Institutional Review Board and the University of Albany responsible for monitoring the study may inspect these records. I don't anticipate any risk in filling in the questionnaire other than you may feel uncomfortable answering some of the questions.

If you are interested in contacting me for any reason (after or before you fill in the questionnaire), please feel free to email yisacao@hotmail.com (the easiest way to reach me), call 0563-3290925, or send letters to: Yingxia Cao, Liangmaoxiang #13, Ningguo, Anhui 242300.

Thanks for your precious help and best wishes to you in 2006!

Section A   Reflection and Report on Your Studied Field and College

A1. The name of the college you graduated: _____

A2. The major you studied in the college: _____

A3. You began your study in the college in _____ (year) and graduated in _____(year)

_____ A4. How much had you known the job prospect of your field of study before you chose it?

   1. A lot   2. Some   3. Little   4. Nothing

_____ A5. What type of programs were you in at the college?

   1. Accredited bachelor degree program

   2. Accredited associate degree program

   3. Unaccredited associate degree program – Certificate & Examination

   4. Unaccredited bachelor degree program - Certificate & Examination

   5. Unaccredited bachelor degree program – Self-Study

   6. Unaccredited associate degree program – Self-Study

A6. Looking back, if you were free to choose again, how likely would you

   1. Very likely 2. Likely 3. Less likely 4. Not likely

____ a. choose the same institution of higher education or private institution with similar nature?

____ b. choose the same filed of study?

____ c. choose to go back to high school?

____ d. decide not to study at all?

__ A7.Given the money you spent, how do you value the education you have received in college?

   1. Highly valuable 2. Valuable . A little valuable 4. Not valuable at all

A8. Please indicate the degree to which each of the following considerations were reasons you chose your major.

   1. Strongly agree 2. Agree 3. Disagree 4. Strongly disagree

___ a. I chose my major because *I was interested in the subject matter.*

___ b. I chose my major because *jobs are available in this field.*

___ c. I chose my major because *salaries are high in this field.*

___ d. I chose my major because *I was advised to take this major by my family.*

___ e. I chose my major because *this field offers highly respected career positions.*

___ f. I chose my major because *I have friends/relatives majoring or working in this field*

__ g. I chose my major because *it will allow me to make a meaningful contribution to society.*

A9. Please put the number that best describes your experiences in the college in front of each statement.

   1. Strongly agree 2. Agree 3. Disagree 4. Strongly disagree

___ a. I am satisfied with *the field of study I chose.*

___ b. I am satisfied with *the course I took.*

___ c. I am satisfied with *the interaction with other students.*

___ d. I am satisfied with *the qualifications of faculty in my department.*

___ e. I am satisfied with *information provided about internship, practicum, or co-op experiences.*

___ f. I am satisfied with *information provided about job vacancies.*

___ g. I am satisfied with *opportunities to participate in internship, practicum, or co-op experiences.*

___ h. I am satisfied with *opportunities to be recommended or provided for job placement.*

___ i. I am satisfied with *opportunities to receive advice about planning my career.*

___ j. I am satisfied with *opportunities to receive advice about obtaining a job.*

Section B   Job Search and Initial Graduate Employment Outcomes
(If you haven't taken any job after graduation, skip Section B).

B1. You got the first job offer in __ month ___ year (before or after graduation). The total number of employers you contacted before you took up the first job was _____. The total months you have taken for searching the first job was _____ months. The approximately monthly salary of your first job was _____. The location of your first job was _____ province and _____ (rural/urban/suburban) area. And the monthly salary of your current job is_____. I have changed my jobs ____ times after graduation. (*Note: Please think back if you have changed your jobs. By using "the first job", I mean the initial job that you chose with serious consideration after your graduation).*

___ B2. How would you characterize the relationship between your field of study and the area of your first job?
1. Closely related   2. Related 3. A little bit related   4. Not related at all

____ B3. To what extent did you use the knowledge and skills acquired in courses studied for the first job?
1. To a very high extent   2. To some extent   3. To a low extent 4. Not at all

____ B4. How difficult do you think for getting a job in your field?
1. Very difficult   2. Difficult   3. A little difficult   4. Not difficult at all

____ B5. What was the nature of the employer of your first job?
1. State company or government 2. Joint adventure or sole foreign company
3. Private Chinese firm   4. Self employed   5. Others (please specify) _____

_____ B6. What was your occupational responsibility on your first job?
1. Senior manager, official   2. Professional, middle/low level manager, supervisor
3. Technician 4. Clerk   5. Skilled worker   6. Unskilled workers

____ B7. How were/are you satisfied with your first job after graduation?
1. Very satisfied   2. Satisfied   3. Dissatisfied 4. Very dissatisfied

____ B8. What was the minimum education do you think appropriate for your first job?
    1. Middle school graduates or lower
    2. High school graduate or technical secondary education graduates
    3. Associate degree graduates
    4. Bachelor degree graduates
    5. Master or doctoral degree graduates

B9. According to your perception, how important were the following aspects for your employer in recruiting you for your first job after graduation and how satisfied are you with relevant work to train you in the college?
1. Very important/satisfied   2. Important/satisfied   3.Unimportant/dissatisfied   4. Not important at all/very dissatisfied

Importance		Your satisfaction
_____	a. Field or course studied	_____
_____	b. GPA	_____
_____	c. Professional/Vocational Certificates	_____
_____	d. Practical/work experience	_____
_____	e. Reputation of the institution of higher education	_____
_____	f. Foreign language proficiency/certificates	_____
_____	g. Computer skills/certificates	_____
_____	h. Recommendations/references	_____
_____	i. Personality	_____

_____B10. How did you find your first job (please select the one number that best describes your situation)?

1. I applied for the job all by myself
2. The company came to recruit at the college and I was selected or recommended
3. I got information or help from the career service center, faculty, or staff and then applied by myself
4 I used other personal connections/contacts, such as parents, relatives, friends, or other acquaintance
5. I started or worked on my own business/self-employment
6. I participated in government arranged job fairs or contacted governmental employment agencies
7. Other, please specify _____.

B11. Please think back to the week 7/3-7/9/2005 and week 1/1/-1/7/2006? Put the number that best described your situation on the line under each week.

7/3-7/9/2005	The Description of Your Situation	1/1/-1/7/2006
_____	1. I had a job offer or one job	_____
_____	2. I had no job offer or job, and was still searching	_____
_____	3. I was self-employed	_____
_____	4. I had no job offer/unemployed, but was not searching.	_____
_____	5. I haven't graduated or I was preparing for Examinations	_____
	6. I was preparing for or was in further education	

B12. Please indicate whether the college or the faculty of your graduated college had provided the following career services (put "Yes" or "No" on the line before each service) and how satisfied you are with each service (by 1, or 2, or 3, or 4 on the line after each service) in obtaining your first job.

1. Very satisfied   2. Satisfied   3. Dissatisfied   4. Very dissatisfied   5. Not Provided

Provision (Y/N)	Career Services	Your Satisfaction
_____	1. Provide career counseling, e.g. planning, assessment, etc.	_____
_____	2. Teach job-search courses	_____
_____	3. Invite employers or alumni to report on employment	_____
_____	4. Inform job vacancies	_____
_____	5. Hold on-campus or institutional-sponsored job fairs	_____
_____	6. Provide job placement	_____
_____	7. Arrange internship, practicum, or co-operated training	_____
_____	8. Contact employer for you	_____
_____	9. Support job hunting via web	_____

Section C   Background Information

C1. Your Gender is _____ (Male/Female). You were born 19 ___ (Year).

C2. Your hometown is in _____ province and _____ (rural/urban/suburban) area. Your family annual income is ___.

C3. Your college entrance examination total score was ___; College average GPA was ___. You worked ___ months before entering college, and have worked ____ months after entering college.

___ C4. Regarding your high school education, did you graduate from
        1. General higher school
        2. Vocational higher school
        3. Technical secondary school
        4. Others, please specify _____

C5. What are your mother (or female guardian)'s and father (or male guardian)'s highest level of education?

Mother/female-guardian	Education Level	Father/male-guardian
_____	1. No education	_____
_____	2. Elementary school	_____
_____	3. Middle school	_____
_____	4. High or vocational secondary school	_____
_____	5. College or University	_____

C6. Do you have anything else to say regarding your job or Alma Mater (please kindly write in the back if the blank is not enough).

Thanks for completing the survey. Your participation is greatly appreciated. Please SIGN and mail it by the enclosed postage-paid envelope immediately or by 2/15/06.

Appendix I: Questionnaire for Graduate Survey in Chinese

民办高校毕业生调查问卷

中国民办高等教育与劳动力市场：高校经营管理与毕业生初期就业状况的视角

亲爱的毕业生：

您好！

我名叫曹迎霞，现为纽约州立奥尔伯尼大学（SUNY at Albany）博士候选人和加州私立拉文大学（University of La Verne）研究员。我来自安徽的偏僻农村，曾因家境贫寒上不起高中；所幸中专毕业后获得上大学的机会，和您一样接受了一般大学的高等教育。后来由于得到众多人的帮助，在厦门大学读完硕士之后来到美国。现在正为题为"中国民办高等教育与劳动力市场：高校经营管理与毕业生初期就业状况的视角"的毕业论文收集数据，以完成博士论文并结束长达六年之多的博士学习。在此特别恳请您回答此调查问卷，为我收集数据和顺利获得博士学位提供至关重要的帮助。

通过本研究，我试图弄清中国民办高校如何在提供高等教育机会的同时能够确保其毕业生获得满意工作。根据您提供的信息，希望能够为您的母校在提高毕业生就业方面提供有用的意见和建议。这不仅将有助于在校生，也有可能对已毕业的毕业生有所帮助。因此在问卷中，您会被问及一些关于您所学专业和学校、您的工作和就业、家庭和个人背景的问题（所有问题的提出都有着重要的原因）。回答这些问题大约需要10分钟；您有可能对有些问题的回答感到不自然，但回答本调查不会对您有任何害处；您可以选择不回答其中的某些问题。此研究从几千毕业生中挑选您代表您的校友和中国民办高校毕业生，因此您的答卷对此研究极重要。

回卷是自愿和不署名的。您提供的信息将得以保密：我收到您的回卷后会将其输入个人计算机并加上密码；除法律、奥尔伯尼大学及其研究监管会的检查和我之外，其他任何人不得以查看您和其他毕业生的回卷。

若有兴趣（有关毕业生就业以至于进一步求学和出国问题），您可以和我联系与交流。我的联系方式为：电邮ycao@ulv.edu（因为居无定所，这是和我联系最快捷、最可靠的方式), 电话0563-4037981, 邮寄地址为：安徽省宁国市城北路江南综合楼1楼，恒瑞房地产评估有限公司（曹迎霞收，邮编242300）。

非常感谢您的帮助，*请尽快（或在2006年8月15日之前）寄出您的回卷*！祝愿找到自己理想的职业！

请在接下来两页问卷的的27个问题旁的横线上填上相关内容或写上您所选选择的前面代表数字：

例一：我对问题23的回答为：

23．您出生于__1975__年，性别是___女___、家乡在__安徽___省/市/自治区___3___（1)城市2)乡镇3)农村）

例二：我对问题26的回答为：

26．您妈妈或女监护人所接受的最高教育程度是___1___；您爸爸或男监护人所接受的最高教育程度是__2__

1) 没有受教育　2)小学　3) 初中　4) 高中或中专　5) 大学专科或本科　　6) 研究生

第一部分：所学专业及民办高校的反馈

（问题1-3：请在横线上填上相关内容；问题4-9：请在横线上填上您所选选择的前面代表数字）

1．您毕业的高校的名字是：＿＿＿＿＿＿＿＿＿＿＿＿＿＿＿＿＿＿＿。

2．您在校所学的专业是：＿＿＿＿＿＿＿＿＿＿＿＿＿＿＿＿＿＿＿＿＿。

3．您＿＿＿＿＿＿＿年开始在此校学习，并在＿＿＿＿＿＿＿年结束在此校的学习？

4．在您选择所学专业之前，您对其就业前景的了解程度是：＿＿＿＿＿＿

　　　1）很了解　　2）了解　　　3）不怎么了解　　　4）一点都不了解

5．您是＿＿＿＿＿＿＿类型学生：

　　　1)国家承认普通或高职本科　2)国家承认普通或高职专科　3）专升本或成人教育本科

　　　4)学历文凭试点或成人教育专科　　5）自学考试本科　6）自学考试专科　7）其他

6．就所花费的钱而言，您认为您所受的民办高等教育是：＿＿＿＿＿＿

　　　1）很值得　　2）值得　　　3）不怎么值得　　4）不值得

7．假如能重新选择，您在大学入学前会

＿＿＿＿＿选择同一所或相同性质和类型的高校　＿＿＿＿＿选择同一专业

＿＿＿＿＿＿选择复读　　　　　　　　　　　　＿＿＿＿＿＿选择不读书

　　　1）很大可能　　2）可能　　　3）很小可能　　　4）不可能

8．您对以下关于您选择所学专业原因的阐述的态度是

＿＿＿＿＿＿因为我喜欢所学专业学科　　　　＿＿＿＿＿＿因为所学专业领域有工作机会

＿＿＿＿＿＿因为所学专业的工资相对较高　＿＿＿＿＿因为我的家人建议我学此专业

＿＿＿＿＿＿因为所学专业领域的工作受人尊敬　　＿＿＿＿＿＿因为所学专业领域工作挑战性强

＿＿＿＿＿＿因为有朋友或家人在所学专业领域工作　＿＿＿＿＿因为所学专业对社会有益

　　　1）非常赞成　　　2）赞成　　　3）不赞成　　　4）极不赞成

9．您对以下关于您在所毕业民办高校经历的阐述的态度是：

＿＿＿＿＿＿我对所学专业满意　　　　　　　　　　＿＿＿＿＿＿我对在校所学课程满意

＿＿＿＿＿＿我对在校与其他同学的交流满意　　＿＿＿＿＿＿我对老师的水平和资格满意

＿＿＿＿＿＿我对学校提供的实习和见习信息满意　　＿＿＿＿＿＿我对学校提供的就业信息满意

＿＿＿＿＿＿我对学校提供的实习和见习机会满意　＿＿＿＿＿我对学校提供的就业机会满意

＿＿＿＿＿＿我对学校提供的职业规划指导满意　　＿＿＿＿＿＿我对学校提供的择业指导满意

　　　1）非常赞成　　　2）赞成　　3）不赞成　　　4）极不赞成

第二部分 择业及就业情况

10．　以下最能代表您2006年毕业时状况的是：＿＿＿＿＿＿

　　　1）已经在工作或获得了工作录用　　　2)在找工作　　　　3)没有工作录用也没有找工作

　　　4)没有毕业或准备毕业 文凭考试　　5)自我创业或就业　　6)在深造或为进一步深造准备

（若您对第10题的回答是1以外的其他选择，请跳过以下第二部分的问题，直接回答第三部分的问题）

11． 您在_____年____月获得第一份工作录用的（从毕业高校毕业前后），获得录用前大约共与_____个用人单位联系过，共花了_____个月找这份工作。您当前被录用工作的起薪大约是每月_____元，这份工作在_____省市自治区的_____（1)都市 2)县乡镇 3)农村）。

12． 您当前被录用工作与您所学专业的相关程度是：_____

   1)紧密相关 2)相关 3)几乎都不相关   4)一点都不相关

13． 您当前被录用工作会用您所学课程的知识和技能的程度可能是：_____

   1)非常多   2)有一些   3)很少   4)根本用不上

14． 您所学专业领域找到工作的难度是：_____

   1)容易   2)不怎么难   3)难   4)很难

15． 您当前被录用工作的用人单位的性质是：_____

   1)国有、公办企事业单位 2)外资或合资企业 3)私、民营企业 4)自我创业或就业 5)其他

16． 您当前被录用工作的工作职位是：_____

   1)官员或高层管理人员   2)中层管理人员、独立自由职业人或分部门主管和工头

   3) 一般职员   4) 熟练工人   5) 非熟练工人

17． 您对当前被录用工作的满意程度是：_____

   1)很满意   2)满意   3) 不满意   4)很不满意

18． 您认为适合做您当前被录用工作人的教育程度是：_____

   1)初中或以下学历 2)高中或中专学历 3)专科学历 4)本科学历 5)研究生学历

19． 在以下的阐述中，最能够代表您找到当前被录用工作的途径是：_____

   1) 从校就业指导或其他教职员工处获得信息后自己申请被录用   2)全靠自己申请被录用

   3)用人单位到学校找人，我被推荐并录用 4)我利用个人关系（父母、亲戚、朋友或熟人）

   5) 自我创业或就业   6)由政府就业扶助机构安排就业   7)其他，请介绍_____

20． 您认为以下各方面对您获得当前被录用工作的重要程度分别是：

_____专业和课程   _____学习成绩   _____学校推荐 _____实践经验

_____外语证书及能力 _____职业 专业证书 _____计算机证书和能力 _____性格和人格

   1)很重要   2)重要   3) 不重要   4)很不重要

21． 您对您毕业高校的以下教育或指导工作对您找到工作的满意程度分别是：

_____专业和课程   _____学习成绩   _____学校推荐   _____实践经验

_____外语证书及能力 _____职业 专业证书 _____计算机证书和能力 _____性格和人格

_____提供职业咨询（如规划和测量等）   _____开设就业指导课程

_____邀请用人单位或毕业校友到校现身报告   _____提供用人信息

_____ 召开在校或校际间的人才交流会   _____ 提供就业安排联系

_____ 通过学校电子网络支持您找工作   _____ 安排实习或见习

        1)很满意   2)满意   3)不满意   4)很不满意   5)没有此类服务

第三部分 您的背景情况

22. 您出生于_____年，性别是_____（1)男 2)女）；家在_____省/市/自治区_____（ 1)都市 2)县乡镇 3)农村），家庭平均年收入大约为_____元。

23. 您大学入学前共大约工作_____月；您大学学习期间共大约工作(包括见、实习)_____月。

24. 您大学入学高考成绩总分大约是_____分；您大学学习期间总平均每科成绩大约_____分。

25. 您毕业中学的性质是：_____

        1)普通高中   2)职业高中   3) 中专   4) 其他，请介绍_____

26. 您妈妈或女监护人所接受的最高教育程度是_____；您爸爸或男监护人所接受的最高教育程度是____

        1)没有受教育   2)小学   3)初中   4)高中或中专   5)大学专科或本科   6)研究生

27. 请在以下空白处写下您对您工作或母校的任何建议和想法（若空白不够，请附纸或写在介绍页反面)：

Appendix J: Universities & Colleges Analyzed in This Research

PRIVATE	PUBLIC
Shanghai	
College A – Accredited three-year college The college was established in 1993 and accredited in 2002. Its 28 programs cover fields of study in foreign languages, arts, and engineering. It has over 6000 students (Translated from college website)	**Shanghai Xing Jian Polytechnic College (Public #A)** In 2001, the college was transformed to higher vocational postsecondary college from being adult-oriented college with a history of twenty years. Now it has a total staff of 306 and the majorities are professional teachers with titles of lecturers or professors. http://www.shxj.cn/english/english.htm.
College B: Accredited three-year college The college was established in 1984 and part of an educational group that has educational provision from kindergarten to college. In 2006, it has about 4300 students in 17 programs and over 200 faculties (Translated from college website)	**Shanghai College of Science & Technology (Public #B)** It was established in 2001 from a merge of one college and one university campus with 40 years' history. It has over 20 programs, which covers engineering, business, and social sciences. The college has a capacity of having about 3,000 students (Translated). http://www.scst.sh.cn/xygk/jsh.shtml
College C: Accredited four-year college The college was established in 1992, accredited by Ministry of Education in 1994, and promoted to four-year college in 2002. It is a comprehensive university with over 9000 students (In English, excerpted from college website)	**Shanghai Institute of Technology (4-year) (Public #C)** It is result of a merge of three institutions with history of over fifty years in 2000. It has over 11,000 students and over 1800 faculty and stuff (about 600 full-time teachers). While conducting the three-year vocational education, SIT is mainly devoted to the running of the bachelor's degree programs. The Institute provides education in arts and sciences, engineering, and business. (http://www.shict.edu.cn/english/index.htm).
College D: Accredited four-year college The college was established and accredited in 2000 and promoted to four-year college in 2005. It has over 8000 students and 600 faculty (about 300 are full-time), with 26 program provision in six departments: Information Technology Department, Trade and Commerce Department, Management Department, Foreign Languages Department, Art Design Department, and Mechanical and Electronic Engineering Department (In English, excerpted from college website) .	**Shanghai Second Polytechnic University (Public #D)** The university was established in 1960 and transformed into a higher vocational education institution from adult education college in 2000. It was merged with another vocational education college in 2001 and now mainly provides polytechnic fields while also having educational provision in humanities and social science, administration, economics, and sciences (Translated from http://www.shspu.edu.cn/introduce/suit/index.shtml)
College F: Unaccredited three-year college The college was founded in 1964 and has over 80 types of professional development programs in science, technology, foreign languages, and business. In addition, it also provides associate degree programs education in 21 programs for cooperated local universities. It also has over 10,000 professional development students each year (Translated from college website)	**Shanghai City College ((Public #F)** The college was established in 1956 as a part-time higher educational provision college and transformed in full-time higher vocational educational provision college in 2001. Its faculty and staff are over 400; its degree-seeking students are over 6000; and its professional development students are over 13,000 annually (Translated from http://www.umcollege.com/file/about.asp).
College G: Unaccredited three-year college The college was established in 1983 and mainly provides professional	

209

development in foreign languages, such as English, German, French, and Spanish. It also provides some professional development programs in computer sciences. In addition, it has educational provision in six programs for cooperated local universities for associate-degree-seeking students (Translated from college website).

Other Cities in the Middle and West of China: Xi'an, Zhengzhou, and Hefei

College E: Accredited four-year college
The college was established in 1985, accredited in 2001, and promoted to grant bachelor-degrees in 2005. It has about 30 programs, 20,000 students, 800 faculty and staff (Translated from college website).

Xi'an University of Finance & Economics (Public #E)
It is a merge of several colleges and schools (the college dated back to 1950s). The comprehensive university mainly focuses on fields of study in economics and administration, but also has educational provision in arts & sciences, engineering, and law. Its 24 bachelor-degree programs and 18 vocational higher education programs have a total of over 23,000 students and 800 faculties. (Translated from http://www.xaufe.edu.cn/General/Introduction.html)

College I: Unaccredited three-year college
The College was established in 1999. It focuses on radio, broadcasting, and movie related fields, and has over 400 students (Translated from college website)

College J: Private Affiliated College to Public University
Under the ownership of Education Corporation of a Key University, the college was established after a merge of three colleges that had functions in self-study facilitating, adult education, and continuing education in 2000 (Its mother university has a history back to 1956). It provides self-study facilitating higher education, vocational higher education, adult education, and long-distance education. Its fields of study in self-study facilitating programs are over 40 and have several thousand students (Translate from college website)

College K: Accredited four-year college
Established in 1995, it is a comprehensive university with 52 programs that covers 8 major fields of study in sciences, Engineering, Agricultural, Arts, Economics, Administration, law, and education. Its student population reaches 25,000 and faculty population reaches 1,200 (Translated from college website)

Henan Institute of Science & Technology (Public #K)
The college was transformed from colleges back to 1949. It has 5 master's degree programs and 38 bachelor's degree programs, which covers Sciences, Engineering, Agricultural, Arts, Economics, Administration, law, and education. It also provides adult and online education. Its total student population is over 20,000 (Translated from http://www2.hist.edu.cn/news/jianjie.htm)

College L: Accredited three-year college
It was established in 2000 and has 28 programs in engineering, computer sciences, foreign languages, communications/mass media, and arts. Its student population is over 6,000 (Translated from college website).

Anhui Vocational and Technical College (Public #L)
It was formed in 2003 following the merge of three vocational schools, one of which began vocational higher education in 1999. Its student population reaches 9,000 and faculty and staff population reaches 491(Translated from http://www.ahtu.ah.cn/intro.asp)

Note: All internet information was accessed on 1/6/2007; the cited websites for private colleges are omitted to make the private colleges anonymous.

Appendix K: Analyzing the Mission Statements of Interviewed Private Colleges and Selected Public Colleges

	Economic/Labor Development	Private Colleges	Cultural/Human Development
College A: Three-year college			
The College has very clearly and uniquely defined mission statements, as published in one of its brochures for public relations.			
Individual /Local/Re gional	The college has formulated its educational philosophy, which is to be responsible for students, for their parents, and for society. Three responsibilities: Responsible for specialty choice, overall development and career. Five channels: Channels for … career, entrepreneurship and practice. Six combinations: The combination of career orientations between recruitment and career guide & recommendations; the combination of practical learning between diploma education and professional qualification certificate education; the combination of college-enterprise cooperation between theoretical education and practical training... (excerpted from brochure)		The college has formulated its educational philosophy, which is to be responsible for students, for their parents, and for society. The college puts passion first, bases on development, promotes creativity, and uses creative education to cultivate creative talents. Five channels: Channels for further education, study abroad... Six combinations: …the combination of human-focus between strict-management and customized administration; the combination of overall development between intelligent and emotion...
College B: Three-year college			
Its statements are rather vague and the wordings are more close to slogan or politically-correct claims.			
Individual	It helps students to master basic knowledge and skills for life and career, and enables them become a knowledgeable whole. It emphasizes multiple certificates, comprehensive appraisal, administrator rotation, cooperative educational provision (note: with industry/enterprises) (Translated from its website).		Provide students for further education opportunity through transfer (interview and translated). It promotes the education principle of being "comprehensive, creative, and personality/ethical" and insists on the motto of "being cooperative, practical, perseverant, and progressive". The college has its distinguished features in centralizing on people, enabling students to learn to how to learn and how to act. (Translated).
College C: Four-year-college			
While most of its mission statements are clear and some are even unique, some generally follow popular claims about higher education or about private higher education.			
Global/Int ernational	The distinguished feature of the university is … … to produce labors that are ready to facing new challenges for … economic globalization.		The students of the university are encouraged to become professionals … with a sense of global responsibility.
National/Ge neral	The principle of the University is to faithfully follow the guidelines set up by the state for developing the country through enhancing education, science and technology, and to persist in its non-profit orientation".		The students of the university are encouraged to become professionals with a sound moral grounding and to carry forward fine Chinese traditions with a sense of

	The students of the university are encouraged to become professionals.... and to meet the needs of ... developing the economy (excerpted website)	global responsibility, to be accountable to both themselves and society, and to meet the needs of enhancing social civilization...(excerpted website)
Individual/Local/Regional	The distinguished feature of the university is to enable its students "to have a solid command of English and be good at computer skills", (excerpted website) and thus to produce labors that are ready to facing new challenges for the economic development in Shanghai, Shanghai Pudong, Yangzi River Delta and economy globalization (Translated from website)).	

College D: Four-year college
The college does not clearly define its mission, goals, and objectives. It only makes vague claim about human/cultural development.

National/General	The vocational college's niche is set by Ministry of education as cultivating front-line professionals for product, service, and construction (Translated from interview notes). Its educational provision is to meet demands and be distinctive as well as multi-disciplinary, applied, and comprehensive. The college aims to contribute to the development of the country through education, science and technology (Translated from interview notes).	
Individual/Local/Regional	The college focuses on Shanghai in its market-oriented educational provision and aims at establishing bridges for the society on producing human resources, and for students to be successful, and for faculty and staff to have a career (Translated from brochure).	The College is characterized with regulated operation and high academic standard by sticking to the principle of human orientation, nurturing with virtue... (Translated from brochure)

College E: Four-year college
The goal of the college is clearly defined.

Individual/Local/Regional	The strategic goal of the college development is to "focus on students, cultivate their employment ability, and improve campus living and study quality". The college emphasizes experiencing education and graduate employment services. The college has over 500 business and corporations to come here for graduate recruitment each year, 8 employment career service offices in the country, and over 100 practicum bases (translated from website).	The strategic goal of the college development is to "focus on students... and improve campus living and study quality".

College F: Unaccredited three-year college
Most of the statements are clearly expressed.

Global/International	Its objective is to education various types of labors to meet the needs of ... the world... (Translated from its website)	
National/General	Its objective is to education various types of labors to meet the needs of the society, its science and technology, product and producing, and the world... (Translated from its website)	
Individual/Local/Re	The college is responsible for each student and to help each student to be successful in producing professional and practical labor with both ability and	

gional	virtue. The college is structured to make XXX (note: the local community of the college) as a computerized, modern, and learning community. Its objective is to education various types of labors to … to serve the regional economy. Directed by market demand, it aims at producing intermediate and advanced labors/talents with practical and various skills. It tries to have a niche in educational provision by having new fields of study, quality faculty, strict management, high quality, and broad employment opportunities. (Translated from college website)	

College G: Unaccredited three-year college
The statement is clearly and unique, with strong job-orientation.

Individual /Local/Re gional	Our mission and goals are: to utilize our strengths in foreign language and produce various types of inadequately-produced but urgently-needed advanced technical professionals who master both fields of profession and foreign languages as well as meet the demands of international communications and economic construction in the 21st century (Translated from Brochure for Admissions).	

College I: Unaccredited three-year college
The college mission is clearly defined primarily for individual students.

National/ General		Its mission is to … and thus to contribute to the development of socialistic mass media.
Individual /Local/Re gional	Its mission is to strict management, enhance education, emphasize practicality, and cultivate competent talents with skills and ethics for the fields of movie, TV, and broadcasting… The college encourages students to also pursue a minor to become multi-disciplinary artists for broader employment opportunity and better employment ability. (Translated from College Brochure for Admissions).	It emphasizes cultivate students' artistic aptitudes and creativity (College Brochure for Admissions)

College K: Four-year college
Its mission is very general and somewhat follows governmental slogans

Global/Int ernational		It also competes in the international education market and has extensive international communication and exchanges.
National/ General	The mission of the college is to help in what the county and the people concern, and serve in the construction of socialism modernization and open policy reform. The strategic slogan is to strive to be better, distinctive, and compete to have brand names. Its curriculum changes and establishments are directed by the society's demands and tuned to market demand from market economy and social development. (Translated from website)	Its curriculum changes and establishments are directed by the society's demands and tuned to market demand from market economy and social development. (Translated from website).
Individual	It has first class educational facilities, famous faculties, distinctive educational	

/Local/Re gional	provision, as well as individualized student career planning. (Translated from website). It enhances experiments, apprenticeship, and internship. While having cooperative agreements with over 3000 employers in recruiting our graduates, it has established more than 510 employment and internship bases in Beijing, Shanghai, Tianjing, Guangzhou, Shenzheng, Xiamen, and Zhengzhou.
College L: Three-year college	Its mission is clearly defined.
Global/Int ernational	It cooperates with foreign and other Chinese higher education institutions for education and pedagogy. (Translated from website).
National/ General	It cooperates with foreign and other Chinese higher education institutions for education and pedagogy. (Translated from website). The college adheres to the demands of economic and social development, and establishes hot fields of study with good employment prospects in the labor market. Its educational provision emphasizes self-study ability, creativity, practicality, and to produce advanced practical professionals. It has established various training and internship bases in Tianjin, Guangdong, and Hefei, and some of its fields of study are provided on specific orders. (Translated from website).
Individual /Local/Re gional	The college adheres to the demands of economic and social development, and establishes hot fields of study with good employment prospects in the labor market. (Translated from website).
College J* (Private College Affiliated to Public College)	
National/ General	'In the journal of realizing great rejuvenation of Chinese people in the new century, the institute will explore new trails through practice, and make greater contribution to the cultivation of competent talents for the cause of socialistic modernization. (Translated from College Brochure for Public Relations)
Individual /Local/Re gional	The cultivation of students' comprehensive quality has been of great importance in the educational policy of the Institute.

Public Colleges

Shanghai Institute of Technology (Public #A)	
Individual /Local/Re gional	SIT has been making determined effort to cultivate its students in an all-round way, namely, morally, intellectually, physically…. SIT has been making determined effort to cultivate its students in an all-round way, namely, morally, intellectually, physically, and train them to become advanced engineering and technological personnel who are armed with knowledge of modern science and a remarkable ability in application and

	problem-solving undertaking. SIT endeavours to build the university into a high-leveled, application-oriented, multiple-disciplined university of higher learning with its outstanding features and into "a cradle for engineers".	
Shanghai Second Polytechnic University (Public #B)		
Global/Int ernational	... the college tries to serve Shanghai, face the nation, and interact with the world.	
National/ General	It focuses on society's demand, professional norms, and labor requirements. Its educational provisions are guided by market demand, based on scientific management, assured by quality curriculum, and developed by distinguished niches. ... the college tries to serve Shanghai, face the nation, and interact with the world. (Translated from website).	
Individual /Local/Re gional	Resident in East Shanghai, the college tries to service Shanghai, face the nation, and interact with the world. Directed by society demands and centering on the local, it will consistently cooperate with industry/business, and achieve "zero distance" in college networking with corporations. (Translated from website).	The college values life, ethics, as well as skills. It provides general and theoretic education, emphasizes experiment and practices. By connecting theories with practices, it tries to improve student creativity in science and technology. (Translated from website).
Shanghai Xing Jian Polytechnic College (Public #C)		
Individual /Local/Re gional	The college adheres to the educational principle "Based on the students' demand, assist the students to be successful". To enable students to become indispensable applied technicians in the society, the college emphasizes applied technological ability in teaching and cultivating student ability in practice and operation (Translated). http://www.shxj.cn/xjgk/index.asp	
Shanghai College of Science & Technology (Public #D)		
Individual /Local/Re gional	Guided by market demand, the college is to cultivate high vocational and practical front-line professionals for production, construction, administration, and service. Its objectives are: resident in Jiading, serve shanghai, face Yangze River Delta, focus on higher vocational education, produce "blue collar" professionals for shanghai and Yangze River Delta.... The College also has networked with foreign and Chinese universities as well as business/industry for its educational provision.	...make Jiading a learning and life-long education community.
Shanghai City College (Public #F)		
Global/Int ernational		The college selects excellent students to participate in field exhibition and academic activities in Singapore, Hong Kong, as well as in China.
National/ General		The college selects excellent students to participate in field exhibition and academic activities in Singapore, Hong Kong, as well as in China.
Individual	It provides equipment and facilities to enable students to acquire "one diploma	Its motto is: Education people, cultivate abilities, and

/Local/Regional	multiple certificates".	promote morale and ethics. … The college emphasizes cultivating student comprehensive quality and ability.
Xi'an University of Finance & Economics (Public #E)		
Individual/Local/Regional	The college consistently sticks to the principle of "strengthening the effectiveness, enhancing the reforms, improving the quality, and assure continuous development". It prioritizes quality, focus on educational provision, and aims at developing distinguished characteristics. Directing its activities by society's demands, it strives to cultivate advanced applied labors/talents, who have practical and creative abilities as well as been able to adapt to social, economical, technical, and science development.	
Henan Institute of Science & Technology (Public #K)		
Global/International		It also actively participates in international communications and exchanges.
National/General	Its educational provisions, such as curriculum and pedagogies are in accord to labor demands from social and economic development.	It has produced well-recognized scientific research.
Individual/Local/Regional		It tries to associate theories with practices in its educational provision while emphasizes practicality and improves students' comprehensiveness and creativity.
Anhui Vocational and Technical College (Public #L)		
National/General		Its goals are …to conduct applied and technical research.
Individual/Local/Regional	The college's mission is to provide satisfying vocational higher education and produce applied and technical talents/labors with high abilities. It posits its educational provision to be around vocational higher education, to face various fields and professions, to target at the local, to be distinctive, and to assure quality. Its goals are to cultivate high vocational and practical front-line professionals for production, construction, administration, and service…	

Source: The main source of the data is the same as

Appendix J. Mission statements of some private colleges are also from brochures.

Appendix L: Number of Programs Provided by Field of Study in 8 Private and 8 Public Colleges: Fall 2006

Fields of Study	A	B	C	D	F	E	K	L	Private Total		SH Sec. Poly. Coll.	SH Xing Jian Coll.	SH Coll. of Sci & Tech	SH City Coll.	XA Uni. of Fin. & Eco.	HN Sci. & Tech. Coll.	AH Voc. & Tech. Coll.	SH Sec. Poly. Coll.	Public Total	
Foreign Language	7	2	2	2	1	2	2	2	20	10.9%	1	0	4	2	0	1	1	1	10	4.8%
Arts	4	2	0	6	0	4	7	5	29	15.8%	3	3	2	2	1	1	5	4	21	10.1%
Others	0	4	0	2	0	3	0	4	13	7.1%	0	1	1	1	0	3	1	1	8	3.9%
Literature	11	8	3	10	1	9	9	11	62	33.9%	4	4	7	5	5	5	7	6	39	18.8%
Administration	5	3	6	4	7	7	5	3	40	21.9%	4	2	4	3	6	7	3	7	36	17.4%
Economics	6	1	4	2	1	2	3	1	20	10.9%	3	2	1	0	1	9	1	2	19	9.2%
Computer	3	2	3	4	0	5	2	3	22	12.0%	2	4	3	4	1	3	1	5	23	11.1%
Science	4	2	3	5	0	6	3	5	28	15.3%	2	6	4	7	2	3	8	7	39	18.8%
Engineering	2	2	0	4	1	4	3	4	20	10.9%	20	9	0	4	6	1	4	19	63	30.4%
Law	0	0	1	0	0	2	2	0	5	2.7%	0	0	0	0	0	2	0	0	2	1.0%
Education	0	0	0	0	0	0	3	0	3	1.6%	0	0	1	0	0	0	4	0	5	2.4%
Agriculture	0	0	0	0	0	0	0	0	0	0.0%	0	0	0	0	0	1	1	0	2	1.0%
Health Science	0	1	0	0	0	0	4	0	5	2.7%	0	0	0	0	0	0	1	1	2	1.0%
Grand Total	28	17	17	25	10	30	32	24	183	100.0%	33	23	17	19	16	28	29	42	207	100.0%

Source: admission plan of relevant colleges in Fall 2006 and field of study introduction of their websites (A-K represents private colleges).

Note: In the private sector and by field. literature includes foreign languages (English, Japanese, Germany, French, Spanish, Korean, and Arabian), arts (art & design, advertisement design & practice, "advertisement, conference, and exhibition", jewelry arts & appraisal, movie & animation, TV & radio. music and acting, broadcasting & hosting, dance and directing, apparel/clothes design, human & image design, movie & TV acting, fine arts), and other literature programs (journalism, secretary, publishing and computer technology, publishing and distribution, public relation, social works, Chinese & literature). Administration includes business/public administration, marketing, logistics, customs & transportation, tourism & management, hotel management, labor and social security. financial management/investment, supply chain management, conference & exhibition management, city planning & management. human resource management. Economics includes international economics/trade, finance or international finance, accounting & auditing, e-commerce, real estate, stock & bond, economics, taxation, insurance. Science includes computer sciences and information technology, electronics, applied electronics, audio & video technology, communication, information appearance and light & electronic technology, applied electronics education, animal product, mathematics & applied math, chemistry & pharmacy, environmental science, and biology. Engineering include programs such as engineering (construction & management), automation, automobile use & technology, engineering project appraisal, building automation, electronic engineering, mechanic design, producing, & automation, environment controlling and management technology, industry and environment projection & safety technology, biological technology and application, mechanic engineering & automation, industry engineering, industry design, industry appraisal, environmental engineering, electronic controlling technology, material science and engineering, metal extraction & engineering, processing equipment & control engineering, safety engineering, chemical engineering, light chemistry & engineering, food science & engineering, chemical & material processing, light industry, cloth/waving, and food, gardening arts & engineering, mechanic and electronic technology, cloth waving process, appraisal, management, and technology, modeling and producing. The field of law includes law, paralegal studies, politics and bureaucracy. Education includes physical education, national & traditional physical education, athletic training, pre-school education, general education, educational technology, social physical education, cook and nutrition education. Agriculture includes general agriculture, agricultural economics & management. Health sciences includes nursing, medical test, nutrition & food hygiene, pharmacy, clinic health/medicine, and animal health.

Appendix M: Planned New Enrollment by Field of Study in 7 Private and 7 Public Colleges: Fall 2006

Fields of Study	A	B	C	D	E	K	L	Private Total	SH Sec. Poly. Coll.	SH Xing Jian	SH Coll. of Sci. & Tech	SH City Coll.	XA Uni. of Fin. & Eco.	HN Sci. & Tech. Coll.	AH Voc. & Tech. Coll.	Public Total
Literature	560	605	776	666	1375	1504	1262	35.1%	300	410	285	70	590	460	924	16.5%
Foreign Language	360	188	402	140	560	282	441	12.2%	170	225	170	0	100	80	222	5.2%
Arts	200	150	111	387	395	1090	515	15.1%	90	155	80	70	100	300	557	7.3%
Others	0	267	263	139	420	132	306	7.8%	40	30	35	0	390	80	145	3.9%
Administration	300	298	740	445	645	352	925	18.9%	337	290	140	405	1222	317	678	18.4%
Economics	200	200	937	176	1030	437	211	15.2%	220	40	0	40	1667	82	225	12.3%
Science	160	50	270	262	700	516	572	13.1%	523	140	350	80	1085	872	749	20.6%
Computer Science	120	50	270	196	605	516	320	10.7%	423	140	230	40	835	120	340	11.5%
Engineering	80	130	0	276	110	732	298	8.6%	614	100	370	405	0	819	2221	24.5%
Law	0	0	67	0	380	197	0	3.4%	0	0	0	0	196	70	0	1.4%
Education	0	0	0	0	0	230	0	1.2%	0	480	0	0	0	165	0	3.5%
Agriculture	0	0	0	0	0	0	0	0.0%	0	0	0	0	0	180	0	1.0%
Health Science	0	120	0	0	0	707	0	4.4%	0	0	0	0	0	335	0	1.8%
Grand Total	1300	1403	2790	1825	4240	4675	3268	100.0%	1994	1460	1145	1000	4760	3300	4797	100.0%

Source: admission plan of relevant colleges in Fall 2006 (A-K represents private colleges).

Appendix N: Fields of Study Provision in China's Regular Undergraduate Higher Education: 1997-2005

	1997	1998	1999	2000	2001	2002	2003	2004	2005
Philosophy	1636	1341	1763	1847	1805	2175	1520	4067	1797
Economics	153367	159207	237129	363379	138746	182416	221410	240100	264219
Law	41527	48102	69048	114682	146782	160618	185999	195638	199521
Education	46681	50295	67257	107259	158283	178223	218575	264251	315638
Literature	143080	161862	230175	343418	417604	509315	612021	724402	760475
Foreign Language							263490	302534	302174
Art								236900	295497
History	16329	16383	19070	22003	16082	15351	16330	17128	13379
Science	110443	120531	155880	202466	258201	294867	329656	357070	270147
Engineering	380946	412393	607597	832124	892356	1057241	1242426	1466459	1809426
Agriculture	35959	38325	52251	68966	62952	69247	81619	88281	97188
Health Sciences	70425	75188	108384	149928	174156	207909	257681	299314	338563
Administration					415823	527614	654464	816712	974228
Total	1000393	1083627	1548554	2206072	2682790	3204976	3821701	4473422	5032581

Source: China Education Statistics, Education Database at http://www.stats.edu.cn/

Appendix O: Niche Programs Designated by Investigated Private Colleges

	Programs/Majors/Specialties	A	B	C	D	E	F	K	Total
Literature:									
Foreign Language	English	1		1			1		3
	Japanese	1		1					2
	Germany, French, Spanish, Korean, Arabian	5							5
Arts	Art & Design				2			1	3
	Music and Acting							2	2
Other	Journalism		1						1
	Publishing and Computer Technology		2						2
	Literature Total	7	3	2	2	0	1	3	18
Administration:									
	Business/Governmental/Industry Administration						2	1	3
	Logistics					1	1		2
	Hotel Management						1		1
	Financial Management/Investment						1		1
	Supply Chain Management					1			1
	Community Management		1						1
	Administration Total	0	1	0	0	2	4	2	9
Economics:									
	International Economics/Trade		1					1	2
	Accounting & Auditing						1	1	2
	Insurance					1			1
	Economics Total	0	1	0	0	1	1	2	5
Science:									
	Computer & Information Science and Technology			3	4				7
	Science Total		0	3	4	0	0	0	7
Engineering:									
	Automation		1		3				3
	Engineering Subtotal	0	1	0	3	0	0	0	3
Education:									
	Physical Education							1	1
	National & Traditional Physical Education							1	1
	Athletic Training							1	1
	Education Subtotal	0	0	0	0	0	0	3	3
Health Science:									
	Nutrition & Food Hygiene		1						1
	Health Science Subtotal	0	1	0	0	0	0	0	1
	Grand Total	7	6	2	5	3	6	10	39

Source: Interviews and brochures.
Note: A-K represents private colleges.

REFERENCES

Aamodt, Per Olaf, and Clara Ase Arnesen. "The Relationship between Expansion in Higher Education and the Labor Market in Norway." *European Journal of Education* 30, no. 1, March (1995): 65-77.

Agelasto, Michael. "Social Relationships and Job Procurement by Graduates: Case Study of a Chinese University." Ph.D. Dissertation, University of Hong Kong, 1996.

Akoojee, Salim. "Private Further Education and Training." In *Human Resources Development Review 2003: Education, Employment and Skills in South Africa*, 396-415. Cape Town, South Africa: HSRC Press, 2003.

AL-Omari, Aieman, and Osamha Obeidat. "University Missions/Goals in the Context of Globalization: Public and Private Institutions in the Middle East." *International Journal of Private Higher Education*, no. 1 (2006).

Allen, J., P. Boezerooy, E. de Weert, and R. van der Velden. "Higher Education and Graduate Employment in the Netherlands." *European journal of education* 35, no. 2 (2000): 211-220.

Allen, Jim, and Egbert De Weert. "What Do Educational Mismatches Tell Us About Skill Mismatches? A Cross-Country Analysis." *European Journal of Education* 42, no. 1 (2007): 59-73.

Allen, Jim, and Rolf van der Velden. "Education Mismatches Versus Skill Mismatches: Effects on Wages, Job Satisfaction, and on-the-Job Search." *Oxford Economic Papers*, no. 3 (2001): 434-452.

Altbach, Philip. G. (ed.). *Private Prometheus: Private Higher Education and Development in the 21st Century*. Westport, CT.: Greenwood Press, 1999.

Banya, K. "Are Private Universities the Solution to the Higher Education Crisis in Sub-Saharan Africa?" *Higher Education Policy* 14, no. 2 (2001): 161-174.

Bao, Wei. *The Function and Structure of Private Higher Education in China*. Beijing: Peking, 2005. Reports on her doctoral dissertation.

_____. "The Development of Private Higher Education in China: Change and Response." In *International Seminar on Frontier of Private Higher Education Research in East Asia*. Tokyo: Organized by Research Institute of Independent Higher Education and collaborated with Program of Research on Private Higher Education, 2006a.

_____. *Private Higher Education and the New Market of Graduate Employment*. Beijing: Peking University, 2006b.

Bennett, Neville, Elisabeth Dunne, and Clive Carré. "Patterns of Core and Generic Skill Provision in Higher Education." *Higher Education* 37, no. 1 (1999): 71-93.

Bernasconi, Andres. "External Affiliations and Diversity: Chile's Private Universities in International Perspective." PROPHE Working Paper No.4., November., Program for Research on Private Higher Education (PROPHE), State University of New York at Albany. Available online at http://www.albany.edu/~prophe/publication/paper.html, 2004a.

_____. "Organizational Diversity in Chilean Higher Education: Faculty Regimes in Private and Public Universities." Doctoral Dissertation, Boston University, 2004b.

Boesel, David, and Eric Fredland. *College for All? Is There Too Much Emphasis on Getting a 4-Year College Degree?* Washington, DC: U.S. Department of Education, Office of Educational Research and Improvement, National Library of Education, 1999, accessed December 12 2003; Available from http://www.ed.gov/pubs/CollegeForAll/.

Bollag, Burton. "Private Colleges Reshape Higher Education in Eastern Europe and Former Soviet States." *Chronicle of Higher Education* 45, no. 40, 44 (1999): 43-44. June 11.

_____. "Private Universities Bloom in Chile." *Chronicle of Higher Education*, June 27 2003, 34.

Bosker, R.J., R. van der Velden, and P. van de Loo. "Assessing Institutional Effects of Colleges: The Labour Market Success of Their Graduates." In *The Dynamics of Vet and Hrd Systems*, ed. L.F.M. Nieuwenhuis and W.J. Nijhof, 153-168. Enschede, Netherland: Twente University Press, 2001.

Brender, Alan. "South Korean Government Cracks Down on Troubled Private Universities." *The Chronicle of Higher Education*, September 24 2004, 38.

Breneman, David. *Liberal Arts Colleges: Thriving, Surviving or Endangered*. Washington, DC: Brookings Institution, 1994.

Brennan, John. *Graduate Employment: A Review of Issues*. London: Centre for Higher Education Research & Information, Open University, 2000.

_____. "Graduate Employment: Issues for Debate and Inquiry." *International Higher Education*, Winter (2004).

Brennan, John, Brenda Johnston, Brenda Little, Tarla Shah, and Alan Woodley. *The Employment of UK Graduates: Comparisons with Europe and Japan*. London: Centre for Higher Education Research and Information, Open University, 2001.

Brennan, John, Maurice Kogan, and Ulrich Teichler. *Higher Education and Work* Higher Education Policy Series; 23. London; Bristol, Pa.: J. Kingsley Publishers, 1996.

Brookman, Jennie. "Jobless Graduates Get Money Back." *Times Higher Education Supplement*, 09/12/97 1997, 9.

Brown, Phillip, and Richard Scase. *Higher Education and Corporate Realities*. London: UCL press, 1994.

Brunello, Giorgio, and Simona Comi. "Education and Earnings Growth: Evidence from 11 European Countries." *Economics of Education Review* 23, no. 1 (2004): 75-83.

Brunner, José Joaquín, Paulo Santiago, Carmen García Guadilla, Johann Gerlach, and Léa Velho. *Thematic Review of Tertiary Education: Mexico Country Note*. OECD, 2006.

Bryant, Alyssa N. *The Economic Outcomes of Community College Attendance*. ERIC Clearinghouse for Community Colleges Los Angeles CA, 2001. Eric Digest.

Burke, Dolores L., and Ahmad A. Al-Waked. "On the Threshold: Private Universities in Jordan." *International Higher Education*, no. 9 (1997): 2-4.

Business/Higher Education Round, Table. *Enhancing the Learning and Employability of Graduates: The Role of Generic Skills*: Business/Higher Education Round Table, 2002.

Cao, Yingxia. "A Study of the Employment of Graduates from Four Private Colleges in China (Minban Gaoxiao Biyesheng Jiuye Wenti Yanjiu) [in Chinese]." Unpublished master thesis, Xiamen University, 2000.

Cao, Yingxia, and Daniel C. Levy. "China's Shifting Private Higher Education Development: Impacts from Public Sector Privatization." *International Higher Education*, Fall (2005).

Caplánová, Anetta. "Does the Institutional Type Matter? Slovak Higher Education on Its Way to Diversity." *Tertiary Education and Management* 9, no. 4 (2003): 317-340.

Cappellari, Lorenzo. *High School Types, Academic Performance and Early Labor Market Outcomes* 2004, accessed on 10/10/2004 http://www.ncspe.org/publications_files/OP89.pdf.

Castro, Claudio de Moura, and Juan Carlos Navarro. "Will the Invisible Hand Fix Private Higher Education?" In *Private Prometheus: Private Higher Education and Development in the 21st Century*, ed. P. Altbach, 45-63. Westport, CT: Greenwood Press, 1999.

Catterall, J. S., and R. McGhee. "The Emergence of Private Postsecondary Education in the Former Soviet Republic of Azerbaijan." *International Higher Education*, no. 5 (1996): 3-5.

Chesler, Herbert A. "Proof of Worth: Career Services' Help Leads to Better Jobs Faster." *Journal of Career Planning and Employment* 55, no. Jan (1995): 47-50.

Chevalier, Arnaud. *Graduate over-Education in the UK*. London: Centre for the Economics of Education, London School of Economics and Political Science, 2001.

Clanchy, John, and Brigid Ballard. "Generic Skills in the Context of Higher Education." *Higher Education Research & Development* 14, no. 2 (1995): 155-166.

Cohen, David. "The Worldwide Rise of Private Colleges." *Chronicle of Higher Education*, 3/9/2001 2001, A47.

Cohen, de Clemencia Consentino. "Diversification in Argentine Higher Education: Dimensions and Impact of Private Sector Growth." *Higher Education* 46, no. 1 (2003): 1-34.

Coimbra Group of Universities. *Raising Employers' Awareness about the Bologna Process: Findings Survey 2006.* 2006. Accessed on 11/01/2007, online from http://www.coimbra-group.eu/reabp/document/Coimbra%20DEF_LASTREV.pdf.

Correia, Fernanda, Alberto Amaral, and António Magalhães. "Public and Private Higher Education in Portugal: Unintended Effects of Deregulation." *European Journal of Education* 37, no. 4 (2002): 457-462.

de la Fuente, Gloria. "Higher Education and Employment in Spain." *European Journal of Education* 30, no. 2 (1995): 217-34.

De La Harpe, Barbara, Alex Radloff, and John Wyber. "Quality and Generic (Professional) Skills." *Quality in Higher Education* 6, no. 3 (2000): 231-243.

Deil-Amen, Regina, and James E. Rosenbaum. "Charter-Building and Labor-Market Contacts in Two-Year Colleges." *Sociology of Education* 77, no. 3 (2004): 245-265.

Denzin, Norman Kent. "Sociological Methods: A Sourcebook." Aldine Transaction (2006).

Di Pietro, Giorgio, and Peter Urwin. "Education and Skills Mismatch in the Italian Graduate Labour Market." *Applied Economics* 38, no. 1 (2006): 79-93.

Dima, Ana-Maria. "Tribune - Romanian Private Higher Education Viewed from a Neo-Institutionalist Perspective." *Higher Education in Europe* 23, no. 3 (1998): 10.

Directorate for European and International Relations and Cooperation. *Bologna Process 2005-2007: Report for France for the Bologna Follow-up Group* 2006, accessed on 10/27/2007 at http://www.ond.vlaanderen.be/hogeronderwijs/bologna/links/National-reports-2007/National_Report_France2007.pdf.

Dolton, Peter, and Anna Vignoles. "Is a Broader Curriculum Better?" *Economics of Education Review* 21, no. 5 (2002): 415.

Dolton, Peter, and Mary Silles. *Over-Education in the Graduate Labour Market: Some Evidence from Alumni Data*. London: Centre for the Economics of Education London School of Economics and Political Science, 2001.

Duczmal, Wojciech. "Polish Private Higher Education: Expanding Access." *International Higher Education*, no. 38 (Winter) (2005): online at http://www.bc.edu/bc_org/avp/soe/cihe/newsletter/News38/text008.htm.

Eisemon, Thomas. *Private Initiatives and Traditions of State Control in Higher Education in Sub-Saharan Africa*. Washington D.C.: Education and Employment Division, Population and Human Resources Development, World Bank, 1992. SAREC. PHREE Background Paper Series Document No. PHREE/92/48, 10534.

Eisemon, Thomas Owen. "Private Initiatives in Higher Education in Kenya." *Higher Education* 24, no. 2 (1992): 157-175.

Ellerinton, Kerry. "Melbourne University Private: A Coarse Dandelion on the Manicured Lawn of Higher Education?" *International Journal of Private Higher Education* (2004): 1-9.

Fehnel, R. "The Role of Private Higher Education in Professional Development: Private Providers." *Outcomes* 2, no. 4 (2001): 18-20.

Finnie, Ross. *Earnings of University Graduates in Canada by Discipline: What You Study Matters - an Econometric Analysis of Earnings Differences of Bachelor's Level Graduates*. Ontario, Canada: Applied Research Branch, Strategic Policy, Human Resources Development Canada, Statistics Canada, 1998.

_____. *Earnings Differences by Major Field of Study: Evidence from Three Cohorts of Recent Canadian Graduates*. Ontario, Canada: Queen's University and Statistics Canada, 1999a.

_____. *Earnings of Postsecondary Graduates in Canada: Changes in the Structure of Earnings in 1980s and 1990s*. Ontario, Canada: Queen's University and Statistics Canada, 1999b.

_____. *Fields of Plenty, Fields of Lean: The Early Labour Market Outcomes of Canadian University Graduates by Discipline*. Ontario, Canada: Queen's University and Statistics Canada, 1999c.

_____. "Holding Their Own: Employment and Earnings of Postsecondary Graduates." *Education Quarterly Review* 7, no. 1 (2000): 21-37.

Fiorito, Jack. "The School-to-Work Transition of College Graduates." *Industrial and Labor Relations Review* 35, no. 1 (1981): 103-114.

Fitzgerald, Robert A., and Shelley Burns. *College Quality and the Earnings of Recent College Graduates*. Washington D. C.: National Center of Educational Statistics, 2000. Research and Development Report, NCES 2000–043.

Fuller, Alison, and Lorna Unwin. "Creating a 'Modern Apprenticeship': A Critique of the UK's Multi-Sector, Social Inclusion Approach." *Journal of Education & Work* 16, no. 1 (2003): 5-26, March.

Galbraith, Kate. "Towards Quality Private Higher Education in Central and Eastern Europe." *Higher Education in Europe* 28, no. 4 (2003): 20.

Gereffi, Gary, and Vivek Wadhwa. *Framing the Engineering Outsourcing Debate: Placing the United States on a Level Playing Field with China and India*. Duke University, 2005.

Giesecke, Hans. "Legitimacy Seeking among New Private Institutions of Higher Education in Central and Eastern Europe." *Higher Education in Europe* 31, no. 1 (2006): 11.

Giesecke, Hans C. "Expansion and Development of Private Higher Education in East Central Europe." *International Higher Education* 16, no. Summer (1999a): 2-4.

_____. "The Rise of Private Higher Education in East Central Europe." *Society and Economy* 21, no. 1 (1999b).

Gong, Zi. "Enrolment Gimmicks Come Bottom of Class." *China Daily*, 08/07/2004, 4.

Goodman, Peter S. "College Degrees Lose Their Magic in China: Graduates Flood the Job Market." *Washington Post*, Tuesday, August 19 2003.

Gottschalk, Peter, and Michael Hansen. "Is the Proportion of College Workers in Noncollege Jobs Increasing?" *Journal of Labor Economics* 21, no. 2 (2003): 449-471, April.

Griffin, Peter, and Philip T. Ganderton. "Evidence on Omitted Variable Bias in Earnings Equations." *Economics of Education Review* 15, no. 2 (1996): 139-148.

Gulosino, Charisse. "Evaluating Private Higher Education in the Philippines: The Case for Choice, Equity and Efficiency." Occasional Paper No. 68. Available online at http://www.ncspe.org/publications_files/537_OP68.pdf (1/10/2005), Teachers College, Columbia University, 2003.

Haapakorpi, Arja. "The Recession in Finland and the Labour Market for Academic Degree Holders." *European Journal of Education* 30, no. 1 (1995): 105-110.

HEFCE. *Graduate Employment: A Review of Issues*. A Report to the HEFCE by the Centre for Higher Education Research and Information, Open University. 2000.

_____. "Indicators of Employment." Accessed on 10/30/2006. Available online at http://www.hefce.ac.uk/pubs/hefce/2001/01_21.htm, 2001.

Hopper, Ricker. "Emerging Private Universities in Bangladesh." *International Higher Education*, no. 10 (1998): 5-6.

Huong, Pham, and Gerald Fry. "The Emergence of Private Higher Education in Vietnam: Challenges and Opportunities." *Educational Research for Policy and Practice* 1, no. 1-2 (2002): 127-141.

Jalowiecki, Bohdan. "Prospects for the Development of Private Higher Education in Poland." *Higher Education in Europe* 26, no. 3 (2001): 421-425.

James, Estelle. "The Public/Private Provision of Responsibility for Education: An International Comparison." *Economics of Education Review* 6, no. 1 (1987): 1-14.

_____. "College Quality and Future Earnings: Where Should You Send Your Child to College?" *The American Economic Review* 79, no. 2 (1989): 247-252.

_____. "Why Do Different Countries Choose a Different Public-Private Mix of Educational Services?" *The Journal of Human Resources* 28, no. 3 (1993): 571-592.

Johnson, Burke, and Larry B. Christensen. *Education Research: Quantitative, Qualitative, and Mixed Approaches*: Allyn & Bacon, 2004.

Ke, Youxiang. "A Study on Profit-Making Private Higher Education [in Chinese]." Ph.D. Dissertation, Xiamen University, 2001.

Kelly, Kathleen F. *Meeting Needs and Making Profits: The Rise of for- Profit Degree-Granting Institutions* Washington D.C.: Education Commission of the States, 2001, accessed 6/24 2002; Available from http://www.ecs.org/clearinghouse/27/33/2733.htm.

Kinser, Kevin. "Sources of Legitimacy in U.S.: For-Profit Higher Education." In *In Search of Legitimacy: Private Higher Education in Post-Communist Countries*, ed. Snejana Slantcheva and Daniel C. Levy: Palgrave/MacMillan, 2007.

Kinser, Kevin, and Daniel C. Levy. "The for-Profit Sector: U.S. Patterns and International Echoes in Higher Education." In *The International Encyclopedia of Higher Education*, ed. J. Forest and P. G. Altbach: Kluwer Publications, 2005.

Kivinen, Osmo, and Sakari Ahola. "Current and Future Demand for Graduates: Problems of Comparative Analysis." *European Journal of Education* 30, no. 2, June (1995): 187-203.

Kolasinski, Maciej, Arkadiusz Kulig, and Piotr Lisiecki. "The Strategic Role of Public Relations in Creating the Competitive Advantages of Private Higher Education in Poland: The Example of the School of Banking in Poznan." *Higher Education in Europe* 28, no. 4 (2003): 15.

Koskinen, Katariina. *Graduate Employment and Quality Assurance* 2005, accessed on June 16, online at http://www.utwente.nl/cheps/documenten/susukoskinen.pdf.

Krejecie, R.V., and D.W. Morgan. "Determining Sample Size for Research Activities." *Educational and Psychological Measurement* 30, no. 3 (1970): 608.

Kruss, Glenda. *Chasing Mobility and Credentials: Private Higher Education in South Africa*. South Africa: HSRC (Human Science Research Council), 2004.

Kwong, Julia. "The Reemergence of Private Schools in Socialist China." *Comparative Education Review* 41, no. 3 (1997): 244-60.

Lang Research., and Canadian Millenium Scholarship Foundation. *Meta-Analysis of Institutional Graduate Surveys* Millenium Research Series. Montreal, QC: Canadian Millenium Scholarship Foundation, 2002.

Levy, Daniel C. *The Rise of Private Universities in Latin America and the United States* Sociology of Education Expansion: Take- Off Growth, and Inflation in Educational Systems, ed. Margaret Archer. London: Sage, 1982.

———. *Higher Education and the State in Latin America: Private Challenges to Public Dominance*. Chicago, Illinois: University of Chicago Press, 1986a.

———. ""Private" and "Public": Analysis amid Ambiguity in Higher Education." In *Private Education: Studies in Choice and Public Policy*, ed. Daniel C. Levy, 170-236. Oxford and New York: Oxford University Press, 1986b.

———. *A Comparison of Private and Public Education Organizations* the Nonprofit Sector: A Research Handbook, ed. Walter W. Powell. New Haven, Conn.: Yale University Press, 1987.

_____. "Accountability and Private-Public Comparisons." *Educational Policy* 5, no. 2, Jun (1991): 193-99.

_____. "Private Institutions of Higher Education." In *The Encyclopedia of Higher Education*, ed. Burton Clark and Guy Neave, 2. New York, NY: Pergamon Press, 1992.

_____. "Recent Trends in the Privatization of Latin American Higher Education: Solidification, Breadth, and Vigour." *Higher Education Policy* 6, no. 4 (1993): 12-19.

_____. "When Private Higher Education Does Not Bring Organizational Diversity: Argentina, China, Hungary." In *Private Prometheus: Private Higher Education and Development in the 21st Century*, ed. Philip Altbach, 17-50. A translation of the book is to be published by FLACSO. West Port, Conn.: Greenwood Press, 1999.

_____. "Profits and Practicality: How South Africa Epitomizes the Global Surge in Commercial Private Higher Education." In *Understanding Private Higher Education in South Africa*. Benoni, South Africa. April 9-10, 2002a.

_____. "Unanticipated Development: Perspectives on Private Higher Education's Emerging Roles." PROPHE Working Paper No.1, April 2002, Program for Research on Private Higher Education (PROPHE), State University of New York at Albany. Available online at http://www.albany.edu/~prophe/publication/paper.html, 2002b.

_____. "Where Reality Defies the New Institutionalism: Implications from Private Higher Education's Global Growth." In *Advancing the Institutional Research Agenda in Education*. Albany, NY: University at Albany, SUNY. September 20-22, 2002c.

_____. "Expanding Higher Education Capacity through Private Growth: Contribution and Challenges." *The Observatory*, no. 11 (2003a): 1-15, January.

_____. "Profits and Practicality: How South Africa Epitomizes the Global Surge in Commercial Private Higher Education." PROPHE Working Paper No.2., March., Program for Research on Private Higher Education (PROPHE), State University of New York at Albany. Available online at http://www.albany.edu/~prophe/publication/paper.html, 2003b.

_____. "The New Institutionalism: Mismatches with Private Higher Education's Global Growth." PROPHE Working Paper No.2., March., Program for Research on Private Higher Education (PROPHE), State University of New York at

Albany. Available online at
http://www.albany.edu/~prophe/publication/paper.html, 2004.

_____. "Analyzing a Private Revolution: The Work of PROPHE." *International Higher Education*, Spring (2005).

_____. "The Unanticipated Explosion: Private Higher Education's Global Surge." *Comparative Education Review* 50, no. 2 (2006a): 217-240.

_____. "The Unanticipated Explosion: Private Higher Education's Global Surge." *Comparative Education Review* 50, no. 2 (2006b): 217–240.

Lin, Jing. *Social Transformation and Private Education in China*. Westport. CT: Praeger, 1999.

Little, Brenda. "Reading between the Lines of Graduate Employment." *Quality in Higher Education* 7, no. 2 (2001): 121-129.

Liu, Lili. *A Study of China's Private Higher Education Development [in Chinese]*. Jilin, China: Jilin People's Press, 2002.

Lofland, John. *Analyzing Social Settings*. Belmont, CA: Sage, 1971.

Mabizela, Mahlubi. "Whither Private Higher Education in Africa?" *International Higher Education*, Winter (2004).

Maldonado, Alma, Yingxia Cao, Philip Altbach, Daniel Levy, and Hong Zhu. *Private Higher Education: An International Bibliography*. Greenwich CT.: Information Age Publishing, 2004.

Maoscati, Robert, and Michele Rostan. "Higher Education and Graduate Employment in Italy." *European Journal of Education* 35, no. 2, June (2000): 201-10.

Mason, Geoff. "High Skills Utilization under Mass Higher Education: Graduate Employment in Service Industries in Britain." *Journal of Education and Work* 15, no. 4 (2002): 427-456.

McGrath, Gary L. "The Emergence of Career Services and Their Important Role in Working with Employers." *New Directions for Student Services*, no. 100, Winter (2002): 69-83.

McMahon, Walter W., and Alan P. Wagner. *Returns to Investment in Higher Education: Expected and Realized Rates of Return by Occupational Objective, Degree Level, Type of Institutional Objective, Race, and Sex* Faculty Working Papers; No. 301. Urbana: College of Commerce and Business Administration University of Illinois at Urbana-Champaign, 1976.

_____. "Expected Return to Investment in Higher Education." *Journal of Human Resources* 16 (1981): 274-285.

_____. "Monetary Returns to Education as Partial Social Efficiency Criteria." In *Financing Education*, ed. Walter W. McMahon and T. G. Geske, 161-169: University of Illinois Press, 1982.

Merrow, John, American Community Service Network., South Carolina Educational Television Network., and Learning Matters Inc. *Is College Worth It?* videorecording. United States: Learning Matters? 1993.

Miller, Margaret A. "The Marketplace and the Village Green." *Change* 32, no. 4, Jul/Aug (2000): 4.

Min, Weifang, Xiaohao Ding, Dongmao Wen, and Changjun Yue. "Survey on 2005 College Graduate Employment [in Chinese]." *Economics of Education Research (Peking University)*, no. 12 (2005).

Mok, Ka-Ho. *Private Challenges to Public Dominance: The Resurgence*, 1997a.

_____. "Privatization or Marketization: Educational Development in Post-Mao China." *International Review of Education* 43, no. 5/6 (1997b): 21.

Mok, Ka-Ho, and King-Yee Wat. "Merging of the Public and Private Boundary: Education and the Market Place in China." *International Journal of Educational Development* 18, no. 3 (1998): 255-67.

Monks, James. "The Returns to Individual and College Characteristics: Evidence from the National Longitudinal Survey of Youth." *Economics of Education Review* 19, no. 3 (2000): 279-289.

Moses, Oketch. "Costing and Financing Higher Education for Development in Sub-Saharan Africa: Kenya's Case." *International Education Electronic Journal* 4, no. 3 (2000): September.

Nagy-Darvas, J. "Private Higher Education in Hungary." *International Higher Education*, no. 9 (1997): 6-8.

Nagy-Darvas, Judit, and Peter Darvas. "Private Higher Education in Hungary: The Market Influences the University." In *Private Prometheus: Private Higher Education and Development in the 21st Century*, ed. Philip G. Altbach, 161-180. Westport, CT: Greenwood, 1999.

National Centre for Vocational Education Research. "Defining Generic Skills: At a Glance." NCVER, 2003.

Newman, Frank, and Lara K Couturier. "The New Competitive Arena: Market Forces Invade the Academy." *Change* 33, no. 5 (2001).

Nicolescu, Luminita. *Private Higher Education in Romania: Success or Failure?* Open Society Institute, Budapest, Hungary, 2001, accessed 1/8. OSI Project 2000 Final report. 2005; Available online at http://www.policy.hu/nicolescu/.

_____. "Reforming Higher Education in Romania." *European Journal of Education* 37, no. 1 (2002): 91-100. Available also at http://www.policy.hu/nicolescu/.

_____. "Higher Education in Romania: Evolution and Views from the Business Community." *Tertiary Education and Management* 9, no. 1 (2003): 77-95. Available also at http://www.policy.hu/nicolescu/article_3.htm.

_____. "Private versus Public in Romania: Consequences for the Market." *International Higher Education*, Spring (2005).

_____. "The Legitimacy of Private Higher Education in Romania: Between Legislative Recognition, Institutional Efforts and Market Acceptance." In *In Search of Legitimacy: Private Higher Education in Post-Communist Countries*, ed. Snejana Slantcheva and Daniel C. Levy: Palgrave/McMillan, 2007.

OECD. *From Higher Education to Employment: Synthesis Report*. Paris: OECD, 1992.

_____. "OECD-France Seminar: The Labour Market Orientation of Tertiary Education in France and in OECD Countries: Assessment and Prospects." Paris, 2007.

Patton, Michael Quinn. *Qualitative Research and Evaluation Methods*. 3 ed. Thousand Oaks, Calif.: Sage Publications, 2002.

Paul, Jean-Jacques, and Jake Murdoch. "Higher Education and Graduate Employment in France." *European Journal of Education*, no. 2, June (2000): 179-177.

Paul, Jean-Jacques, Ulrich Teichler, and Rolf Van Der Velden. "Editorial." *European Journal of Education* 35, no. 2 (2000): 139-140, June.

Person, Ann E., and James E. Rosenbaum. "Educational Outcomes of Labor-Market Linking and Job Placement for Students at Public and Private 2-Year Colleges." *Economics of Education Review* 25 (2006): 412-429.

Porter, Kathleen, and ERIC Clearinghouse on Higher Education Washington DC.BBB15669. *The Value of a College Degree. Eric Digest*. U.S.; District of Columbia: ERIC, 2002.

Porter, Stephen. "Raising Response Rates: What Works?" *New Directions for Institutional Research* 121, no. 5 (2004).

Praphamontripong, Prachayani. "Thai Private Higher Education: Diversification or Homogenization." In *Private Higher Education: China and Beyond*. Xi'an, China. December 14-16, 2004.

Pritchard, Rosalind M. O. "Principles and Pragmatism in Private Higher Education: Examples from Britain and Germany." *Higher Education* 24 (1992): 247-273.

Qin, Guozhu. *A Dream of Private Universities: The Past, Presence, and Future of Private Higher Education in China [in Chinese]*. Xiamen, China: Lujiang Press, 2000.

Roane, Warren. "Impediments to Private Higher Education in Uruguay." *International Higher Education*, no. 19 (2000): 13-14.

Rosenbaum, James E., Takehiko Kariya, Rick Settersten, and Tony Maier. "Market and Network Theories of the Transition from High School to Work: Their Implication to Industrialized Societies." *Annual Review of Sociology* 16 (1990): 263-299.

Rubb, S. "Overeducation in the Labor Market: A Comment and Re-Analysis of a Meta-Analysis." *Economics of Education Review* 22, no. 6 (2003): 10.

Rubb, Stephen. "Overeducation: A Short or Long Run Phenomenon for Individuals?" *Economics of Education Review* 22, no. 4 (2003): 6.

Rumberger, Russell w. *Overeducation in the U.S.Labor Market*. New York: Praeger, 1981.

Sapatoru, Dana, Luminita Nicolescu, and Snejana Slantcheva. *The Growth and Labor Market Impact of Private Higher Education: The Cases of Bulgaria and Romania*. Bulgraria: PROPHE's Regional Center for Central and Eastern Europe. Research Report for IREX 2002-2003, The Black And Caspian Sea Collaborative Research Program. http://www.prophecee.net/irex%20final%20report.pdf. Accessed on December 1, 2003, 2003. Research Report.

Schomburg, Harald. "Higher Education and Graduate Employment in Germany." *European Journal of Education* 35, no. 2 (2000): 189-200.

_____. "The Professional Success of Higher Education Graduates." *European Journal of Education* 42, no. 1 (2007): 35.

Schomburg, Harald, and Ulrich Teichler. "Increasing Potentials of Alumni Research for Curriculum Reforms: Some Experiences from a German Research Institute." *New Directions for Institutional Research* 2005, no. 126 (2005): 31.

Sharvashidze, George. *Private Higher Education in Georgia* International Institute for Educational Policy, Planning and Management, 2002, accessed 1/7 2005; Available from http://www.eppm.org.ge/pdf/Private%20HE%20in%20Georgia%5B1%5D.pdf.

Silver, Irving, Laval Lavallée, and Bert Pereboom. *Labour Market Transitions of Graduates*. Ontario, Canada: Applied Research Branch, Strategic Policy, Human Resources Development Canada, Statistics Canada, 1999, R-00-1-9E.

Slantcheva, Snejana. "Private Higher Education in Bulgaria and Its Role in Providing Alternative Educational Opportunities." In *23rd EAIR Forum*. 9-12 September, Porto, Portugal, 2001.

Slantcheva, Snejana, and Daniel C. Levy. *In Search of Legitimacy: Private Higher Education in Post-Communist Countries*: Palgrave/McMillan, 2007.

Smyth, Emer, Markus Gangl, David Raffe, Damian F. Hannan, and Selina McCoy. *A Comparative Analysis of Transitions from Education to Work in Europe (CATEWE)*. Economic and Social Research Institute (ESRI), Dublin, 2001. TSER Programme Project Report, ERB142 PL97/2100.

Sosale, Shobhana. *Trends in Private Sector Development in World Bank Education Projects*. Washington D.C.: The World Bank, 1999. Economic development paper.

Sperling, John. *Rebel with a Cause: The Entrepreneur Who Created the University of Phoenix and the for-Profit Revolution in Higher Education*. New York: John Wiley & Sons, 2000.

Sperling, John, and Robert Tucker. *For-Profit Higher Education: Developing a World-Class Workforce*. New Brunswick, NJ: Transaction Publishers, 1996.

Stetar, Joseph, and Elena Berezkina. "Evolution of Ukrainian Private Higher Education: 1991-2001." *International Higher Education*, Fall (2002): Available online at http://www.bc.edu/bc_org/avp/soe/cihe/newsletter/News29/text009.htm (1/10/2005).

Suspitsin, Dmitry. "Russian Private Higher Education: The Quest for Legitimacy." Doctoral Dissertation, Pennsylvania State University, 2007.

Tait, Hilary, and Helen Godfrey. "Defining and Assessing Competence in Generic Skills." *Quality in Higher Education* 5, no. 3 (1999): 245-253.

Team of Economic Research Foundation of Turkey. *Higher Education and the Labor Market in Turkey*. Washington D.C.: World Bank, 2007.

Teichler, Ulrich. "Research on Higher Education and Work in Europe." *European Journal of Education* 24, no. 3 (1989): 223-247.

_____. "Students and Employment - the Issues for University Management." *Higher Education Management and Policy: [Journal of the Programme on Institutional Management in Higher Education]* 6, no. 2 (1994): 217 - 225.

_____. "Research on Higher Education and Employment and Its Implication for Higher Education Management." *Higher Education Policy* 8, no. 1 (1995): 11.

_____. "Higher Education and Employment - Twenty-Five Years of Changing Debates and Realities." *Higher education management: [journal of the Programme on Institutional Management in Higher Education]* 8, no. 3 (1996): 14.

_____. "Graduate Employment and Work in Selected European Countries." *European Journal of Education* 35, no. 2 (2000): 16.

_____. "Graduate Employment and Work in Europe: Diverse Situations and Common Perceptions." *Tertiary Education and Management*, no. 8 (2002): 199?16.

_____, ed. *Careers of University Graduates: Views and Experiences in Comparative Perspectives*. Dordrecht: Kluwer, 2003.

The Institute for Research on Higher Education. "Understanding Employer's Perceptions of College Graduates." *Change* 30, no. 3, May/June (1998): 47-51.

Tooley, James. *The Global Education Industry: Lessons from Private Education in Developing Countries*. London, IEA Education and Training Unit, and IFC: World Bank, 1999.

UNESCO. "Thematic Debate: The Requirements of the World of Work." In *Higher Education in the Twenty-First Century - Vision and Action*. Paris: UNESCO, 1998.

_____. "Higher Education in Asia and the Pacific: 1998-2003." In *Meeting of Higher Education Partners*. Paris, 2003.

Villar, Esperanca, Jaume Juan, Enric Corominas, and Dolors Capell. "What Kind of Networking Strategy Advice Should Career Counselors Offer University Graduates Searching for a Job?" *British Journal of Guidance & Counseling* 28, no. 3, August (2000): 389-410.

Vincens, Jean. "Graduates and the Labour Market in France." *European Journal of Education* 30, no. 2 (1995): 133-26.

Wang, Yongyang, and Margaret Secombe. "A Study of People-Run Tertiary Education in South and West China." *International Education Journal* 4, no. 4 (2004).

Wielers, Rudi, and Arie Glebbeek. "Graduate and the Labor Market in the Netherlands: Three Hypotheses and Some Data." *European Journal of Education* 30, no. 1, March (1995): 11-31.

Wolbers, Maarten H. J. "Job Mismatches and Their Labour-Market Effects among School-Leavers in Europe." *European Sociological Review* 19, no. 3 (2003): 249-266.

Wolff, Laurence, and Claudio de Moura Castro. *Public or Private Education for Latin America? This Is the (False) Question?* Washington, DC: Inter-American Development Bank. Sustainable Development Department Technical Papers Series, 2001.

Wu, Shujuan. "A Comparison of Students' Costs and Employment between Gongban and Minban Colleges [in Chinese]." *Economics of Education Research (Peking University)*, no. 1 (2003).

Yan, Fengqiao, and et. al. *Minban Education in China.* Beijing and Shanghai: School of Education, Peking University and Shanghai Institute of Education Research, 2003. World Bank Funded Project.

Yan, Fengqiao, and Peijuan Wu. "Research of Private Higher Education in China: Retrospect, Comparison and Prospect." In *Qifang Seminar on Minban Higher Education.* Xi'an Foreign Affairs College, 2004.

Yonezawa, Akiyoshi, and Masateru Baba. "The Market Structure for Private Universities in Japan." *Tertiary Education and Management* 4, no. 2 (1998): 145-152.

Yoshimoto, Keiichi, and Akiyoshi Yonezawa. "The University Employment Governance and the Labor Market of New Graduates (Daigaku Shushoku Shido Soshiki to Daigaku Rodo Shijo) [in Japanese]." *Bulletin of the National Institute of Multimedia Education (Hoso Kyoiku Kaihatsu Center Kenky Kiyo)* 10 (1994): 129-150.

Yue, Changjun, and Juan Yang. "Overeducation or Undereducation: Some Evidence from Chinese Graduates." In *International Conference: Economy of Education: Principal Contributions and Prospects.* Dijon, France, 2006.

Zhou, Junbo. *Skills, Credentials, or the Chances to Enter More Advanced Higher Education after Graduation: What Have Minban Colleges Given Their Students?* Peking University, 2003. Unpublished graduate student group project.

www.ingramcontent.com/pod-product-compliance
Lightning Source LLC
Chambersburg PA
CBHW061402210326
41598CB00035B/6069